D1518222

Crusade *for* *the* Children

Crusade *for the* Children

A HISTORY OF
THE NATIONAL
CHILD LABOR
COMMITTEE AND
CHILD LABOR
REFORM IN AMERICA

BY

WALTER I. TRATTNER

CHICAGO

Quadrangle Books: 1970

Photographs by LEWIS HINE, from the collection
of the Library of Congress.
Typography and binding design by VINCENT TORRE.

Library of Congress Catalog Card Number: 76-116090
SBN 8129-0141-X

FOR JOAN

Declaration of Dependence by the Children of America in Mines and Factories and Workshops Assembled

WHEREAS, We, Children of America, are declared to have been born free and equal, and

WHEREAS, We are yet in bondage in this land of the free; are forced to toil the long day or the long night, with no control over the conditions of labor, as to health or safety or hours or wages, and with no right to the rewards of our service, therefore be it

RESOLVED, I—That childhood is endowed with certain inherent and inalienable rights, among which are freedom from toil for daily bread; the right to play and to dream; the right to the normal sleep of the night season; the right to an education, that we may have equality of opportunity for developing all that there is in us of mind and heart.

RESOLVED, II—That we declare ourselves to be helpless and dependent; that we are and of right ought to be dependent, and that we hereby present the appeal of our helplessness that we may be protected in the enjoyment of the rights of childhood.

RESOLVED, III—That we demand the restoration of our rights by the abolition of child labor in America.

ALEXANDER J. MCKELWAY, 1913

Preface

It has been said that human progress can be measured by the extent that children's rights are protected. Today in the United States we hold that children comprise the nation's most valuable resource, and that the most productive thing they can do—for themselves and for society—is to complete their education. Yet this was not always the case. In fact, as the history of child labor in America indicates, it was not very long ago that the opposite was true. Even during the present century, the labor of young children in factories, mines, streets, and fields, which aborted healthful growth, schooling, and self-fulfillment, was not only condoned but approved. Only after a long and hard fight were these harsh conditions altered, in principle at least, if not always in practice.

As knowledge of the needs of children increased and more emphasis was placed upon the importance of education, the criteria of what constituted child labor naturally underwent change. Generally, however, child labor was defined as the work of children under conditions that interfered with their physical development and their education, and thus prevented them from becoming happy and socially useful adults; it was the employment of children at unsuitable ages, for unreasonable hours, under unhealthful or hazardous conditions, or while school was in session. (Work around the home or farm, or elsewhere for that matter, which was not unsuited to the child's strength, which was carefully supervised by parents or others, and which did not necessitate absence from school or loss of needed recreation, was always considered part of the child's upbringing.) A program to combat child labor therefore had to include both restrictive measures to keep young children out of industry, and positive schemes to insure them good health and an education or training for suitable work in later life.

Although largely a success story, this chronicle of child labor reform is not an account of a task fully accomplished: child labor is still with us today. It exists among migratory children—underpaid, undernourished, diseased, uneducated sweaty ciphers who, hustled from place to place, sleep in tar-paper shacks and bend their backs day after day picking fruits and vegetables for people they never see. It exists for those children who carry too heavy a load of part-time work while attending school; and it exists for thousands who are unlawfully employed each year, many of whom are killed or crippled as a result of injuries suffered at work. Too, it exists for the millions of children who each year drop out of high school before graduating, ill prepared for a productive or rewarding future. Nevertheless, viewed in contrast to conditions existing in 1904, when the National Child Labor Committee was organized, the improvement in child labor conditions is striking. At least we have traveled far along the road toward eliminating one of the gravest social injustices in American life.

The factors responsible for this, as any other social change, were numerous and complex; many forces converged during the twentieth century to mitigate or abolish child labor. State and local laws and improved enforcement agencies were important, as was a growing knowledge of the nature and needs of children. So, too, was the mechanization of industry, which eliminated many of the hand processes for which children were used.

The growth of labor unions, the development of widows' pensions and Social Security, the passage of minimum-wage legislation, the growing demand by industry for high school graduates—all these and many other factors helped to alleviate abuses. To single out the precise role which the National Child Labor Committee played in achieving this result obviously is impossible. Yet, as this study will demonstrate, many children who today enjoy freedom as well as good health and the benefits of an education would have been denied those rights were it not for the far-ranging services rendered by that body.

When the National Child Labor Committee was born, there were no generally accepted standards of protection against child exploitation. Ten-year-old boys were commonly found in the blinding dust of coal breakers, picking slate with torn and bleeding fingers; thousands of children sweltered all night for a pittance in the glare of the white-hot furnaces of the glasshouses. Young girls toiled in damp, dust-laden cotton mills for long hours, six days a week. Unsanitary factories and tenement sweatshops, canneries, and the street trades, including the night messenger service, all took their toll from the home, the schoolhouse, and the playground while most Americans looked on with approval or indifference. Child labor had few effective opponents.

At the turn of the century, however, conditions were ripe for child labor reformers to deal with the main causes of the evil—prejudice, greed, and ignorance. This was the so-called period of progressivism, when millions of Americans, concerned about themselves, their neighbors, and the future of their country, seemed willing, perhaps eager, to learn of their sins and to atone for them. The nation's conscience was awakened by a literature of moral protest. The city's squalor and congestion, the poverty and degradation of the industrial order, the waste of the nation's physical and human resources, and the graft and corruption in its political life were exposed and attacked. For each evil there appeared to be a remedy. Full of buoyant optimism, men and women came together in public agencies and in private charitable, rescue, and humane societies to prevent and ameliorate the political and social malaise.

A broad child welfare movement was part of this widespread campaign for social betterment. It embraced many programs: the creation of children's aid societies; the transfer of children from almshouses into good homes; efforts to curtail infant mortality through an improved milk supply and better care for mothers; the establishment of juvenile courts, reformatories, and probation systems; the building of parks and playgrounds; the passage of compulsory school attendance laws; and, above all, a crusade against child labor.

Almost every individual or agency working for social improvement saw in children the opportunity for constructive work. Even the apathetic, or those who might have become hardened to the appeals of suffering adults, frequently were touched and aroused to action by "the bitter cry of children" in distress, by those who were no more responsible for their condition than for their birth—and thus most deserving of sympathy and help. A rapidly declining birthrate had moreover aroused widespread concern and even cries of "race suicide." Above all, the child was seen as the key to social control: if later generations were to possess the strength of mind and body to be good, self-supporting citizens, they had to be protected as children.

So when child labor reformers pleaded for the children, they were concerned not merely with the young ones but with the nation as well. Motivated by pity, compassion, and a sense of patriotism, they argued that, for the child, labor was a delusion; for industry it was a fallacy; and for society, a menace. Child labor meant the spread of illiteracy and ignorance, the lowering of the wage scale and hence the standard of living, the perpetuation of poverty, an increase in adult unemployment and crime, the disintegration of the family, and, in the end, racial degeneracy. As Felix Adler, long the chairman of the National Child Labor Committee, put it: "We are engaged in a 'holy war,' a war having for its object the stability of civilization as well as the welfare of the child." [1]

The National Child Labor Committee was not a palliative or relief-giving agency; nor was it a theoretical or idealistic body. Rather, it was at all times a militant and practical organization made up of individuals who believed that a healthy, happy, normal childhood was not only the rightful heritage of all children but was essential for the development of socially useful adults, and that the premature drafting of youngsters into the labor market denied them this good life. Its members recognized that educating large numbers of apathetic, uninformed, and even hostile citizens and enlisting their support in a child labor program could not be done through a visionary approach; the Committee therefore seldom operated in a climate of rarefied ideals. Concentrating first on those areas which were the most glaring —child labor in factories and mines, for example—it went on to attack some even more widespread and firmly entrenched but less shocking practices, such as child labor in the nation's streets and on its farms.

The National Child Labor Committee was to leave a large constructive imprint on the whole field of child welfare. Thanks to its successful efforts in promoting both restrictive legislation to prevent early or harmful employment, and constructive measures to increase opportunities for good health and education, the door of opportunity has been opened to countless Americans. The Committee's history lives not so much in this or in any book as in the lives of those unnumbered citizens—some grown up, others on the threshold of life, and still others yet to come—released from defenseless bondage through its activities.

I should like to emphasize that this book is neither an exhaustive treatment of child labor reform in America nor a complete history of the National Child Labor Committee. In view of the enormity of the problem, the wealth of material, and the impressive record of accomplishments at the local and state levels as well as the federal, it would take several lengthy volumes to describe and analyze each. I have undertaken the much more modest job of relating some of the more important developments and trends in the history of child labor reform, and the general role the National Child Labor Committee played in bringing them about: Some events and achievements are only alluded to, others are omitted. There is, then, need for further studies of the problem, especially critical accounts of the struggle within the states. Hopefully this book will stimulate interest in child labor as a subject for future historical research.

W. I. T.

Milwaukee, Wisconsin
January 1970

Acknowledgments

F AR too many debts have been incurred in the preparation of this book for me to attempt to list them all here; it is a pleasure, however, to acknowledge my obligations to those persons and institutions who have provided the most assistance.

Like all historians, I have depended on many librarians and curators of manuscripts, most of whom went out of their way to be of assistance. Particularly helpful were the staffs of the Manuscript Division of the Library of Congress and the New York Public Library. My thanks also go to staff members at the Columbia University School of Social Work Library, the University of North Carolina Library, the University of Chicago Library, the Franklin D. Roosevelt Library, the University of Wisconsin–Milwaukee Library, and the Milwaukee Public Library, especially Mr. Orval Liljequist, coordinator of the Humanities Department.

I would like to thank Mr. Benjamin McKelway, editorial chairman of the *Washington Evening Star,* for permission to use and quote from his father's papers at the Library of Congress. The same holds true for those in charge of the Judge Benjamin B. Lindsey and Senator Albert J. Beveridge Papers.

I am particularly grateful to the staff of the National Committee on Employment of Youth of the National Child Labor Committee, especially to Mr. Eli E. Cohen, executive secretary; Mr. Joel Seldin, associate executive secretary; Mrs. Ruth LaVar, administrative assistant; and Miss Jean E. Dulaff, librarian. Their generous cooperation, which went far beyond the bounds of common courtesy, is greatly appreciated.

I should like to pay tribute to the memory of two noted humanitarians and leaders in the field of child welfare, the late Mr. and Mrs. Savel Zimand. Their interest in this project and their suggestions and efforts on the writer's behalf always will be remembered; I deeply regret that they could not see the completed study.

I was fortunate to receive financial assistance in the research and writing of the book from the American Philosophical Society; from the College of Letters and Science, the School of Social Welfare, and the Graduate School of the University of Wisconsin–Milwaukee; and from the Social and Rehabilitation Service, Department of Health, Education and Welfare, Washington, D.C. (grant nos. 421 and 421-C1).

As this work evolved I became increasingly conscious of how much I owe to Professor Emeritus Merle Curti of the University of Wisconsin–Madison, a teacher and adviser of rare humanity and inspiration. While he made no specific contribution to this manuscript, it would never have been written without his earlier encouragement, his useful advice, and his unselfish assistance in numerous ways.

For helpful suggestions and editorial revisions I am most grateful to Freeman Cleaves of Millburn, New Jersey. Another discerning critic to whom I am deeply indebted is Clarke A. Chambers of the University of Minnesota, who also was kind enough to read the manuscript and offer valuable comments. Finally, Ivan Dee of Quadrangle Books read the manuscript closely and suggested stylistic changes that I have been happy to incorporate in the final revision. While these gentlemen are not responsible for my interpretations or omissions, their efforts have improved this book.

To Caroline Dulka, who deciphered my scrawl and typed and retyped the manuscript in its various drafts with commendable accuracy and speed, I offer my sincere thanks.

Last, but certainly not least, I wish to thank my wife, Joan D. Trattner. Even though this book is dedicated to her, it would be quite unfair to omit a special thanks for her constant encouragement, good-natured forbearance, and editorial assistance; all this was far more helpful than she realizes, and it cannot be adequately acknowledged.

Contents

Crusade *for* *the* Children

I

The Problem
Emerges

Children have always worked. During early human history, the young of wandering tribes shared in hunting, fishing, and trapping animals. Later, when tribes and clans separated themselves into families, children continued to work with their elders in the woods and fields and in caring for crops and animals. They also helped in the handicrafts, as these developed. While at times they no doubt suffered abuses, their share of the work in the tribe or family was healthful in the sense that it prepared them for survival in the daily struggle with their fellows and with the forces of nature.

The medieval guild system, with its payless and often hungry apprentices, was preeminently child-employing and thus pregnant with possibilities for offhand child abuse. Under its provisions, young boys were indentured to masters to learn trades, and girls were bound out to serve in the domestic arts. Again, during a stable and orderly period of craftsmanship, the work of children made up a large part of their education and training. Since work was done by hand with the simplest of tools, this advance into artisanship (and homemaking) was well adapted to proper child development.[1]

With the close of the medieval period, the first tangible symptoms of the child labor problem appeared. The breakdown of medieval society, the increase in travel, the triumph of Protestantism, the advance of capitalism, and the rise of nationalism with its sometimes stringent regulation of trade and commerce, all contributed to new social pressures. In 1575, for instance, an English statute provided for the use of public funds to employ children in order to "accustom them to labor" and "afford a prophylactic against vagabonds and paupers." [2]

This statutory provision for keeping children at work for other than educational reasons was clearly written into early poor law provisions. The English Poor Law of 1601, for example, designed in part to banish idleness, authorized the involuntary "binding out" of needy children. This allegedly benevolent gesture usually served the interest not of the child but of the master, who looked upon his charge as a source of cheap labor and compelled him to work long, arduous hours, often at menial tasks, only to cast him loose at the end of his tenure into a strange, competitive world without money and a trade.

So profitable was this arrangement that entrepreneurs opened "spinning schools" and "houses of industry" which were staffed by pauper children; not only were such youngsters cheap sources of labor, but because putting them to work reduced relief expenditures and thus kept the poor rate down, Poor Law officials paid keepers several pounds per head for each child taken off their hands.[3] Child labor thus assumed the stature of a righteous institution. By combating unemployment and vagrancy it embraced a sound measure of social control. It was a source of profit to private citizens and a savings for the realm—a pretty blend of morality and self-interest.

The industrial revolution and the use of power machinery by industry, then, did not create the child labor problem or all of the abuses connected with it. It did, however, provide more opportunities for the further exploitation of the young. Industry now transferred their employment from the home or shop to the factory, which usually worsened the conditions under which they worked and the way in which they were treated; child labor became child slavery.[4] In the cotton, silk, hat, and ribbon trades, for example, children five, six, or

seven years old, deprived of all opportunity for an education, were crowded into airless factories and forced to work all day, or sometimes all night, under tortuous conditions for a tiny wage. In the coal mines, where children might work as many as eighteen or twenty hours a day, the ordinary starting age was eight or nine years, but still younger children were used underground where they were harnessed to carts to pull the heavy loads of coal through long, narrow, dark shafts to the openings. In the words of the British Commission on the Employment of Children and Young Persons (1842):
"Chained, belted, harnessed like dogs in a go-cart, black, saturated with wet, and more than half naked—crawling upon their hands and feet, and dragging their heavy loads behind them—[the children] . . . present an appearance indescribably disgusting and unnatural." [5] Many never survived such degrading and brutalizing conditions; those who did grew up weak, bloodless, miserable, and in many cases deformed cripples victimized by almost every disease.

These appalling conditions coincided with the growth of England's export trade and popular acceptance of the idea that laissez faire was the basis of the nation's greatness and wealth. Hence the prevailing view remained that child labor was good; it benefited those directly involved and society as well, not only by reducing relief expenditures but by furnishing the means to develop the nation's resources. To interfere with it was socially unsound. Parents might be refused work if they did not send their children into the mills and mines to man the machinery especially built to accommodate the youngsters. Years later, when fears of physical degeneracy at last led some people to put humanity before profits, legislative relief finally came. In the meantime, the invention and application of machinery to industry stunted or took far more human lives than it liberated.

Although machine power in the United States lagged behind England and parts of continental Europe, from the outset children labored in America. In a newly settled land there could be little idleness for anyone; the stress and strain of frontier life meant hard work for all. Children thus played their part in clearing the land and building the first settlements in the North American wilderness. Equally important for the children's role, the ways of the colonists were based upon the social habits and traditions of old England. Early Colonial poor laws (which in some cases retained many of the specific provisions of Elizabethan legislation) reflected a belief in the propriety of putting needy children to work. The indenture system, with all of its potential for abuse, was continued, allegedly so that poor children could make their own way and not become a "burden to the community." As in England, youngsters were taken from parents who could not support them, or from public institutions, and were bound out as apprentices.

The conditions of indenture were patterned after those in England. The master was to supply food and clothing and, in the eighteenth century, he was also required to teach the boy to read and write and "to cypher to the Rule of three (if he be capable to learn)." Girls were to be taught only reading and writing "if they shall be capable." The binding out of poor children as apprentices, however, did not necessarily mean teaching them a trade, as an early New England statute reveals. The apprentice, the measure stated, was to serve his master faithfully and "gladly obey" his "lawful commands," for the "person who takes a child off the town shall have him 'to be his servant' until he comes of age." [6]

Perhaps even more important for children's lives was the religious doctrine of some early settlers, especially belief in the virtue of industry and the sin of idleness: "Satan finds some mischief still for idle hands to do," and "It is well for a man that he bear the yoke in his youth," were quotations frequently on the lips of Puritan elders.[7] Thus it was a public duty in Massachusetts to provide for the training of children, not only in learning but in "labor and other employments which may be profitable to the Commonwealth," such as the production of cloth. In a sermon on the "Wonder Working Providence," published in 1638, the people of Rowley, Massachusetts, were commended for building a fulling mill which "caused their little ones to be very diligent in spinning cotton and wool." In 1640 the Massachusetts General Court required town magistrates to see "what course may be taken for teaching the boys and girls in all towns the spinning of yarne." And in 1656 Massachusetts ordered that "all hands not necessarily employed on other occasions, [such] as women, boys, and girls, are hereby enjoined to spin according to their skill and ability." [8]

The employment of children, however, was never merely a Puritan or a New England practice. Quakers also believed that children should be taught to work at an early age, and the Great Law of the Province of Pennsylvania provided that all children "of the age of twelve years shall be taught some useful trade or skill, to the end that none may be idle, but the poor may work to live and the rich if they become poor may not want." [9]

Apparently there were no exceptions. Virginia colonists, the first Englishmen to settle in America (a lonely outpost in Maine excepted), were the first to exploit children. Beginning in 1619, hundreds of English pauper children were kidnaped, sent to Virginia where workmen were badly needed, and bound out to service; youngsters who worked without pay were cheap and useful. The prevailing social ethic was expressed by the framers of a Virginia statute of 1646 who commended the "laudable custom" in England of binding out children, and who believed in work "for the better educating of youth in honest and profitable trades and manufactures and also to avoid sloth and idleness wherewith such young children are easily corrupted."

This same statute noted that parents "through fond indulgence or perverse obstinacy" were failing to put their children to work, and it ordered county commissioners to select poor children seven or eight years old and send them to Jamestown to be employed in the public flax house.[10] Despite such acts, the early introduction of Negro slavery in the South allowed that region to escape, for the time being, the more gross and abusive forms of child exploitation that were common in Europe and in other parts of America.

In the North, hard work for the young continued to prevail, especially in the eighteenth century when a spinning craze swept the region as ties with England became strained. Persistent efforts to expand the early textile industry, with reliance upon children to supply most of the necessary labor, served both the Colonial economy and the growing national impulse. In 1751 the Society for Encouraging Industry and Employing the Poor was organized with the double purpose of promoting the manufacture of woolens and other cloth and of employing "women and children who are now in a great measure idle." In 1767 Governor Sir Henry Moore of New York proudly stated: "Every house swarms with children set to work as soon as they could spin or card." A tax was imposed on carriages to support a linen-making shop which, it was hoped, would provide employment for the poor, "especially women and children and [thus] lessen the burden of caring for them." One manufactory in Boston was cited because it employed "not less than twelve hundred persons chiefly women and children." Such philanthropists as Matthew Carey followed in the wake of this tradition by warmly praising industrial growth precisely because it furnished so large a field of employment for children, sparing men for the essential needs of agriculture.[11]

By the late eighteenth century, with the introduction of power machinery, the substitution of machine for skilled, hand production, the spread of factories, and the growth of mill towns in America, child labor loomed large. As in England, the practice had become more and more profitable for employers, who came to rely on it as a valuable resource with which to offset the relative lack of adult labor in the new nation.

"Friends of industry" nevertheless continued to justify child labor with old moral arguments. In 1789 a petition in behalf of one of the first cotton factories in America (in Beverly, Massachusetts) stated that it would "afford employment to a great number of women and children, many of whom will be otherwise useless, if not burdensome to society." In Pawtucket, Rhode Island, in 1790, Samuel Slater, the "father of American manufacturing," manned his first factory entirely with youngsters from seven to twelve years of age. When the new nation sought ways of developing its infant industries in order to foster domestic manufactures, Alexander Hamilton, in his *Report* of 1791, noted that "children are rendered more useful by manufacturing establishments than they otherwise would be." The influential *Niles Register* asserted that factory work does not demand able-bodied men and is, in fact, "better done by little girls from six to twelve years old."[12] An advertisement in the Baltimore *Federal Gazette* of January

4, 1808, stated: "This [Baltimore Cotton] manufactory will go into
operation this month, where a number of boys and girls, from eight
to twelve years of age are wanted. . . . It is hoped that those citizens
having a knowledge of families, having children destitute of employment, will do an act of public benefit, by directing them to the
institution."

The presence of so many young children in factories often created
discipline problems. To punish youngsters for carelessness or misbe-
havior, or to keep them awake, employers frequently resorted to
corporal punishment; the "whipping room" was an adjunct in most
cotton mills, although sometimes the discipline took more inhumane
forms.[13] Nevertheless, given the choice, most millowners still preferred to hire children rather than adults. Above all, they were
cheaper. But it was also believed they were more tractable, reliable,
and industrious, quicker, neater, and more careful, and, as labor
unions developed, less likely to strike. Equally important was the fact
that child labor depressed the entire wage scale, thus driving adult
wages down as well. So child labor continued to increase in New
England just as it had grown in old England, especially during the
early nineteenth century as roads, canals, and railroads opened the
West to settlement, broadening the market for manufactured goods
while creating adult labor shortages in some Eastern districts.

An editorial in the *Manufacturers' and Farmers' Journal* in 1820
predicted that the certainty of finding employment for all their healthy
children seven years of age and older would lead parents to choose
New England rather than the newer Western states as a place of residence. By that year, according to the *Digest of Manufactures,* children
comprised 43 per cent of the labor force in the textile mills of Massachusetts, 47 per cent in Connecticut, and 55 per cent in Rhode
Island.[14]

In 1829 Frances Wright, the noted English reformer, addressed an
American audience on the subject of child labor and warned: "you
will soon have . . . [your children] as in England, worked to
death." [15] By that time, however, child labor conditions in England,
especially in the textile industry centered in Lancashire, were so bad

that they no longer could be ignored or denied. Protests against the evil began to be heard.

Among the first to record their displeasure and concern was a group of Manchester physicians who, in 1789, aroused by an epidemic of fever which took a frightful toll of child laborers in the noisy, humid cotton mills, denounced what they felt to be mere commercialism fattening off the child slaves.

Later, Lord Ashley (Earl of Shaftesbury), a humanitarian who devoted a great deal of time and self-sacrificing zeal on behalf of helpless children, took up the cause. With Charles Kingsley, Frederic Maurice, Sir Robert Peel, Robert Owen, Michael Thomas Sadler, and others, he demanded a parliamentary investigation of child labor. When carried out and made public, the probe shocked the nation's conscience. Prompted by the obvious evils, Lord Macaulay in 1848 predicted that England's "overworked boys will become a feeble and ignoble race of men, . . . the parents of a more feeble progeny," forcing the nation "to yield the foremost place among commercial nations . . . to some people pre-eminently vigorous in body and in mind." [16]

Charles Dickens satirized the manufacturers of "Coketown" who regarded their property rights as far more sacred than the preservation of human health or life, and who were "ruined" every time restrictive legislation was proposed, periodically threatening to "pitch their property into the Atlantic" rather than submit to any restriction. The poets also contributed their verse on behalf of the children, including Elizabeth Barrett Browning's well-known work "The Cry of the Children," which helped to awaken England's sleeping conscience. As a result, beginning in 1802 and continuing into the next century, Parliament passed a series of acts designed to abolish child slavery.[17]

Although the evil of child labor in the United States was not as widespread as it was abroad, it too came under attack. Yet it was not the employment of young children under horrible conditions, as in England, that aroused concern and a demand for legislative relief. Rather, it was want of education. The religious exercises of New Englanders caused them to place a peculiar emphasis on education.

Puritanism maintained that the individual came into direct contact with God and learned His will through reading the Bible, which was the source of truth, inspiration, and revelation. It was therefore essential that youngsters learn to read. Besides this religious imperative, during the late eighteenth and early nineteenth centuries it was widely assumed that universal education was essential for the welfare of the Republic and, indeed, for the survival of democracy itself.

In 1813 the Connecticut legislature was not so concerned that the very young toiled many hours under unhealthy conditions (for industry was a virtue and idleness a sin); more troubling, a seventy-two- to eighty-four-hour work week left little time or energy to attend school. Thus Connecticut passed a law requiring all children working in factories to be instructed in reading, writing, and arithmetic. The statute did not exclude even the youngest children from industry; rather, it made their labor acceptable by eliminating its one objectionable feature.

Citizens of Massachusetts, the state most involved in the growing textile industry, were also troubled by the fact that work interfered with early education. In 1825 a Committee on Education registered its concern over "the care of young persons engaged in manufacturing establishments whose constant occupation in their daily tasks" was causing them to "gather . . . a crust of ignorance." Eleven years later, Massachusetts passed a law similar to Connecticut's, with the added provision that children under fifteen could not be employed unless they had attended school for at least three months in the preceding year. By 1850 Rhode Island and Pennsylvania had passed similar statutes.[18]

While educational needs provoked an initial concern over child labor, deplorable working conditions also came under attack. At its 1832 convention, the New England Association of Farmers, Mechanics and Other Workingmen condemned child labor because of the evils of the system itself: "Children should not be allowed to labor in the factories from morning till night, without any time for healthy recreation and mental culture," its members declared, for it "endangers their . . . well-being and health"; regulation was needed.[19]

This was a time when labor unions were forming, bringing to

prominence a new phase of the child labor problem. As concerned with the problem of hours as it was with schooling, organized labor demanded a shorter work day for minors, probably in the hope of using it as an entering wedge to limit adult hours. And the unions correctly noted that competition from children depressed wage scales, an argument frequently used by later opponents of child labor. It was not surprising then, that the first proposal to establish a minimum age for factory workers was made at a National Trades' Union convention in 1836.[20]

Responding to such pressure, Massachusetts in 1842 limited the workday for children under twelve to ten hours. In the same year Connecticut passed a similar law, but one that applied to children under fourteen. Not until six years later was the first minimum-age law passed, by the state of Pennsylvania, which in 1848 established a twelve-year-old minimum for work in cotton, woolen, and silk mills. This relatively high standard was followed by a nine-year minimum-age in Connecticut in 1855, and a ten-year limit in Massachusetts in 1866.[21] Thus, while regulation grew, it was still possible for hard-pressed families to move from one state to another to keep all hands at work.

Clearly, no single solution to the child labor problem was evident from the start. But by mid-century, when child labor and education statutes of one kind or another had been enacted in New England and most other Northern states, many of the fundamentals of child labor reform were already present,[22] including public acceptance of the child's right to secure an education and be protected from exploitation —or perhaps a public feeling that the protection of the child was essential to the development of the state.

In actual practice, however, early government measures did little to translate rights into realities. To begin with, they required no proof of age. Most contained no enforcement provisions, and their wording was so ambiguous that employers could easily circumvent them. Typical were the New Hampshire and Maine laws of 1847–1848 which stated that no child could be required to work more than ten hours a day—but which allowed employers to escape these provisions by claiming that extra work was not "required" but voluntary, since a contract, even if it called for a twelve-hour day, was construed as a voluntary agreement. In Massachusetts, New Jersey, and Rhode Island, the only punishable violations of child labor laws were those committed "knowingly," another obvious loophole. And in most states children could legally work at a younger age, or for longer hours, than provided by statute if they had their parents' consent, if they were orphans, or if they were helping to support disabled parents.[23] Thus the laws failed to protect those youngsters most in need of protection.

The inevitable result of these shortcomings was that large numbers of very young children continued to work for long hours under deplorable conditions. The public had little real knowledge of the actual number of employed youngsters because there were no child labor statistics. But as late as 1869 the *New York Times* warned its readers that "a great multitude of the [nation's] youth are growing up, stunted in body, and with not even the rudiments of school training, a prey to the insatiable requirements of industry and capital." [24] The situation worsened as industry grew, as textile cities sprung into being, and as immigrants began to replace Yankee stock for whom mill life had become less attractive.

Post–Civil War America experienced unparalleled industrial growth. Railroad mileage, iron and steel tonnage, agricultural production, and almost every other activity mushroomed. As industry became increasingly mechanized, the output of manufactured goods increased by twenty times by the 1890's, making America, in the quantity and value of her products, the leading industrial nation in the world.[25] The revolution in American life contrasted sharply to the predominantly rural society of the ante-bellum years.

The swift and enormous growth of the factory system and its repetitive processes swept more children into industrial occupations. Not only the entrepreneur but society at large, in fact, sought to reap the economic benefits of using child operatives. Many Americans, not heartless in their grasp for money or power, were caught up in enormous opportunities for personal gain. Neither the dominant laissez-faire economic ethic nor prevailing social attitudes restrained such social practices. The former condemned as unscientific, irrational, and unjust any interference with the "natural harmony" of the economic order; the latter—the Puritan ethic of hard work, the tradition of American individualism with its emphasis on personal initiative and self-reliance, and the Horatio Alger myth with its glorification of youthful labor—were reinforced by the so-called Gospel of Wealth, which emphasized the moral duty of the individual to acquire property and accumulate riches.[26]

Immigration, too, had its effect on child labor. Fourteen million aliens, mostly peasants from southern and eastern Europe, streamed into the United States between 1860 and 1900, settling for the most part in the urban-industrial Northeast. The poorly paid foreigners usually needed extra income to survive, and their wives and children were not unused to work, so immigrant children entered the labor force in large numbers.[27]

The 1870 census, the first to note the number of child workers in America, documented the breadth of the evil and aroused new interest in the subject; at least some consciences were stirred. In 1872 Charles Loring Brace devoted a portion of his *The Dangerous Classes of New York* to child labor and the factory system. Later, Jacob Riis, in *The Children of the Poor,* a sequel to his widely read *How the Other Half Lives,* exposed the gross evasion of New York's child labor laws.

More important, by the 1870's organized groups, such as political parties and a growing number of labor unions, recognized the dangers of premature employment and spoke out against it. Thus in 1872 the Prohibition party included a clause in its national platform condemning child labor—the first political party of any consequence to take such a stand. In 1876 the Working Men's party, a radical labor union, proposed laws barring the employment of children under fourteen in industry. At about the same time the Knights of Labor took notice of children under fifteen laboring in workshops, mines, and factories and urged that such practices be prohibited. In 1880, when the United States census revealed that more than a million children between the ages of ten and fifteen (about one out of every six in that age group) were gainfully employed, the Greenback party demanded that all children under fourteen be prohibited from factory work.[28]

The American Federation of Labor, at its first annual convention in 1881, adopted a resolution calling upon the states to bar children under fourteen from all gainful employment. In 1897 the AFL advocated passage of a constitutional amendment to empower federal regulation of child labor (a position it later reversed and then supported again).[29]

The attack gained force in 1883 when a United States Senate probe into the relations between capital and labor publicized the deplorable conditions under which children worked. The Democratic party adopted the following plank at its 1892 convention: "We are in favor of the enactment by the states of laws for abolishing the notorious sweating system, for abolishing contract convict labor, and for prohibiting the employment in factories of children under fifteen years of age." [30]

The rise and growth of socialism in America during the late nineteenth century directed attention to this as well as to other evils in the industrial order. The 1904 Socialist party platform pledged to "watch and work, in both the economic and political struggles . . . for the complete education of children and their freedom from the workshop." [31] Although most Americans rejected radicalism, the Socialists' revelation of exploitation and industrial abuses, and their indictment of the capitalist order, contained much truth; they helped stir public opinion and develop a reformist attitude even among many who were not personally oppressed, such as members of the nation's women's clubs.

The postwar domestic revolution had accelerated the spread of women's clubs, culminating in 1890 in the creation of the General Federation of Women's Clubs. By the turn of the century the organization could boast of several hundred thousand members, and while its avowed objective was "literary, artistic, or scientific culture," its members often spoke on public issues. At its fourth biennial convention in 1898, the Federation adopted a series of labor resolutions, one of which called for an end to child labor. After the turn of the century, having created a Child Labor Committee, it urged that "every woman in the General Federation . . . be a 'committee of one' to use all possible influences against anything which dwarfs the minds and bodies of the children." Local chapters set up their own child labor committees, and in state after state women's clubs helped fight for binding child labor laws.[32]

The most important body working to regulate child labor during these years was the National Consumers' League. Founded in 1890 as the Consumers' League of the City of New York, it sought to enlist the interest and influence of consumers to improve working conditions through publicity and legislation. From the outset the League engaged in vigorous campaigns against tenement sweatshops, starvation wages, excessive working hours, and child labor.[33]

The League's general secretary and leading spirit was the fiery Florence Kelley, Hull-House resident and chief factory inspector of Illinois. A large woman with a hot temper, Mrs. Kelley was an explosive, determined, and deeply emotional person with strong reasoning power and a deep concern for others.[34] Educated at Cornell and the University of Zurich, she was a licensed attorney, a translator of Friedrich Engels, and an avowed American Socialist. With her radicalism, however, she possessed a unique combination of varied experience and tactical shrewdness. She spoke extremely well and often passionately. When moved by what she believed to be social injustice or callous unconcern for others, she was a terrifying opponent for those who faced her on the public platform. Working children in America had no wiser and more helpful friend than Florence Kelley, who believed that if parents could not provide their children with proper care and education, then the government had to assume the task.

In her annual reports as chief factory inspector of Illinois, she vividly publicized the unhealthy conditions under which many children toiled in the stockyards, glass factories, and garment industry sweatshops. These moving accounts of conditions as they really existed, portrayed for the first time by a public official, were largely responsible for passage of the Illinois Factory Act of 1893, a model law which at the time marked the most advanced state control over industry in America.[35]

When in 1897 she was removed from office for political reasons, Mrs. Kelley began to write more and to travel widely, speaking throughout the country on behalf of better working conditions and sound labor legislation. In 1899 she assumed leadership of the newly created National Consumers' League, located in New York City, a post she held until her death in 1932. In all the industrial states, League chapters had enormous influence in publicizing existing evils and the need for better labor standards, as well as in drafting laws to prohibit child labor and improve other areas of industrial life.

The growing social concern that followed the Civil War bore some fruit. As early as 1867 Massachusetts instituted the nation's first factory inspection, thus marking the beginning of enforcement procedures for labor legislation. Connecticut followed suit two years later. Between 1885 and 1889 ten states passed minimum-age laws, while six prescribed maximum hours for child workers. The first nightwork provision was enacted in 1888 when Massachusetts passed a law prohibiting children under fourteen from working between the hours of 7 P.M. and 6 A.M. In 1889 New York State passed similar legislation, setting an age limit of eighteen for boys and twenty-one for girls between the hours of 9 P.M. and 6 A.M.; Minnesota followed this lead in 1895, Ohio in 1898, and Michigan and Wisconsin in 1899. Seven other states enacted their first child labor laws in the 1890's.[36]

These developments nevertheless failed to stem the tide of child labor. In fact, the number of children at work continued to increase. Trade unions had spoken out against the evil, but they were accused of selfishness. Women's clubs were committed to the abolition of child labor, but they were charged with feminine sentiment. Socialists were without power or much influence, and party platforms, like many laws, were forgotten after they were drafted and adopted.

Except for the National Consumers' League and a relatively few enlightened reformers, society had not awakened to the injustice.

Most Americans still believed that hard work was good for youngsters —it prevented juvenile delinquency and female promiscuity, and it was the first rung on the ladder to success. In any event, it was assumed that only a small number of children were forced to labor, usually in support of needy widowed mothers. The 1890 census, however, showed the extent to which the evil had grown: more than 1,500,000 children between the ages of ten and fifteen were gainfully employed, more than 18 per cent of the youngsters between those ages—a stark revelation of popular indifference.[37] Only an aroused and well-organized public could move state legislatures, whose members were often controlled by powerful economic interests that profited from the practice.

Most important, something had to be done about conditions in the South, a region that by the late nineteenth century desperately needed child labor legislation. Its climate, abundant rainfall, fairly productive soil, and Negro slavery had made the Old South largely an agricultural rather than an industrial community. Beginning in 1820 a few factories (chiefly cotton mills) and mines had been established there, and by 1860 the region contained approximately 450 cotton mills with one million spindles and fifty thousand looms, employing some forty thousand workers.[38] Like its other plants and few iron foundries—indeed, the entire economic structure of the South—these mills were ruined by the Civil War.

After the war and Reconstruction, when the South again fell under the control of conservative Democrats, large social and economic problems remained. Poverty was widespread, and many of the South's young men, those best able to bear the burdens of rebuilding the region, had been killed or maimed. When new political and civic leaders—Henry W. Grady, Francis W. Dawson, Daniel A. Tompkins, Ellison Smyth, and others—exhorted their fellows to build a new and a greater South on a solid industrial foundation, desperate Southerners heeded the call, and industrial progress became almost an obsession.[39] Blessed by proximity to raw materials, especially cotton, easy access to coal fields, and abundant water power (as well as Yankee capital, as it turned out), the new entrepreneurs claimed that prosperity would return to the region once factories were built and employment was provided for its impoverished farm dwellers, who would gladly trade low wages for their wretched rural existence.

During the last three decades of the nineteenth century, manufacturing of various kinds made tremendous advances in the South, especially in Tennessee, Kentucky, and Virginia, where fuel was cheap, and in Georgia, Alabama, and the Carolinas, where the easy harnessing of water power encouraged the building of cotton mills, in some cases as an adjunct to New England corporations. An immense amount of capital and human energy went into the cotton mill campaign, which became a great folk movement. White Southerners in all walks of life were gripped by an almost religious enthusiasm.

In 1880 there were 667,000 spindles in all the Southern states, less than 5 per cent of the national total. Between 1880 and 1890, capital invested in the manufacture of cotton rose from $22,000,000 to $113,000,000, and the number of cotton mills from 180 to 412. In 1900, when the value of Southern manufactured goods surpassed that of agricultural, there were seven million spindles in the area, some 25 per cent of the national total. By 1904 the South operated more than nine hundred mills, and by 1915 it could boast of having over 40 per cent of the nation's spindles and more cotton mills than all the other states combined.[40] In no section of the country was economic progress more rapid. But just as the shadow of Negro slavery had hung over the cotton fields of the Old South, so the shadow of child slavery hung over the cotton mills of the New South.

Almost all Southern mill operatives were native whites; Negroes simply were not hired, and few immigrants settled in the region. It was easy to persuade vast numbers of impoverished white sharecroppers, tenants, and depressed farmers to abandon the exhausted, ruined land for the bright promise of the mill.[41] The pittance wages seemed generous to many of the refugees from the eroded hillside farms and isolated coves of the Appalachian Mountains. In fact, these laborers from rural areas, inured to hard work in which the whole family participated, regarded the factories as institutions created to deliver them and the South from poverty. Entire families cheerfully

expected to work in the mills just as they had on the farms. The inevitable results were paternalistic mill villages and an enormous
growth in child labor.

Company-owned mill villages originated out of necessity: housing
near the mills was inadequate to meet the influx of workers. Since
rural folk were unable to build or buy their own homes, they had no
choice but to live in company-owned houses built along with the
mill.[42] The terms naturally were set by the mill managers, who
favored families with many children, especially widows with youngsters. Mill owners later claimed they were forced to hire children,
that unless they did so, families would go elsewhere to work. In fact,
they usually insisted that each household supply its quota of operatives. Sometimes parents had to sign contracts binding themselves
and their children to mill work; sometimes only their children were
so bound.[43]

Not all villagers, however, were unhappy with mill and village life.
The promise of regular pay and the opportunity to handle even a
little money—a rarity on the farm—plus better homes, more food and
clothing, and contact with other people all made mill life seem more
attractive for many of the former Piedmont tenants and mountain
farmers. But the system obviously exploited children.

Aside from the fact that children worked for lower wages, Southern mill owners preferred them to adults because their speed and
agility were more valuable than adult experience. Adults whose
hands were gnarled by years of farm work allegedly were unfit for
the handling of cotton in process. As a result, families moving to
mill villages might find no work available for fathers, many of whom
thereupon lived off the labor of their children.[44]

While the criticism of Southern operators was similar to that
leveled against the mill owners of New England, there were special
problems in combating child labor in the South. Most Southern cotton
mill operators were rampantly independent and unwilling to submit
to what they considered undue control by the state. Southerners argued
that legislation should not interfere with the authority of the parents
(especially the father) over the family. Furthermore, the laissez-faire

attitude of state officials toward industry was slower to give way in the South than elsewhere, not only because of the long and historic tradition of localism, but simply because manufacturing on any large scale was a recent development.

Southern mill owners and operators usually were the most trusted and respected members of their communities. They looked upon themselves, and they were looked upon by others, as altruists and benefactors despite the working conditions they oversaw. They were the trustees of the economic aspirations of their communities and the whole South. The use of women and children in the mills, it was argued, was not avarice but philanthropy. Were the owners and operators not performing an act of charity by providing a livelihood for families that would otherwise be destitute? In 1880 Francis W. Dawson, a forceful propagandist for child labor in the South, contended that employment in the mills subjected the poor whites "to elevating social influences, . . . and improves them in every conceivable aspect." [45]

Certainly many of the mill owners were not consciously inhumane. Some sincerely felt they were raising the living standards of many of the socially backward people who flocked to the mills. And because for some of the families factory and village life was a distinct improvement over the isolated log-cabin, salt-pork, and peach-brandy existence from which they had come, it was difficult to condemn the system as an unmitigated evil.

Nor was the argument used earlier in New England—that child labor was bad because it deprived youngsters of an education—very effective in the South. Unlike Puritan New England the South had no tradition of free public education; and many of the young mill hands would not have been formally educated had they stayed on the farms. Some of the working children, not knowing better, preferred a job in the mill to school. Perhaps more important, parents who frequently lacked an education themselves, objected to their children "wasting time" by attending school. Seeing no need for education, recognizing no differences between agricultural and factory work, they felt the children should continue to do their part to help support the family, just as they had done on the farm. Some of the most devoted advocates of child labor, then, were the young themselves and their own parents.[46]

Equally important, however, was Southern resentment of "Northern interference." Was not agitation over child labor provoked by Northern meddlers in a concerted attempt to reduce the advantages of Southern mills, ruin Southern competition, and retard Southern production? While in effect an admission that industrial prosperity was more important than the protection of children, the question was nevertheless easily answered in a region still sore from the wounds of the Civil War and Reconstruction. And the prevailing hostility toward organized labor (an advocate of child labor control) naturally strengthened the opposition to restrictive laws. So it was that social customs, economic needs, and public feeling combined to retard the growth of child labor reform in the South.[47]

By 1900 child labor in the South had therefore become the usual practice, especially in the production of textiles. Almost 25,000 children under the age of fifteen worked in Southern factories, an increase of almost three times since 1890. Some 90 per cent of these youngsters were employed in the four leading textile states of North and South Carolina, Georgia, and Alabama, where there were no child labor or compulsory education laws whatsoever, and where the illiteracy rate of children between the ages of ten and fifteen in the mill districts was about three times as high as it was throughout the rest of the states. A former president of the Cotton Manufacturers' Association declared that the adoption of a minimum working age of fourteen would close every mill in North Carolina—simply because 75 per cent of the spinners in that state were under fourteen.[48]

While the total number of working children in the South was far less than in the North, the proportion of child to adult laborers was almost four times greater below the Mason-Dixon line. Between 1880 and 1900 the percentage of children under fifteen in the nation's factory workforce had been cut in half, but in the South it had remained the same.[49]

Yet, despite growing awareness and the passage of various laws, neither North nor South could boast by the turn of the century that much had been done to eradicate the evil. Although twenty-eight states had passed some kind of protective measure for child workers by 1900, legislative remedies remained ineffective. The typical statute was limited to children employed in mining or manufacturing; thus tenement home work and the street trades (newsboys, peddlers, delivery and messenger boys, and so forth), to say nothing of farm and domestic labor, were not affected by the law, which usually set a minimum working age of ten or twelve, fixed maximum hours at ten or more per day, and contained some vague and limited requirements as to school attendance and literacy.

In only eight states were children protected against night labor, 10 P.M. being the retiring hour for those under fourteen years of age.[50] Most of the laws were loosely drawn and full of exemptions, and enforcement was lax.[51] As a result, a great many children throughout the country continued to work, either legally or illegally, for paltry wages and under harsh and demoralizing conditions.

The actual extent of child labor in America was made evident by the 1900 census, which showed that 1,750,178 children between ten and fifteen were engaged in gainful occupations, an increase of over 1,000,000 during the preceding thirty years. This figure did not include the large number of working children under ten who were not recorded by the census.[52] A conservative estimate including these youngsters put the total over two million. Many descended into the dark and dangerous coal mines each day, or worked above ground in the coal breakers, where harmful clouds of dust were so thick that light could scarcely penetrate even on the brightest days. Others were forced to crouch for hours at a time and face the blinding glare and stifling heat of glass factory furnace rooms. Many children spent their days or nights in the dull, monotonous, noisy spinning rooms of cotton mills, where humid, lint-filled air made it difficult to breathe, and where they were kept awake by cold water thrown in their faces. Others, perhaps only five or six years old, shucked oysters and

picked shrimp. Some worked in fruit and vegetable canneries sixteen hours a day, seven days a week, in sheds exposed to the weather.
Some two million American children were in these ways being robbed
of their natural heritage—a healthy and happy upbringing—and even
of life itself.

II

The National Child
Labor Committee

Although reform had been brewing for some time, child labor first became a matter of widespread public concern in the early twentieth century. Since the 1830's, as we have seen, a small but growing number of citizens had complained of the flagrant misuse of children in industry; over the years their efforts to arouse public opinion and end the abuses through legislation were largely unsuccessful. While early statutes acknowledged the inherent malignancy of the evil, they were limited in scope and generally unenforceable. In the early twentieth century, as interest in the problem spread, there was a growing feeling that public attention must be directed to securing more effective laws. To achieve this end it was necessary to create and then coordinate anti–child labor organizations.

The organized child labor movement was not an isolated phenomenon but rather an integral part of the so-called Progressive movement, a broad, general campaign in late nineteenth- and early twentieth-century America to establish minimum standards of public health, social well-being, economic security, and political worth.[1] It was a time when millions of Americans, vitally concerned about themselves, their neighbors, and the future of their country, seemed willing, if not eager, to learn of and atone for their sins.

As Robert Bremner has shown, the appearance of the professional
social worker in the 1890's signalled a new approach to the problem of poverty. Discarding traditional shibboleths about the poor,
pioneer social workers set out to gather the facts. In light of their
findings, the dominant public view of poverty as natural, inevitable,
and a penalty for individual faults was no longer tenable.[2] Poverty
was revealed as a social condition, the result of circumstances beyond
the individual's control. It was due, said Robert Hunter, a pioneer
investigator, "to certain social wrongs that must be put right," including child labor.[3] About and after 1900, social workers demanded
government intervention—municipal, state, and federal—in behalf
of the poor, the weak, and the young.

Social workers were not alone in their quest. Other aroused citizens
probed the nation's political, economic, and social lives and pricked
the public conscience with a literature of moral protest. They exposed
and attacked the city's squalor, the poverty and degradation of the
industrial order, the waste of the nation's physical and human resources, and the graft and corruption in its economic and political life.

Yet for every evil there appeared to be a remedy—the regulation
of big business, the direct election of United States Senators, the
promotion of women's rights, the reform of marriage and divorce
laws, the enactment of pure food and drug legislation, the preservation of the nation's resources, and so on. Full of buoyant optimism,
men and women banded together in public agencies and private
societies to ameliorate and counteract the widespread malaise.

Above all, this campaign for betterment focused upon the child.
For various reasons, including a rapidly declining birthrate that had
aroused universal concern and cries of "race suicide," almost every
individual or agency working for social improvement recognized the
rights and needs of children. In fact, even the normally apathetic,
or those who might have become hardened to the appeals of suffering
adults, were aroused to action by "the bitter cry of children" in distress. If the nation's forests, mines, waterways, and soil were to be
saved for the future, shouldn't the nation's children also be protected? President Theodore Roosevelt, in supporting conservation,

would add: "If you do not have the right kind of citizens in the future, you cannot make any use of the natural resources." [4]

The child was the key to social control; children of the present would become the citizens of the future. And if later generations were to have the strength of mind and body to be good self-supporting citizens, they had to be protected as children. To allow them to be abused was not merely a personal injustice but a social one; to expose the nation's youngsters to evil influences was to endanger the future welfare of the country. No wonder that reports of uneducated, underfed, and overworked children alarmed and even outraged middle-class morality, especially after the census of 1900 revealed a sizable increase in the number of working children.

The child-saving campaign embraced many programs: the creation of children's aid societies; the transfer of children from almshouses to private homes for better care; efforts to reduce · infant mortality; the establishment of houses of correction, juvenile courts, probation systems, parks, playgrounds, and public baths; widows' pensions; improved schools and curricula as well as compulsory attendance laws; and, above all, a crusade against child labor.[5]

Among its many efforts to improve labor conditions, the National Consumers' League in 1902 widely circulated copies of the Massachusetts child labor statute as a "Standard Child Labor Law," recommending it as the best yet attained—"so good, . . . and so reasonable as to serve for some time as a model upon which all other states may well frame their statutes." [6] The American Academy of Political and Social Science, at its 1902 annual meeting in Philadelphia, devoted an entire session to "The Child Labor Problem" and published the proceedings in its *Annals*.[7] Father John A. Ryan, a young liberal Catholic clergyman and student of economics who would later be a leader in the fight for social justice both within and without the Church, advocated a minimum working age of sixteen, contending publicly that until that age "children are not, as a rule, sufficiently strong to work day after day under the direction of an employer. Besides," he went on, "if they are taken out of school at an earlier period, they get less than a fair protection of the educational oppor-

tunities so generally provided by the state for the benefit of all," and
"their share in the industrial opportunities that depend so largely
upon education is likewise diminished." 8

The extent and depressing effects of child labor was revealed
afresh for the public in the anthracite coal strike of 1902. The work
stoppage in the coal fields directed attention both to the number of
child laborers in the Pennsylvania mines and to the way in which they
were so generally exploited, if not abused, in that industry. The
hopeless outlook of the children doomed to such labor provoked a
wave of public indignation against the practice.9

The national magazines began to take up the broad question.
Poole's Index to Periodical Literature listed sixty-nine articles under
the heading of "Child Labor" from 1902 to 1906, whereas only four
such articles were listed for the prior five-year period. Discussions of
child labor appeared in such influential journals as *McClure's*, *The
Independent,* and *The Outlook,* and in a series of articles by Mrs.
John Van Vorst in the widely circulated *Saturday Evening Post.* The
prophet-poet of democracy, Edwin Markham, created a sensation with
his emotional indictment of child labor, "The Hoe-Man in the Making," which appeared in William Randolph Hearst's *Cosmopolitan.*10

There were also the Socialists, who were not only among the earliest
but probably the most persistent and clamorous critics of child abuse
in industry. They contributed important full-length works devoted to
juvenile emancipation. Ernest Poole, Robert Hunter, and John Spargo,
for example, probed child labor conditions, and in their respective
classics—*The Street: Its Child Workers, Poverty,* and *The Bitter Cry
of the Children*—piled fact upon fact with effective moral persuasion,
an appeal to the minds and hearts of the American people.11 They
and others like them, who struck notes to be echoed and reechoed
during the next decade or two, contributed to the spiritual uprising.

At issue was not the performance of odd jobs or chores around the
house or on the family farm. Nor did the reformers oppose employment for wages outside the home so long as it did not interfere with
the child's physical, mental, and moral growth. They did oppose the
employment of children in any occupation at unfit ages, or for un-

reasonable hours, or under unhealthful conditions, or while they should have been attending school. Advocates of regulation argued that child labor was cruel, stupid, and uneconomical, that it was harmful to the child, that it was unnecessary, and that it was costly. To permit it to continue was therefore contrary to the best interests of the community; every dollar spent in preventing such labor and in promoting the health and education of children was not only a humanitarian gesture but essential for society's welfare and progress. The reformers, in other words, appeared to be as concerned with the adverse economic and social consequences of child labor as with its inhumanity.[12]

Earlier, they admitted, there might have been a need for child labor, but that time had passed. The nation, including the South, had long since reached that stage of economic development which did not require the labor of its children to turn the wheels of industry. (Any industry which, in order to live, required children to work all day or night deserved to die.) To continue the sacrifice was stupid and criminal.

Long hours of taxing labor by young children stifled their bodily growth, as evidenced by the high incidence of tuberculosis, heart strain, anemia, curvature of the spine, and permanent bone and muscle injury (and other diseases and physical deformities) among child laborers. It also stifled their mental and moral growth, for work deprived most youngsters of an education and a proper home life. And insofar as their future earning capacity was concerned, daily rounds of monotonous unskilled drudgery did not prepare youngsters for a healthy, happy, self-supporting adult life. On the contrary, it led to a purposeless one, a life frequently plagued by infirmity, dependency, and delinquency. As the reformers often pointed out, to care for the sick and the injured, the delinquent and the criminal, cost the taxpayers millions of dollars each year. It was, therefore, economical and in the public interest to abolish child labor.[13]

To the argument that it was essential for children of the poor to work in order to help support their families, the reformers replied that the burden of such financial responsibility should not be thrust

upon the children, especially those already handicapped by their desti-
tution. Society should bear the cost, for this was basically a relief
problem. A needy family should be helped by "scholarships" or other
forms of public or private assistance, in amounts equivalent to the
child's earnings or based upon his needs. In that way the child could
attend school and the needy family could live according to reasonable
standards. In any case, reformers demonstrated that the number of
poor widows who were supported by the pittance earned by their
children was indeed very small.[14]

It would be unnecessary for young boys and girls to seek employment in the first place, reformers said, if the family's natural breadwinner, the parent, were paid a living wage. One of the main reasons
he did not receive such a wage was that children in the labor market
depressed the wages of adults forced to compete with them for jobs.
Child labor, then, was a leading cause of as well as an effect of
poverty; it lowered the entire standard of living.[15] As one reformer all
too dramatically put it: "Child laborers at the loom in South Carolina
mean bayonets at the breasts of men and women workers in Massachusetts who strive for a living wage." [16]

Advocates of child-labor control in the South, where the situation
was at its worst, spearheaded the organized reform movement. That
25 per cent of Southern cotton mill operatives were under fifteen had
failed to excite much concern in 1890 when the children numbered
less than nine thousand. But when in 1900 there were almost 25,000
of that age working in Southern factories, certain public-spirited
citizens became aroused.

Perhaps the foremost champion of child-labor legislation in the
South was Edgar Gardner Murphy, Episcopal clergyman, author, and
amateur astronomer. Born in 1869 at Fort Smith, Arkansas, Murphy
was graduated from the University of the South, in Sewanee, Tennes-
see, in 1889. He studied at Columbia University and at the General
Theological Seminary in New York City, and after serving in various
Episcopal churches in Texas, Ohio, and New York, he was called to
St. John's Church in Montgomery, Alabama. There, in 1899 and

after, he became concerned with the social problems of the new industrial order in the South.[17]

Living and working in the midst of the great Southern cotton textile industry, he observed the growing use of child labor and its ugly effects. As each day began with the shriek of whistles at 4:45 in the morning, he heard the tramp of small feet trudging to the mills. Long after dusk he saw the children return home—a pallid, ill-clad, ill-fed little horde, some with hands and fingers and even arms missing, dragging their feet to hovels called homes. Once there, according to his testimony, they would eat only a scant meal or, if too tired to eat, would toss all night in restless sleep and rise in the morning as tired as before. Murphy saw more and more of these fresh young children with clear eyes and supple limbs brought from the fields and hills to work in the prison-like factories where, almost overnight, they were converted into "mill children" with typically pallid faces, tired and battered limbs, and pain-ridden eyes. Through this vicious process of depleting, exhausting labor which robbed them of their strength and their education, the nation's children were converted into human waste.

Alabama had been the first Southern state to enact a child labor law when, in 1887, it passed a statute establishing a fourteen-year age limit for factory workers and an eight-hour day for those under sixteen. While the measure contained no enforcement provisions and thus was not very effective, it nevertheless was an achievement for its day. But before long, as industry grew and Northern mill owners erected plants in the state, the measure was repealed.[18] Thereafter, new child labor bills were regularly brought up—and each year, due largely to the influence of the mill owners, Southerners and others alike, were defeated.

In the late 1890's, after all efforts to get a new and effective child labor law in Alabama had failed, the American Federation of Labor took up the cause. An AFL agent, Irene Ashby, came to Alabama to enlist support in a renewed drive for a child labor law. Her preliminary study showed that Alabama had forty-five cotton mills with a total of 9,049 operatives, about 30 per cent of whom (or 2,747) were children between the ages of ten and fifteen. These youngsters worked twelve hours a day, six days a week, for fifteen to thirty cents a day. When Miss Ashby gave these facts to Edgar Murphy he willingly supported the AFL's attempt to secure a new law.[19]

Murphy did more. Astute enough to realize that popular opposition to organized labor and "Northern interference" would kill any child labor bill if it appeared to be either a labor measure or one imposed from outside the state, he persuaded Miss Ashby and the AFL to withdraw from the stage and turn the movement over to him.

Murphy was well suited to lead. He understood the reasons for the existence of factory child labor and the problems involved in remedying it. He saw that the South's industrial progress was no more than a repetition of what had happened elsewhere when work had shifted from home to factory. Unlike some others, Murphy viewed the employer of child labor not as an unfeeling tyrant but as one who had to keep abreast of the competition to survive. Since child labor was simply part of the system, the remedy lay to a large extent in legislation. But that alone would not be enough. The mass of citizens had to be made to feel strongly responsible for the welfare of those children whom the laws were designed to protect; that would have to be done through education.[20]

Murphy had a sharp pen, and in a series of newspaper articles and pamphlets, which he published and circulated at his own expense, he lashed out against the evils of unregulated child labor. Rejecting the frequent contention that children were better off in the mills than in the fields or on the streets, he pointedly inquired: "Are the probable iniquities of little children under twelve so great that we can save them only by the antidote of sustained labor in the factory for ten or twelve hours a day?"[21]

Child labor, he argued, was not only a moral evil but economically unsound. Likening child labor with slavery, both of which, in his opinion, denied human beings their right to self-realization, he asserted grandly:

More than a generation ago it was argued for the system of slavery that there were good plantations upon which the slaves were well treated. That statement was true, but the argument was weak. The presence of the good plantation could not offset the perils and evils of the system any more than the "good factory" can justify the system of child labor. . . . There can be no "good" child labor. And this system is monstrous, not only in principle, but in results.[22]

Murphy was especially concerned with the end result of child labor, both for the youngsters involved and for the welfare of the region in which they lived. He was among the first to recognize that the abnormal straining of muscles and nerves during immaturity meant permanent injury. While the mill operators contended that the work required of children was light, they did not realize or did not care, as Murphy did, that the nervous tension involved in long hours of monotonous repetition was stupefying.

But Murphy fought the evil not only because premature labor often forced youngsters permanently into the lot of the underprivileged. He also loved the South, and he was convinced that as long as child labor continued the entire region would stagnate. He maintained in forceful phrases that it was in the best interests not only of humanity but of the South's own business and economy to protect its future workers and citizens.

What sort of child labor laws were found elsewhere? If Northern states could protect immigrant children, Murphy said, then the Southern states could and should do the same for their own native-born. He appealed to those mill operators who were motivated by a fear of spreading labor unions, warning that the surest way to lose the fight against organized labor was by opposing reasonable working conditions for children. Do not, he warned, underrate the sentiments which would emerge if the region were aroused to defend its children.[23]

Murphy's articles and pamphlets, written in a logical vein by a native Southerner who by birth and profession was allied with the conservative class, succeeded in arousing some public opposition to child labor. But government action was another story. During the 1900–1901 legislative session, Murphy appeared before joint Alabama House and Senate committees to press for the adoption of a twelve-year minimum age for factory work. Opponents effectively argued that the prosperity of the South depended upon child labor, and that Murphy was a tool of New England industrialists seeking to destroy the South's textile mills. The appeal to fear won the day; the proposed child labor bill was defeated.

Murphy, however, had set his sights on victory. After perceiving the nature of the opposition, which appeared rather ill informed and shortsighted, he brought other resources to bear on the problem. He had the gift of rousing others to his cause, and so in 1901 he and his supporters created the Alabama Child Labor Committee, the first such organization in America. Among its members were former governor and judge Thomas G. Jones; J. A. Phillips, Birmingham's superintendent of schools; Erwin Craighead, editor of the (Birmingham) *Daily Register;* Rev. Neal L. Anderson and Judge J. B. Gaston, also of Birmingham.[24]

Murphy and others of his little band resumed the task of writing and speaking. Taken together, the newspaper articles and leaflets that sprang from the leader's sharp pen constituted the first sizable body of printed material favorable to child labor legislation to be found in the South. One of the most effective pieces of propaganda was *Pictures from the Mills,* a pamphlet showing actual photographs of young operatives at work. Murphy had taken them himself by smuggling his camera into the stifling textile plants.

Murphy traced the defeat of the 1901 child labor bill to the lobbying of an agent of the Dwight Mill at Alabama City, a mill owned by a Massachusetts concern which had also figured in the repeal of the 1887 statute. Feeling that the general attitude in New England might require some revision as well, Murphy and his committee addressed public appeals to the people and press of that area through their pamphlets and the columns of the influential *Boston Evening Transcript.* Their telling argument was that legislative progress in the South had been delayed not only by the opposition of its own citizens but by that of the Yankee owners of Southern mills. Murphy hoped to arouse the New England conscience.[25]

Somehow Murphy won. Alabama's 1903 compromise bill, despite its modest provisions, set the highest child labor standards of any of the Southern industrial states. A twelve-year age limit in factories and a sixty-six-hour week were specified. Although ten-year-olds were permitted to work if orphaned, or if they had dependent parents, and while provisions for inspection and enforcement were lacking, at least a beginning had been made. Best of all, public opinion, not only in Alabama but throughout the South and even the nation, had been stirred.[26]

Yet Murphy was not content with his victory in Alabama. To him the problem was not a local one but a pervasive evil to be dealt with in a larger way. He was gratified by the fact that fifteen states in 1902–1903 managed to get child labor laws on the books, and in seven of these states the statutes were the first of their kind.[27] But this general movement would have gained far more ground if efforts had been coordinated, and if acquired knowledge and hard knocks had been shared. Reform, like big business, needed planning and organization; the reformers and the states had to unite against the injustice.

Murphy made his appeal for a joint effort in an address before the National Conference of Charities and Correction which met in Atlanta in 1903. In both its immediate impression and long-range effect, this talk, referred to a decade later as "the greatest speech against child labor ever," [28] had a tremendous impact. Murphy vividly described the seriousness of the child labor situation and called for a nation-wide crusade to obtain uniform legislation against the evil.[29] Clearly he did not mean federal regulation; he explicitly used the term "national" in its geographic sense, explaining, "The conditions of industry vary so greatly and so decisively from State to State, locality to locality, that the enactment of a federal child labor law, applicable to all conditions under all circumstances, would be inadequate if not unfortunate." [30] Above all, Murphy sought to establish a national organization that would coordinate various anti–child labor activities around the country, promote uniform state legislation, and spearhead a broad campaign against the injustice.

Other developments were pushing in the same direction. In the spring of 1902, at the suggestion of Florence Kelley and Lillian D. Wald (founder and head of the Henry Street Settlement in New York City), the Association of Neighborhood Workers, an organization derived from New York City's thirty-one settlement houses, appointed a Child Labor Committee to investigate the problem in New York. The committee, which included Miss Wald, Mary K. Simkhovitch of Greenwich House, and Pauline Goldmark of the National Consumers' League, was headed by Robert Hunter, chief resident of University Settlement.[31]

Hunter, who was born in Terre Haute and graduated from Indiana University, later served with the Chicago Bureau of Charities. He also had been a resident at Hull-House and the Northwestern University Settlement, where he had written on Chicago's housing problem. (Later he would publish his widely read *Poverty*.) Impetuous and outspoken, Hunter had great energy and the ability to organize reform. He quickly got his committee into action. Raising the necessary funds through public appeal, he hired Helen Marot, a young Philadelphia Socialist and labor reformer, as a full-time investigator. Other social workers assisted her by spending part of their time gathering information on child labor. Their findings showed that a large number of children in New York were either beyond the pale of the state's child labor laws or were working anyway, and that new legislation was essential. Hunter and his colleagues were convinced that a permanent child labor committee was needed; in November 1902 the temporary "Child Labor Committee" became an independent organization known as the New York Child Labor Committee, the second such state body in America.[32]

Like the Alabama committee, which preceded it by a year, the New York group was at first made up mainly of social workers, reformers, academicians, and a few well-to-do bankers and businessmen. Besides Hunter and Florence Kelley, some of the charter members of the New York committee were Felix Adler, founder and head of the

Ethical Culture movement in America and a professor at Columbia University; Hunter's brother-in-law, James G. Phelps Stokes, president of a corporation bearing his name and founder of Hartley House Settlement; William H. Baldwin, Long Island Railroad president; V. Everit Macy, director of the Title Guarantee & Trust Company; and Paul M. Warburg and Jacob A. Schiff, partners in the Kuhn, Loeb Investment Banking Company.[33]

The committee at once enlisted the support of other prominent and wealthy persons, of newspapers, and of religious and civic groups. It waged a campaign of education and propaganda, then turned its energy to a fight for legislation, in which it was eminently successful. In the words of the committee's biographer, "Entering the twentieth century with a formidable child labor problem, New York emerged . . . [a few] years later with one of the highest standards in the United States. That it did so was almost entirely due to the efforts of the New York Child Labor Committee." [34] It harmonized the state's incongruous factory and education laws, succeeded in partially regulating some previously undefined areas, put teeth into the law by including provision for documentary proof of age (not merely parents' affidavits), and strengthened the penal code for violators.

In less than a year this fledgling committee was responsible for the passage of five bills that effected more significant changes in New York's child labor laws than had occurred in the preceding century.[35] Yet it became increasingly evident to the committee that the problem required not only a broader attack but some larger organization to coordinate the activities of other state and local groups and spearhead a nation-wide campaign.

Edgar Murphy, meanwhile, had become secretary of the Southern Education Board, based in New York City, and had thus become acquainted with some of the city's leading reformers, including members of the New York Child Labor Committee, especially Felix Adler. He had talked with Adler about the possibility of creating a national organization. At Adler's suggestion, the New York Child Labor Committee set up a provisional committee composed of himself, William Baldwin, and Florence Kelley, which would confer with Murphy and

other interested citizens on this topic. This committee was also to do
the preliminary work toward creating such an organization, which
everyone in fact seemed to encourage.[36]

The plan called for a national committee made up of members
from throughout the country but run by an executive committee composed of people who lived near enough to New York City, where its
office would be located, to attend regular meetings. While the executive committee would determine policy and legislative goals, day-to-day
work would be under the guidance of a paid, full-time secretary. The
drafting committee invited interested people from all over America,
urging them to attend a meeting at New York's Carnegie Hall to
consider the plan and join the new organization. Thus the National
Child Labor Committee convened its first general meeting on April
15, 1904.[37]

Felix Adler presided with Murphy serving as secretary. Several of
the assembled spoke of the need for more aggressive measures to
protect children from premature employment, whether caused by
greedy industrialists or heedless parents. Then, in a speech worth
quoting at length, Adler stated the need for a national body, which,
he said,

shall be a great moral force for the protection of children. It is to
combat the danger in which childhood is placed by greed and rapac-
ity. Cheap labor means child labor; consequently there results a holo-
caust of the children—a condition which is intolerable.

What we have witnessed is that one state after another, as it
swings into line in the introduction of the factory system, repeats
the experience of the older states, allows its children to be sacrificed,
and learns only after bitter experience that protective legislation is
required. If this danger is met at its very inception, the continuance
of such needless sacrifices may be prevented. The existence of a
National Child Labor Committee acting promptly and aiding to form
public sentiment at the critical moment will prevent the repetition of
this experience in communities which have not yet passed through it.
The Committee thus becomes a great moral force to prevent the relapse
of whole communities into the barbarous conditions which we now see
in certain states.

National bodies are sometimes organized simply as a useful mechanism for the co-ordination of various local movements. The Child Labor Committee should be that, but it should be vastly more. It should represent a wise and genuine statesmanship; it should be, as it is from its membership, authoritative, in order to inspire public confidence; it should not appear to represent the most radical position, pressing for something which the public is not yet ready to concede, but rather the opposite tendency. That for which the Committee stands should be the absolute minimum which the enlightened public sentiment of the community demands. It should be plainly said that whatever happens in the sacrifice of adult workers, the public conscience inexorably demands that the children under twelve years of age shall not be touched; that childhood shall be sacred; that industrialism and commercialism shall not be allowed beyond this point to degrade humanity. Thus the function of the Committee will be a preventive one. By no other means than those that have been suggested can the needless sacrifice of child life be prevented.[38]

Among the more important tasks that would fall to the new committee, according to Adler, would be research and investigation conducted by experts, "since a knowledge of the facts will be the most useful of all means of accomplishing results"—effective legislation. The work of the committee would supplement that of local child labor committees, and in those states where such committees did not exist, it would promote their creation. In addition, its members would work to create an enlightened public opinion throughout the United States; they would testify before legislative bodies and work for the passage and enforcement not only of child labor laws but of laws for sound education, public health, and welfare as well. Finally, the committee would be a medium for the interchange of information, opinion, and literature concerning existing child labor conditions and legislation (or pending legislation) and its enforcement in different localities throughout the country. It would, in short, aim to make the fruits of the experience of each the common possession of all, and thus be an important preventive agency in those communities where the worst effects of the injustice had not yet been experienced.[39]

The historic gathering in Carnegie Hall accepted the fact that the committee would not "promote the interests of suggested federal [child labor] legislation; but by properly informing the public mind and quickening the public conscience, . . . [it would] aid in creating and interpreting a National sentiment upon the subject of child labor —a sentiment which may become intelligently operative under the local conditions and through the specific laws of our states." [40]

Appointed to the executive committee were Adler, Baldwin, Kelley, Murphy, V. Everit Macy, and Paul M. Warburg, founding members of the New York Child Labor Commitee; Robert W. de Forest, corporation lawyer and president of the New York Charity Organization Society; Edward T. Devine, general secretary of that society, editor of *Charities,* and the director of the New York School of Philanthropy; John S. Huyler, president of the Huyler Candy Company; Isaac N. Seligman, investment banker; and John W. Wood, secretary of the Missionary Society of the Protestant Episcopal Church.[41] This eminently respectable group, which would be listed on the Committee's letterhead, appeared to promise substantial support, financial and otherwise.

The new organization was announced in *Charities,* the nation's leading social work journal that later became *The Survey* and *Survey Graphic,* on April 23, 1904. Newspaper comment soon followed. On May 4 the executive committee held its first meeting. Homer Folks, executive secretary of the New York State Charities Aid Association and former Commissioner of Public Charities of New York, was added to the committee. Folks also was named acting chairman to replace Adler who was to be away. Because of ill health and the demands of his other work, Murphy resigned as secretary; Edward T. Devine was appointed his temporary successor. The main order of business was the selection of a permanent general secretary, a position offered to Dr. Samuel McCune Lindsay, an industrial relations expert and sociology professor at the University of Pennsylvania who was on leave serving as Commissioner of Education in Puerto Rico.[42]

Although several more months would pass before the Child Labor Committee's office would be established and the full machinery for its work set in motion, by the time the executive committee held its next meeting in July the new organization was well under way. It had temporarily received from the National Consumers' League, without cost, the use of its office in the United Charities Building. Isaac N. Seligman, chairman of the finance committee, was actively at work raising funds. The Committee had decided not to issue a public appeal but had sent a circular letter to a list of prospective donors, each of whom was asked to give $500. Within a few weeks $8,000 had been raised, and by the end of the year the total was substantially more.[43]

Samuel Lindsay's services as general secretary began on September 1. A native of Pittsburgh and a graduate of the University of Pennsylvania who had studied in Europe, Lindsay was just the executive head the Committee needed—a dauntless leader who was both idealistic and practical.[44] A man of integrity, Lindsay would compromise over minor issues of policy but would never sacrifice important questions of principle. He was well known among important people around the country, including Theodore Roosevelt and William H. Taft, and his personal prestige helped the Committee to a good start. Proving himself of good judgment and executive skill, Lindsay would serve the Committee in one capacity or another until 1935.[45]

He began by establishing a library and compiling a complete bibliography on child labor—books, articles, reports, and so forth. He gathered data from all over the country, including local laws and literature on industrial conditions. A heavy correspondence flowed between his office and those of the secretaries of state and commissioners of labor in every state and United States territory. Officials of many scattered organizations soon heard from him about the work they and others were doing in the struggle to combat child labor and protect the young.[46]

To implement its work in the sections, the executive committee named two full-time assistant secretaries. Owen R. Lovejoy for the North and Alexander J. McKelway for the South.[47] Born in Pennsylvania in 1866, McKelway was nevertheless a Southerner by ancestry and upbringing, having moved to the South as an infant. He was prevented from accepting a job as a page in the United States Senate at $75 a month because his mother insisted that he follow his forefathers into the ministry. After graduation from Hampden-Sydney he attended Virginia's Union Theological Seminary and became an ordained Presbyterian minister in 1891. Later he attended Davidson College in North Carolina, where he obtained the degree of Doctor of Divinity. He meanwhile served as a home missionary and as pastor of a church in Fayetteville. Thus he lived close to the people, the so-called poor whites who flocked to the cotton mills for a meager wage.

In 1897 McKelway became editor of the *Presbyterian Standard* in Charlotte, the heart of North Carolina's mill region. The stodgy *Standard* soon became a dynamic instrument for reform, as McKelway seized the opportunity offered him to awaken the South to its faulty economic practices, especially its blind acceptance of child labor. He made many enemies, but certain friends also, including Edgar Murphy, who stoutly supported his work. It was Murphy's suggestion that the executive committee hire McKelway, and he then urged the cleric-editor to accept.[48]

So Alexander McKelway came to his work—it was to be a lifetime position—as a successful preacher and missionary organizer, and as editor of both a religious weekly and a local daily (the *Charlotte News*). He had traveled throughout the South and had lived in several large cotton-mill towns where he had observed local conditions from top to bottom. In addition to his wide-ranging experience, McKelway had the knack of working well with legislators; he would be an efficient and skillful lobbyist in the states and in the nation's capital.

Like McKelway, Owen R. Lovejoy was born in 1866, came to the National Child Labor Committee from the ministry, and apparently found in social work a medium for the exercise of his passion for service and humanity which the church did not offer. Known as the "children's statesman," Lovejoy became an extremely effective public speaker and propagandist whose name was synonymous with child labor reform.

Born and brought up in Jamestown, Michigan, Lovejoy was graduated from Albion College in 1891; later he received a Master's degree and entered the ministry. He held several Methodist pastorates in Michigan and in 1899 was called to the First Congregational Church of Mount Vernon near New York City. A man of broad interests with a passionate concern for human rights and dignity, he was interested in more than just religious affairs. A Sociological Club which he created often invited noted speakers to its bimonthly meetings at which social and industrial problems were discussed.

During the anthracite coal strike of 1902, Lovejoy and his wife were sent to Pennsylvania by a group of Mount Vernon citizens to observe conditions there. He traveled through the coal regions and came to know the miners and their families, their homes, their work, their pressing ills. He returned to Mount Vernon with a graphic view of the scene. In July 1904 he was asked by the newly formed National Child Labor Committee to return to the coal fields to make a special report on child labor in the coal breakers. Three months later he left his comfortable parish to become the Committee's assistant secretary, a decision he never regretted.[49] In many ways it became another pulpit for him, especially after 1907 when he became its chief executive, traveling throughout the nation to take the child labor problem to the American people.

Lovejoy knew a great deal about child labor both first- and second-hand. One arm bore the scar of an accident he suffered as a boy tending a machine in a Michigan factory. He had seen child labor and its effects in Pennsylvania's coal mines in 1902, and again in its breakers in 1904. And, as he wrote in one of his later reports, "After I had seen those little boys day after day carrying their lunch pails to the breakers every morning like grown men, bending all day over dusty coal chutes, and finally dragging themselves home in the dark at night, I couldn't think of anything else. Sights like that cling to you. I dreamed about those boys." [50]

By the time of the National Child Labor Committee's second general meeting, on November 28, 1904, it had taken its own space in the United Charities Building at 105 East 22nd Street, New York. Permanent officers were elected, and the executive committee was succeeded by a board of trustees. Added to the board was James H. Kirkland, chancellor of Vanderbilt University in Nashville, Tennessee. Felix Adler was chosen chairman, Homer Folks vice-chairman, V. Everit Macy treasurer, and Samuel Lindsay secretary.[51]

Felix Adler (1851–1933) appeared quiet and unobtrusive, yet he was an amazingly energetic and resourceful man driven by a sense of social responsibility. After abandoning the rabbinate, for which he was trained, he began his life's work—formulating and applying "the principles of good living." Dedicated to establishing social justice for all, he became a highly respected leader, whether as head of the Ethical Culture movement or as a social and educational reformer. Thus Adler was not only a founder of the kindergarten movement in America, a professor of social and political ethics at Columbia University, and an author of several books on ethics, politics, and social work, but an outstanding and renowned national figure.[52]

Homer Folks, a true social statesman, was equally respected among his peers. Like Adler a man of tremendous energy and many interests, Folks had become an expert on state and municipal charities, child welfare, public and mental health, and almost every other field of social welfare. He was a man of authority and decisiveness, and the National Child Labor Committee would benefit enormously from his counsel and support as well as his recognized prestige.[53] V. Everit Macy, a banker who would serve as treasurer until 1926, was a man of wealth who gave generously of himself and his money to numerous good causes in education and social welfare.[54]

As a group, the Committee's leaders were widely respected, highly capable, and genuinely interested in the cause. They recognized the need for constructive change but did not allow themselves to be influenced by extreme policies. Research, public education, and minimum-standards legislation would be their initial weapons in the fight for change.

The Committee's general membership was equally impressive. Social workers, church and labor leaders, businessmen, bankers, lawyers, educators, and government officials appeared on its rolls. Robert Hunter; Lillian Wald; Mrs. Emmons Blaine, well-known reformer-philanthropist; Graham Taylor, founder and head of Chicago Commons Settlement House and editor of *The Commons;* Jane Addams, the noted humanitarian; and Ben B. Lindsey, famed Juvenile Court judge of Denver, were members. His Eminence James Cardinal Gibbons of Baltimore and the Right Rev. David H. Greer, Bishop Coadjutor of the Episcopal Diocese of New York, were listed. Organized labor was represented by Edgar E. Clark of the Railway Conductors, and J. W. Sullivan of the International Typographical Union. The Committee also included Alexander J. Cassatt, president of the Pennsylvania Railroad; Stanley McCormick of International Harvester; Adolph S. Ochs, publisher of the *New York Times;* former president Grover Cleveland; Gifford Pinchot, the noted conservationist; Charles W. Eliot, president of Harvard University; John G. Brooks, noted economist and president of the American Social Science Association; Talcott Williams, journalist and chief editorial writer of the *Philadelphia Press;* and Mrs. Sarah S. Platt Decker, president of the General Federation of Women's Clubs.[55]

Although over a third of the forty-six members were from New York, five Southern states and ten others were represented in the membership. About a third of the members were from below the Mason-Dixon line. In addition to board members Murphy and Kirkland, other Southerners included Senator (Pitchfork Ben) Tillman of South Carolina; Hoke Smith, former Secretary of the Interior and a future Georgia governor; Samuel Spencer, president of the Southern Railroad; Clark Howell, editor of the *Atlanta Constitution;* and Judge Noah Feagin of Birmingham, Alabama, a leader in penal reform.[56] As finally constituted, the NCLC emerged as a fairly well balanced and nonpartisan body. In some ways, however, it represented a new approach to social reform, for by obtaining so prominent and influential a national membership it would command a respectful hearing despite its attack upon so controversial an issue.

From the beginning, the Committee was, as Felix Adler stated at its initial meeting, a group of people brought together to become "a moral force" in the land to help safeguard children from the harmful effects of premature labor. Its members did not hope to effect public control over the nation's industrial life or to reshape its social order. Rather they sought to eliminate the injustice of child labor in order to create happier citizens and a more efficient use of the nation's human and physical resources. The object was thus to strengthen and preserve the American system.

Those who joined (like those who get involved in any important movement) did so, no doubt, for various reasons. Wealthy businessmen who did not depend for their livelihood upon cheap child labor could afford to sponsor its regulation. Others may have lent their name to the Committee simply because it was another "good cause," or because it seemed fashionable. The great majority, however, were motivated largely by sympathy for the abused child and a patriotic concern for the nation's future—sentiments deeply held by many Americans during the so-called "Progressive Era." [57] The prevailing passion for self-aggrandizement ought, they felt, to be limited; hence the desire to substitute an ideal of service for that of personal profit and power. As Felix Adler once said, "It is because the chief end of life is money-making that the young child cannot too soon be induced or forced to dedicate himself to the chief end of life. Once Americans realize that life's purpose is not personal aggrandizement but service, not only child labor but every form of social and economic injustice would disappear." [58]

Committee members firmly believed that all people had a right to maximum physical, mental, and cultural development, that society was responsible for the welfare of individuals who were deprived of that right by rapid industrialization (or anything else), and that men could alter their environment and improve society by using knowledge and reason. They were pragmatists in method, convinced that if social issues were brought into focus through research and public education, progressive social change could come about piecemeal through the legislative approach. Enlightened governmental activity was possible. In the words of Samuel McCune Lindsay, to whom fell the task of getting the Committee's work under way:

With the muck-raker and the socialist who gloats over the indecencies revealed by child labor as evidences of the unalterable rottenness of our industrial society, and with the mere sentimentalist who sees none of the practical difficulties or underlying causes of the Child Labor problem, North or South, the National Child Labor Committee has no sympathy. . . . I think I may safely say that the National Committee [members] are meliorists, one and all, that is persons who have a sincere faith in the power of a united effort to ameliorate the conditions brought about by any industrial development or situation, however bad, through the better guidance and application of the laws of natural and economic evolution.[59]

In short, the Committee stood for pure and simple reformism.

III

A Slow Start

THE National Child Labor Committee began its work deeply committed to the cause and hopeful that, with hard work, child labor could be abolished within ten years. The task was to be more arduous than expected.

The first step was the gathering of data. Some general knowledge about child labor was already fairly widespread; it was known that about two million American children under sixteen years of age were at work, that some of them were only six, seven, or eight years old, and that many of them worked for long hours and small wages under adverse conditions. But there had been very little detailed study of child labor—its exact nature, extent, distribution, and, above all, its consequences. Vague general ideas had to be made concrete and specific; unsavory truths had to be publicized by every available means in order to effect legislation to keep children in school and out of shops, factories, and mines.[1]

Where should the Committee begin? Inasmuch as no region or community of the nation was exempt from child labor, the field seemed limitless. Country and city alike were infested with the blight. Little children worked in beet fields and in berry fields, in city tenements and on city streets, in coal mines and in factories, in canneries and in cotton mills. All such enterprises were far-ranging or in widely separated areas.

As one of its earliest activities, the Committee drew up a model bill based on the best features of the Massachusetts, New York, and Illinois child labor statutes. The bill prescribed a minimum working age of fourteen in manufacturing and sixteen in mining; a maximum working day of eight hours; no night work (from 7 P.M to 6 A.M.) for children under sixteen; and documentary proof of age. In 1904 not a single state met all those standards.[2]

McKelway, Lovejoy, and Lindsay then began some scouting trips to observe general conditions in order to plan future detailed investigations. On the basis of their findings, the Committee's early attention focused on the industries where abuses seemed most glaring—in the anthracite mines of Pennsylvania, in the widely scattered glass factories, and in the Southern cotton mills. Next it would concentrate on the Atlantic and Gulf Coast canneries and the street trades, including the night messenger service.[3]

The trio lectured on child labor as it traveled. They talked with elected officials, passed out literature, helped to draft bills, and attended legislative hearings on child labor measures. Lindsay alone traveled more than fifty thousand miles during the first year of the Committee's existence. Besides working with the National Consumers' League and with various women's clubs and other interested groups, McKelway, Lovejoy, and Lindsay devoted a great deal of time to organizing child labor committees in the Carolinas, Georgia, Florida, Ohio, Michigan, Rhode Island, Missouri, Iowa, the District of Columbia, and elsewhere; by September 1905 they had set up seventeen state and local bodies throughout America.[4] Lindsay meanwhile sailed for England to study child labor conditions there. In terms of national and municipal legislation against child labor, England and continental Europe, especially Germany, were far ahead of the United States. It was therefore essential for the Committee to keep abreast of European social legislation, which could be used as a model to improve American standards.[5]

The Committee decided to make the first sustained attack on child labor in Pennsylvania's coal mines. With more than two million school-age children in 1900, Pennsylvania was one of the nation's leading industrial states. And its industries were the very ones in which child labor was most profitably employed—in the production of cotton and silk goods, of glass and, above all, the mining of coal. As many children were employed in Pennsylvania as in New York, Illinois, and Massachusetts combined, or in all the Southern states. Nowhere was there a greater need for strict child labor laws—and in few states were the laws more lax.

The most serious problem was in coal mining, which utilized more children than any other branch of mining or quarrying. Coal, especially anthracite, required preparation before shipment, while other minerals as a rule did not; in preparing the coal for market, children were used in large numbers. In Pennsylvania, where the coal output was greater than that of any other state, a boy could work in an anthracite mine at sixteen, in the breakers at fourteen, and in a bituminous mine, if he was with his father, at twelve. Of the 24,000 children under sixteen employed legally in the mines throughout the country, according to the Census of 1900, more than fourteen thousand worked in Pennsylvania. A weakness in the Pennsylvania law—that no binding proof of age was required—made it almost useless;[6] thus thousands of others worked in the mines illegally.

When the Committee began its attack, the great anthracite coal strike of 1902, with its portrayal in the press of child employment in Pennsylvania's mines, was still fresh in the public mind. Lovejoy already had studied conditions there, and his personal connections with workers, employers, labor leaders, school officials, and others made it possible for him to obtain information that was not always available in the public records. He made further studies of Pennsylvania's mines in 1905 and again in 1907. As expected, he found that in addition to thousands of fourteen- and fifteen-year-olds legally employed, more than ten thousand youngsters worked illegally in the mines. Some of these children, only ten or eleven years old, were found working as mule drivers, couplers, runners, spragers, and gate tenders. Most of them, however, were employed in the breakers.[7]

Working conditions in the mines were probably as harmful to young children as those in any other industry. The unnatural restraint of being underground and held to one repetitive task for eight or nine hours a day was combined with several dire hazards. For example, it was not unusual to read accounts of young boys in the mines being buried by tons of coal. Accidents to children occurred about as frequently in coal mining as in other industries, or about three times as often as to adult workers; [8] but the chances of surviving a serious accident in the mines were much less than in many other industries.

Those lucky enough to survive often bore the telltale scars of the mines, which robbed them of sunlight, health, and sound bodies; many were anemic, underdeveloped, or physically disabled. Lovejoy found one fourteen-year-old boy in a mine shaft who for three years had been helping his father pick coal and load it on the cars. One of his legs had been so badly crushed that he had spent a year in the hospital.[9]

The coal breakers, where none younger than fourteen could work legally but where many younger boys actually did much of the work, were in some ways even more dangerous. The boys sat for ten or eleven hours a day in rows on wooden boards placed over chutes through which tons of coal constantly passed. Their task was to pick out from the passing coal the slate, stone, and other waste that came from the mine. The slate so closely resembled the coal that it could be detected only by close scrutiny. The boys had to bend over the chute and reach down into it. Even if they wore gloves, which was not always possible because they frequently had to rely on a sense of touch, the moving material was so sharp that it could cut and tear their hands. The position in which the boys sat was not only tiring but backbreaking, causing obviously round shoulders and narrow chests. If a boy reached too far and slipped into the coal that flowed beneath him, he stood little chance of surviving intact. The air was so laden with coal dust that the only light in the area came from the mine lamps attached to the boys' caps. As one foreman put it: "There are twenty boys in that breaker, and I bet you could shovel fifty pounds of dust out of their systems." In front of the chutes was an empty space reserved for the "breaker boss" who watched the boys as intently as they watched the coal. Armed with a stick, he would rap the head and shoulders of those who, in his opinion, were not working hard enough.[10] The boys delighted in fooling the inspectors. As one child put it: "When the inspectors came de boss puts the drivers nippin' and the runners drivin' and the laborers runnin' and hid us away in the gob." Lovejoy found that the lives of the small boys "were so tainted by vicious habits that an almost unsuperable obstacle to maturity, . . . virtue and intelligence was formed." [11]

Little in the way of a real education was available. Night schools were maintained, but they were poorly staffed and equipped. More important, after spending eight to twelve hours a day in the mines or breakers the children had little or no strength left for the schools. Lovejoy was impressed by the evidence presented by an eighteen-year-old boy who took him through the breakers. Having worked in the mines and breakers since he was twelve, the boy knew the meaning of "jogs" and "bony," "nippin" and "scraggin," but little else. On his coat were two badges—one a picture of United Mine Workers' president John Mitchel, the other a small cross. Under Mitchel's picture were the words "Labor's Best Friend"; under the cross was "Thy Kingdom Come!" The boy was unable to read a single word.[12]

To a large extent, Pennsylvania law was responsible for these sad conditions. The problem was twofold. First, the sixteen-year age limit for anthracite miners should have been extended to the breakers and to the bituminous miners. Second, and far more serious, a defect in the statute practically nullified even those provisions—the only proof of age required of working children was a parent's affidavit, described by Lovejoy as "a scheme for promoting perjury by process of law." [13] The validity of a parent's affidavit had been discredited many times in the past. Obviously, a parent willing to permit his child to work from eight to twelve hours a day in a mine would be just as willing to perjure himself as to the child's age. Such parents usually had little difficulty obtaining the aid of a notary who, usually for a fee of twenty-five cents, was willing to be a party to the transaction.[14]

As coroners' inquests revealed, children of ten or eleven years were often victims of mine disasters. Witness the court record of a boy named Patrick Kearney, a child laborer who lost his life in the mines in 1907. At an inquest following his death, the foreman testified that he did not know the age of the boy, but that the company had a certificate showing him to be fourteen. Yet he had appeared to be only about ten years old. He was "kind of a small boy," said the foreman, "but I thought he might be older than he looked." In any event, since the boy's parents had told him that the youngster was fourteen, there was no need to question the work certificate. The father then testified that the boy had been born in June 1898 and that he was only nine and a half when he died. The parent admitted that he had sworn under oath before the local justice of the peace that the boy was fourteen; he had wanted to get work for the boy.[15]

As in all its campaigns, the Committee published and circulated reports of its investigations in Pennsylvania, and they provoked bitter opposition. State labor officials as well as mine operators fought proposals to require documentary proof of a working child's age. The State Commissioner of Labor declared that most mine accidents occurred because children were careless or because they left their posts. Rather than advising that the young be prohibited from such work, however, he recommended that the careless and errant be fired. In short, children working in the mines and breakers were surrounded by so many dangers that for their own protection they must act like adults while on the job. Yet all adolescents were (and are) awkward, careless, curious, experimental, and, in varying degree, irresponsible. Unprepared for the physical and mental strain of confining work for eight or more hours a day in a mine or factory, children in their early teens were easily fatigued and had such poor muscular coordination that they were inevitably subject to greater risks than were mature workers, whether in the mines or in most other forms of industrial employment. Industrial injuries to young boys often meant death or lifelong physical handicaps that blighted their lives.

Conditions so flagrant could not be tolerated indefinitely. In 1905, thanks mainly to Secretary Lindsay who handled affairs at the state capital, the Pennsylvania legislature passed a statute which removed

some of the chief defects of the existing law; the new measure required documentary proof of age of working children and prescribed
educational standards. But the courts declared the law unconstitutional,[16] and the fight went on. Finally, in 1909, the Committee assisted in the passage of a similar measure which stood the test of
judicial review. Two years later the sixteen-year age limit was extended
to the state's bituminous mines.[17]

The Committee meanwhile was expanding its efforts. Early in 1906
it changed its financial policy and listed three categories of members
—guarantor (a contribution of $100 or more annually), sustaining
member ($25 to $100), and associate ($2 to $25). By the end of its
next fiscal year, September 30, it had enrolled 981 associate members
in forty states. This group contributed a good part of the Committee's
income, and still more would enroll. In 1909, when as many as
twenty-seven state and local committees were at work, some five
thousand members were counted.[18] The Committee never really
gained a strong foothold in the South, but only about 5 per cent of
its funds came from New England.[19] Thus it was not, as certain
Southerners charged, a Northern group in the pay of Yankees who
competed with Southern mill owners. To help dispose of the charge
that it was sectional in aim and support, the Committee asked to be
incorporated through a special act of Congress, and this was done in
February 1907.[20] Its federal charter also appeared to give the organization a stamp of national approval.

For several years the *Proceedings* of its annual conferences were
published in the influential *Annals of the American Academy of
Political and Social Science* as well as by the Committee itself in separate volumes. More than four thousand copies of the *Annals* devoted
to the first annual conference were circulated, and 48,500 pamphlets
plus some 35,000 pieces of other literature and announcements were
distributed. In all, nearly two million pages of printed matter on
child labor, besides much that was circulated through the daily press,
came from the Committee's offices in one year;[21] each succeeding year
there was more. Compiled with scrupulous regard for the facts, this
literature, including a yearly *Handbook of Child Labor Legislation,*

comprised the most notable collection of information on the subject of child labor ever assembled.

Beginning in 1907 the Committee also sponsored an annual Child Labor Day. Its use as a propaganda medium was reflected in the thousands of letters and other pieces of literature sent to clergymen and educators. All were urged to advance the cause in their churches, synagogues, and schools in the hope of setting in motion the machinery for local reform.[22] Everywhere there was fallow ground.

The National Child Labor Committee's next major campaign was waged against the glass-making industry which, as we shall see, like the coal mining industry was responsible for some of the worst child employment practices in America. While substantial correction was eventually achieved, it took the Committee's steady and unremitting effort from 1905 to 1919 to remove many thousands of misused child workers from most of the nation's glass factories.

The glass industry was one of the oldest and at the same time one of the youngest of America's great enterprises. As early as 1609 a glass factory had been built at Jamestown, Virginia, from which came some of the colonies' first exports. Jamestown disappeared, and until the mid-nineteenth century glass-making failed to gain a foothold in America. In 1865, however, when a Bostonian produced flint glass comparable to the best made in England, successful glass production and sale was stimulated, and by the 1890's domestic glass-making had become a big business.

Night work in the nation's glass plants began in 1888 when a producer in Jeannette, Pennsylvania, used a continuous tank to replace the pot system of heating glass to a molten state. The tank removed the need to halt work in the early evening in order to place small clay pots or containers inside furnace openings where they would sit all night to warm the batch for the following day. The new method was a boon: it usually was cooler after dark anyway, and more economical to keep the factory running all the time. As a result, about two-thirds of the more than 7,500 boys under sixteen years of age employed in America's glass houses at the turn of the century were kept at work after dark, at least every other week.[23]

The four leading glass-producing states were New Jersey, Indiana, Pennsylvania, and West Virginia, all rich in the raw materials essential to glass-making—silica sand and limestone. All allowed children under sixteen to work in glass factories, night or day. New Jersey prohibited those under sixteen from working in certain industries, but not in glass factories; Pennsylvania and West Virginia had no night work provisions at all, while Indiana prohibited only girls under sixteen from working at night.[24]

Actually, only a few girls were employed in the industry, and they usually worked at decorating and packing the finished goods. Some of the boys were employed in the manufacture of plate and window glass; but as many as 98 per cent of them worked in the furnace rooms, where they performed a variety of tasks. Most worked as blowers' assistants. "Mold" boys either had to squat in an awkward, cramped position or, if they stood, had to stoop to their work in order to get close to the mold which was kept near the hot furnace. "Carrying-in" boys were required to remain on their feet for hours at a time, while "snapping-up" boys were forced to endure intense heat and the bright, glaring light of the glory hole which kept the glass molten.

The heat was intense all over. The temperature of the molten glass was 2,500 degrees Fahrenheit; the temperature in the factories (which had to close during July and August) usually ranged between 100 and 130 degrees. Stiff necks, colds, pneumonia, rheumatism, and other throat and lung ailments were common. So were heat prostration, headaches, sleeplessness, and exhaustion, especially in warmer weather.

Because of heavy fumes and dust, many glass-house employees also suffered from injury to the tracheal passages, which induced respiratory diseases. Tuberculosis was common and skin irritation frequent, as was eye trouble, caused by the intense glare. The most common injuries, however, were cuts and burns, for the floors were always littered with broken glass. Glass houses usually operated on a piecework basis so that speed and efficiency counted; yet most factories were crowded and movement quite restricted. Nervous tension, especially since there were few rest periods, made some workers accident prone.

Besides the severity of the regimen there were the usual evils of night work, especially during the winter. The sudden change from the hot air inside the factory to the cold outside air was hardly conducive to good health. And there was usually a transportation problem. The night shift began at 5 P.M. and streetcars were not running at 3 A.M. when it ended. The overheated, sleepy boys had the choice of a nap on the factory floor with a packing box as a pillow (until five or six o'clock when the cars began running) or a long walk in the small hours to their homes.

These conditions were reflected in high mortality figures for workers in the glass-making industry. The life expectancy for employees was forty-one to forty-two years. It was not surprising that very few children of adult glass-house workers could be found in the factories. One worker who had spent much of his life in the industry was heard to remark: "I would rather send my boys straight to hell than send them by way of the glass house." [25]

Glass-house operators used the same arguments as other employers of child labor: that the life of their industry was dependent upon the labor of children; that workers over sixteeen were too slow and clumsy to work in glass houses; that the training required to make good glass workers had to be acquired at an early age; that they would be forced to close down their plants and leave the state should child labor and night work be prohibited; and that such labor was a godsend in helping to relieve poverty. [26]

To answer these arguments the NCLC conducted a series of searching studies. Investigators looked at the factory children themselves; a photographer was employed to take pictures of the youngsters and of the plant environment. The regulations of different states were studied and compared. Owen Lovejoy then prepared a report which discussed the alleged necessity of child labor. In terms of productivity, he noted, greater growth of the industry had occurred in the states that forbade the employment of children at night. [27] In respect to child labor as an economic necessity, Lovejoy concluded that the wages (about sixty-five cents a day) were too small to contribute significantly to a family's earnings. Altruism, he found, played but a small part in the hiring of children in the glass industry. Finally, in proving that the glass industry was not compelled to employ children, either for its own sake or for the sake of the children, Lovejoy cited the *National Glass Budget,* a leading trade journal, which in the fall of 1905 stated that the introduction of machinery "changed modern factory requirements to such an extent that it can be truthfully said that, as a rule, the glass factory of today which still requires the work of the small boy is operated in the crudest, most primitive, most expensive and antiquated manner." [28]

Despite this testimony, for years the glass manufacturers continued to fight—and defeat—every attempt to remedy the evil. Five times a Committee-sponsored bill aimed at establishing a sixteen-year minimum for night work failed in New Jersey. Similar bills introduced in three other offending states met the same fate. The Pennsylvania statute enacted in 1909 (which did away with some of the worst abuses in the coal mining industry) prohibited night work for those under sixteen "with certain exemptions," one of which was the glass industry.

Finally, in 1910 New Jersey established a sixteen-year minimum for night work.[29] After a lively campaign in Indiana, led by Lovejoy, that state passed a similar law in 1911. Pennsylvania and West Virginia, however, continued to exempt themselves from night-work provisions for the glass industry; not until 1915 and 1919, respectively, did those states fall into line.[30]

While the battle against child labor in the Southern cotton mills paralleled that in the glass factories in certain respects, in others it was markedly different.[31] The glass-making industry utilized children under sixteen as a valuable adjunct, as it were, but the Southern cotton mills employed more children under sixteen in proportion to the total number of employees than any other manufacturing industry in America.[32] The cotton industry, moreover, presented a more impregnable front. Unlike glass-house operators, Southern cotton mill employers usually owned the villages in which their operatives lived, and thus almost absolutely controlled their lives. Then too, most Southern states were controlled by Democratic party machines which invariably catered to the large mill owners who controlled a great many votes. As a result, state laws were their laws.[33]

What were the legal standards in respect to child labor? No group of states in the Union had lower standards than the four leading textile-producing states of Alabama, Georgia, North Carolina, and South Carolina. Georgia had no age limit at all. The other three states had a twelve-year limit, but South Carolina and Alabama allowed children under twelve to work if they could prove that it was necessary for them to do so. Alabama and North Carolina allowed a sixty-six-hour week; Georgia had no regulations whatever. South Carolina forbade night work in factories for children under twelve, but none of the other states had any night-work regulations. The feeble child labor laws that did exist were not enforced; factory inspection was almost entirely neglected, and none of the states had any compulsory school attendance laws.[34]

Employed mainly in the spinning rooms, the children of the mills worked as spinners, doffers, and sweepers. Girls employed as spinners walked constantly up and down long aisles brushing lint from the frames and watching the whirling bobbins for breaks in the cotton. When a break occurred, they had to mend it quickly by tying the ends together. Each spinner tended six or eight "sides," as the long rows of spindles were called; consequently, she had to be on her feet nearly all the time.

When the bobbins were filled with thread, boys who worked as doffers replaced them with empty ones. (The boys also were used as sweepers, although others might be hired for that job.) Often the children—boys and girls—were so small they had to stand on boxes to reach the bobbins or broken threads. Thus they were dangerously exposed to severe injury through falling into the moving machinery or being caught by it.

In defending the use of children in the mills, employers frequently pointed out that the work was light, that it required little physical exertion; at most, it only called for close attention. Mill conditions, it was claimed, were generally good. The Pelzer mills in South Carolina and the Parker plants at Greer and Pacolet—mills that presented unusually favorable conditions—were cited as examples.[35]

That the mill work was relatively light was about all that could be said for it. Many of the factories were filthy and unsanitary. But even under the most favorable conditions, the atmosphere in the mills was incredibly bad, often inducing nervous excitability, disease, mental retardation, and even death. The noise in the weaving rooms was so loud that it was almost impossible to be heard above it. More important, because heat and moisture were helpful in preventing the cotton from breaking, the windows were always kept closed and the air moist. As a consequence, the stale air was filled with so much dust and lint that it not only covered the workers' clothes but quickly filled their lungs as well. The death rate for cotton mill hands, adults and children, from tuberculosis, chronic bronchitis, and other respiratory diseases was unusually high. The boy working in the cotton mill had only half as good a chance to reach twenty years as the boy outside the mill; girls had even less chance. And though children generally worked at the less hazardous tasks and were not required to handle the whirling machines, the accident rate in Southern cotton mills was more than twice as high for those under sixteen years of age than for the older group. For youngsters who worked among shafts, belts, and gears, the rate was 133 per cent higher.[36]

The work was long, usually eleven or twelve hours a day, five and a half days a week, and frequently there were night shifts. So another serious effect of the work was the loss of an education. Children in the mills eleven and twelve hours a day simply could not go to school. The average mill child quit school at age twelve; many stopped much earlier or never attended school. To be sure, many of the mill owners (like the mine operators) built schoolhouses and provided night classes for their employees, but the illiteracy tables for the cotton mill states spoke very plainly on this subject.[37]

In 1905 the NCLC began its investigation of the cotton mill states by sending Secretary Lindsay on what was described as a "scouting trip." Lindsay tried to discover not only the exact nature of the problem but also, through conferences with state authorities, labor leaders, industry people, and local residents, the general sentiment toward child labor. Above all, he sought to determine the role the National Child Labor Committee should play in promoting legislation in the South. He concluded that unless the Committee "could aid the cause with the services of an Assistant Secretary, there was nobody to undertake the work of organizing public sentiment, and harmonizing the different agencies interested in passing . . . child labor bill[s]." [38]

Thus Alexander J. McKelway was sent south to conduct a more detailed investigation. Union leaders with whom he talked agreed not to make public statements on child labor that would embarrass him or other reformers. He also spoke before a variety of audiences, interviewed local and national officials who would give him a hearing, wrote letters to influential citizens, continued to organize local child labor committees, drafted new legislative bills, and revised others that were pending. [39]

The first real legislative battle occurred in North Carolina when, in 1905, a McKelway-drafted bill was introduced in the legislature. A moderate measure, it merely sought to raise the minimum working age in factories from twelve to fourteen for girls and illiterate children, and to prohibit night work for those under fourteen. It appeared that the bill would be unopposed inasmuch as North Carolina's two United States Senators and state legislative leaders seemed to favor it. There was also a good deal of popular approval of the measure. More and more Southerners, it appeared, had had their fill of child labor. Physicians were beginning to protest its harmful physical effects. Farmers were complaining about the loss of tenants flocking to the mills. Some educational leaders were beginning to show concern about the widespread illiteracy in factory districts. More and more ministers were inveighing against the system's inhumanity, and the press was becoming concerned over what was termed "racial degeneracy." The politicians, of course, began to sense the mood of this public indignation.

But a delegation of some seventy manufacturers appeared at Raleigh to oppose the North Carolina bill. Leading the group was R. M.

Miller of Charlotte, a future president of the American Cotton Manufacturers' Association. Miller argued that since 75 per cent of the
state's spinners were under fourteen, the measure would cause irrep-
arable harm to the mills. Besides, since Georgia had no child labor
law, why should North Carolina have one? He accused the NCLC of
being a Northern organization in the pay of New England mill interests seeking to destroy Southern competition; speaking for the
manufacturers, he urged defeat of the measure.

The bill was reported unfavorably by the House committee to
which it had been sent, and it died without even reaching a vote.[40]
At one stroke the nature of the opposition which the Committee
would have to reckon with had clearly shown itself. The pattern was
set; a long, hard fight lay ahead.

Many of the same arguments were heard throughout the South as
the textile industry mustered a defense of child labor on various and
sometimes conflicting grounds. In every legislative campaign, claims
were sure to be advanced that the number of working children was
small, that factory conditions were not injurious, and that Northern
agitators were intent on smothering Southern industry. Reformers
were charged with trying to take away the only means of support for
widowed, destitute mothers. (There seemed to be a remarkable concentration of widows in Southern cotton mill villages.) [41] It was declared of course that children were better off in the factory than on
the isolated, mountainous farms from which they had come, an argument that would soon become the main weapon in the arsenal of
those who opposed regulation.

To prove their point, mill owners frequently gathered petitions,
signed by their operatives, that denounced child labor legislation. On
one occasion a petition with three thousand signatures was brought
to the South Carolina legislature. It read: "We are not overworked,
and are satisfied, and only ask to be let alone." Upon close examination it was clear that hundreds of the signers could not even write
their own name. Anyone could sign the petition—and many did—
merely by marking it with an "X." [42]

In the legislative struggles it was often difficult to tell which opponents of child labor legislation were self-interested and which were not. Some manufacturers, convinced that child labor was evil, were nevertheless reluctant to have it made the subject of legislation for constitutional or perhaps for other reasons. In the words of one Raleigh employer, "We think all the mills should run not over eleven hours a day and avoid, if possible, taking children under twelve or thirteen years, but we deem legislation on the subject bad policy; let the employer and the employee settle these things, this is a free country for all." [43]

Was this a real concern about the legal principle involved in the question of government interference between capital and labor? Or was it the fear that organized labor, an advocate of reform, was behind the movement, seeking to use it as an entering wedge for further labor legislation? In fact, it could well have been both.[44] Those Southerners who claimed to oppose child labor in theory yet fought attempts to restrict it in practice continued to hire youngsters, allegedly against their better wishes; otherwise the children would fall prey to the temptations of idleness. They argued, in effect, that if children were removed or barred from the mills before the several states passed compulsory public education laws, they would become juvenile delinquents. As the *News and Courier* of Charleston, South Carolina, felt prompted to say, "The cotton mill people do not want to employ little children any more than some people want to keep them out of the factories. If some way could be devised to make these and other children go to school when kept out of the mills a decided step forward would be taken. The chief point is rather to have the children go to school than to keep them out of the factories." [45]

Whatever their real feelings may have been, the mill men knew of course that compulsory public education would be slow in coming to the South; in fact, in many instances and for various reasons they opposed it themselves. It could be argued—and was—that there were not enough schoolhouses to hold all the children to be accommodated in a public school system. And to be effective it would require an expensive army of truant officers. It would also be an invasion of parental rights. Worst of all, young Negroes, who at one time had been barred from education by statute, would have to be sent to free public schools with white children. If the mill owners could insist that compulsory schooling precede child labor legislation, the reform could be indefinitely postponed.[46]

In this respect, as McKelway readily admitted, he and other child labor reformers in the South were radicals. They considered education far more important—both for the children and for the economic development of the region—than the right of parents to exploit their children. It is interesting, however, to explore McKelway's thinking in this respect. "Our southern people must realize," he declared, "concerning the Negro (what New England, especially Massachusetts recognized concerning the foreigner) that the education . . . [of the Negro] is essential to the prosperity and peace of the native whites, that we must find out the kind of training that is needed for the Negro, and that the strong hand of the masterful race to which we proudly belong shall compel him to receive that training." [47]

And since "when all the people are educated the dominant race . . . has nothing to fear from any other race, least of all . . . from the African race," the South had more to lose from the failure of the Negro than from his success.[48] In any event, whatever one's views on the "Negro question," white youngsters should not be sacrificed in neglecting the children of the former slaves. To do so, to deprive them of an education and to interrupt their period of growth, of tutelage and dependence, was not only to injure them personally, "but, so far as the interruption extends," it "halt[s] the race in its progress" and "turn[s] it toward degeneration and extinction." [49]

This was not a pose for popular Southern consumption. Like many other progressives of his day, McKelway was an ardent defender of white supremacy, and a nativist.[50] Repeatedly he voiced the theme that child labor imperiled the Anglo-Saxon or native racial strain in this country. He therefore visualized the child labor problem as far more serious in the South than in the North, for Southern mills hired native white youngsters while Northern ones employed immigrant children from Canada and central Europe. McKelway went so far as to recommend the importation of a large number of immigrants to work in the Southern mills.[51]

In the long run, the fact that he shared this racial prejudice with the Southerners with whom he dealt may have helped McKelway in his efforts to regulate child labor: he put the issue in terms they understood and cared about. He and his colleagues struck the right note when they pointed out that while poor white children worked in the mills, black youngsters were either going to school or were engaged in so-called wholesome farm labor. To continue the system would jeopardize white supremacy in the South if not in the entire nation.[52]

In 1905 McKelway had reactivated the dormant Georgia Child Labor Committee, assuming the secretaryship himself. The next year he came to Atlanta to establish a branch office there. The argument of Northern interference, however unreasonable, had to be reckoned with; anything that would weaken Southern prejudice against the organization would be helpful. A Southern office headed by a Southerner would better identify the Committee with the cause in that region. Too, it was more practical to distribute literature from a Southern office than from New York. And because Georgia was the most backward state in the area (and it now had an active child labor committee), Atlanta was chosen as the site.[53]

Operating out of Atlanta, McKelway and others aroused reform sentiment throughout Georgia. During the 1906 gubernatorial campaign, candidate Hoke Smith, a founding member of the National Committee, took up the cause, promising child labor regulation if elected. Smith was elected, and even before he took office Georgia enacted its first child labor law. A brief speech on the floor of the House by the only Negro member of the legislature brought a storm of applause from friends of the measure when he declared:

Mr. Speaker, as you know, my people are not particularly interested in this bill. Our children are not employed in the cotton factories. . . . But we have been here for some time legislating for the protection of the birds of the air and the beasts of the field and the fish of the sea, and I for one am in favor of doing something for the protection of the little white children of Georgia.[54]

The Georgia statute prohibited night work for children under fourteen and established a twelve-year minimum age for work in factories, except for youngsters with dependent parents. Children under ten were forbidden from gainful employment under any circumstances. Despite the exceedingly low standards and the lack of enforcement machinery, the measure, for which McKelway received most of the credit, was notable as the first victory for the Committee in the South.[55]

Suddenly, however, the NCLC was faced with its first severe internal crisis, one that split its ranks and almost wrecked the young organization. The Knights of Labor had called for federal action against child labor as early as 1880, but it was not until late 1906 that the first national child labor bill was introduced in Congress. It was sponsored by Senator Albert J. Beveridge of Indiana, who declared: "We cannot permit any man or corporation to stunt the bodies, minds, and souls of American children. We cannot thus wreck the future of the American Republic." [56] Convinced that a federal law was required to deal with the nation-wide evil, Beveridge drew up a bill designed to prohibit the interstate transportation of articles produced in any factory or mine that employed children under fourteen years of age. Stiff penalties were prescribed for violations or for the filing of false affidavits. Enforcement was left to federal district attorneys.

Beveridge naturally turned to the National Child Labor Committee for support. On November 23, 1906, he appeared in person before a special meeting of its board of trustees to explain his bill and ask for the Committee's support. After some animated talk the board decided to take no action but to send a copy of the bill to corporate members of the Committee with a questionnaire asking for an opinion for the board's guidance on "what action, if any, should be taken in this matter by the National Committee." On December 5 Beveridge introduced the bill in the Senate, and on the next day Congressman Herbert Parsons of New York brought up an identical measure in the House.[57]

The next day the board met to again consider the bill. The discussion was heated. Robert W. de Forest, wealthy corporation lawyer-philanthropist, led the opposition. He questioned the effectiveness of a bill that did not provide for on-the-spot inspection by government agents; he doubted its legality; he warned that support of federal legislation in a field which, in his opinion, properly belonged to the states, would handicap the Committee in its work in the South, where the worst abuses existed. But de Forest's arguments failed to convince the trustees, who voted to endorse the Beveridge bill in the belief "that it will establish a National standard to correct the evils of child labor in their important National aspects . . . and will tend to establish equality of economic competition without minimizing state responsibility." [58]

By supporting federal legislation the Committee did not intend to abandon its efforts to secure state laws or to educate the public. In fact, it was involved in several state campaigns which it intended to continue. But Lindsay and some others felt that progress had been dishearteningly slow, especially with regard to enforcement. Opposition by manufacturers who feared interstate competition, and the lack of necessary machinery for state inspection were thorny barriers to success. Even before Beveridge raised the question, some Committee members had begun to doubt the advisability of relying solely upon state action, and introduction of the federal measure deepened this feeling. Here was an opportunity to strike at child labor nationally with a single blow. If Washington could only establish a uniform national standard that would equalize competitive conditions, the Department of Justice had ample resources to enforce the law and prosecute violators.[59]

As the principal speaker at the National Child Labor Committee's annual meeting in December, Senator Beveridge made a stirring appeal for his bill. Child labor, he declared, is "a crime against humanity and a treason against liberty itself." Time and time again he was interrupted by applause. "When the lords of gold tremble for the

safety of their widespread investments," he warned, "let them
remember that child labor is daily creating an element in the Republic
far more dangerous to their physical property itself than ever was
packed in dynamiters' bombs." It was inevitable that the gathering of
more than four thousand people, the largest group ever assembled to
discuss the problem of child labor, would resolve to support the
measure. McKelway, it was decided, should go to Washington to
lobby for the proposal.[60]

McKelway did talk with Senators, Congressmen, and with President Roosevelt in gaining some support, but organized labor refused
to rally behind the measure. Distrustful of federal action, Samuel
Gompers, the American Federation of Labor's doughty leader, maintained that it would set a dangerous precedent and that further government interference in labor relations might follow.[61] Nor would
President Roosevelt lend his support for national legislation, for he
doubted that such a bill was constitutional. Concerned also with the
public mood, Roosevelt realized that organized labor was at best
lukewarm and that even child labor reformers were divided over the
issue. Certainly the bill would face strong opposition in the House
and Senate. As an alternative, the President asked Congress to authorize an investigation by the Bureau of Labor into the working conditions of women and children throughout America.

The idea for this tactic had originated in Chicago among the
pioneer social workers associated with Jane Addams and Hull-House.
While it was felt that the regulation of working conditions was essentially the concern of each state, a thoroughgoing probe of the
subject and widely circulated results would greatly help to arouse the
public conscience and obtain uniform state action.[62] The idea was then
laid before the President. Twice Roosevelt urged Congress to authorize
the investigation—in 1904 and 1905—but no action was taken. In
1906 he reiterated his plea, although, he said, "each state must ultimately settle the question in its own way." Finally, in late January
1907 Congress authorized the study and later appropriated $300,000
for the purpose.[63]

But Roosevelt went a step further by urging passage of a model child labor law for the District of Columbia, which was governed by Congress. Legislation of this scope, he argued, would help provide a standard for state legislators to follow.[64]

Unlike the National Child Labor Committee, which actively supported both of the President's proposals, Beveridge scorned them as meaningless sops to an outraged public opinion. It was time to act, he declared, not to investigate. He was equally unimpressed by the call for a model child labor bill for Washington, D. C., for the District had no cotton mills, shrimp canneries, mines, or glass-making factories. How ridiculous to think that the twelve-hour day for children in North Carolina's cotton mills would be abolished because of a law with such limited applicability.

Beveridge continued to press for his bill, which had been pigeonholed in the Committee on Labor and Education. On January 23, 1907, he took the Senate floor when the District of Columbia bill, which the NCLC drafted, was under consideration. Offering his bill as an amendment to that measure, he kept the floor for almost three days (January 23, 28, and 29). Hour after hour he read descriptions, supported by affidavits obtained by Lovejoy and McKelway, of the extent and inhumanity of child labor in the United States. Behind the organized opposition, Beveridge charged, stood "the cruel and greedy interests that were fattening off the blood of American children—the cotton mills of the South, the anthracite interests of Pennsylvania, . . . the sweatshops and the railroads that carry their products. . . ." Time after time he was answered with spontaneous applause from the crowded galleries.[65] But Beveridge lacked votes, and without any further discussion of the matter the 59th Congress ended with no action on child labor other than expediting the District of Columbia bill.

Although the National Committee had been a mainstay of support, many of its members remained opposed to Beveridge's federal bill. Some weeks before the Senator took the floor in its behalf, Edgar Murphy resigned from the Committee in protest against its endorsement of the measure. The board, Murphy wrote, in reversing the

Committee's original agreement to exclude federal legislation from its aims, had "departed from a compact which I regarded as inviolable." Reflecting his Southern viewpoint, Murphy expressed fear of federal intervention in a sphere that he felt belonged to the states. Recent gains at the state level, he argued, had been substantial, and there was no need for federal action. Besides, the bill's effectiveness was highly doubtful. And finally, by endorsing the bill the Committee hampered its own cause in the South. "You do us an . . . almost incurable injury," he wrote Felix Adler, "when you mix up the cause of the children with the bitter issues of coercion. . . ." [66]

Murphy not only left the Committee, announcing his resignation in the *Montgomery Advertiser* before it had been accepted, but he now publicly opposed federal child labor legislation and raised money to fight the measure nationally. He even wrote President Roosevelt urging his continued opposition to the Beveridge bill. His arguments were published in the press and then expanded into a pamphlet entitled *The Federal Regulation of Child Labor, a Criticism of the Policy Represented in the Beveridge-Parsons Bill.*[67]

Murphy's resignation from the National Committee naturally came as a shock. More than anyone else, he had been its founder. Robert de Forest promptly renewed his attack on the Beveridge measure, warning that continued support would further disrupt the organization. (There was under way, Florence Kelley told Beveridge several months later, "a very active subterranean propaganda against your bill . . . and lukewarm friends tend to grow chilly.")[68] At a board meeting in the fall, de Forest offered a resolution calling for withdrawal of the Committee's endorsement of the bill. After a lengthy, bitter debate, the board voted to poll the entire Committee before acting. An angered Lindsay wrote to Beveridge, "We have reactionaries in corporations not for profit as well as in corporations [for profit]. . . . I am fighting for all I am worth . . . against obstacles, the strength of which you can scarcely appreciate. The whole business may cost me my job . . . but I am ready to walk the streets for a while if necessary." [69]

Supporters of the bill rushed to its defense. Alexander McKelway prepared a memorandum answering its critics. Claiming to be in closer touch with Southern public opinion than Murphy, he argued that most residents of the South were appalled by the injustice of child labor and were well aware of its detrimental effects. They would, in his opinion, support the measure. And even if they did not, little would be lost: the Committee already had been tarred in the South as a tool of New England textile interests. The states were no match for the corporations; only federal legislation could end the evil. It was not a question of states' rights but of human welfare. The health and character of its future citizens was the nation's most pressing business.[70]

Beveridge joined in the battle, personally pleading with the Committee not to abandon him in midstream. "The worst enemies . . . [of] the reform are those that say they want to stop [the evil] . . . but are always against any effective means" of doing so, he wrote.[71] Yet the Committee finally voted 18 to 10 to reverse its earlier stand in favor of a national bill. As if to reconcile the Beveridge faction and hopefully reunite the board, a revised resolution was worded so as to withdraw endorsement of the bill without mentioning it by name. Unanimously adopted by the trustees on November 26, 1907, it provided that "the National Child Labor Committee will for the present take no other action with reference to National legislation" until the federal Bureau of Labor's investigation was completed. Individual members of the Committee, however, were free to do as they chose.[72]

Lindsay, still angry, sent Beveridge a copy of the resolution with the comment: "I don't like it but it was the best we could do. . . . I had to fight for every inch conceded." He then stepped down as executive head of the Committee. "You have won out," de Forest notified Murphy, who also heard from Owen Lovejoy, the organization's new secretary. "The practical effect of the resolution . . . is to bind the National Committee to take no action in the matter of Federal legislation," Lovejoy wrote to Murphy. "My own feeling is that the less said about the matter of . . . Federal legislation, the better." [73]

Now, under new leadership, the Committee would bind up its wounds and seek to exploit a greater popular interest in the cause. It planned to continue its program for the enactment of favorable legis-- lation by the states, especially in the South and, above all, for the establishment of a federal children's bureau.[74]

IV

Broadening the Field

WHILE the National Child Labor Committee did not support federal child labor legislation, it did favor a federal children's bureau. That idea sprang from the minds of Florence Kelley and Lillian Wald of New York's Henry Street Settlement. As early as 1900 Mrs. Kelley had pointed out the desperate need for a central agency to collect the information on child labor gathered by private and government agencies. In the fall of 1903 Miss Wald made the first specific suggestion for a children's bureau. A *federal* agency was needed, she told Mrs. Kelley, to collect and disseminate information on the needs of children. Such a bureau, located in Washington and staffed by experts, would function as a clearing house and an educational agency. It would address itself not only to questions of child labor but to all matters related to child health and welfare. Miss Wald thought that only the federal government could "cover the whole field and tell us of the children with as much care as it tells us of the trees or the cotton crop." Such was the keynote, to which she added: "Let us bring the child into the sphere of our national care and solicitude." [1]

At Mrs. Kelley's suggestion, Miss Wald went to Edward T. Devine, secretary of the New York Charity Organization Society, who in turn wired President Theodore Roosevelt. "Bully," the President wired back, "come down and tell me about it." So Devine and Miss Wald went down to Washington to see Roosevelt who, as an alleged conservationist of human as well as natural resources, promised his support.[2]

When the proposal was laid before the National Child Labor Committee's board of trustees, it too endorsed the plan. Investigating child labor and its related problems throughout the country was an enormous task. Only the national government could finance and properly carry out such a venture, and information it collected would be beyond suspicion. Inasmuch as Washington was already collecting and circulating information in many other fields, there could be no constitutional objections to the proposal.[3]

After further discussion with several interested parties (including two Cabinet members and the Director of the Census) the NCLC drafted a bill which provided for the creation of a federal bureau whose purpose would be "the collection of information and the dissemination of the results of the latest scientific work on the care and protection of children—thus furnishing to the several states the basis for wise legislation and to the officers of state boards the information necessary for efficient administration of laws relating to the welfare of children." [4] When the plan was submitted to Roosevelt, who discussed it at the White House with Lindsay, the President said plainly that the bureau was just what he wanted to see established. He promised to urge Congress to act. The bill itself, which then topped the National Committee's list of legislative goals,[5] was introduced in the Senate on January 10, 1906, by Murray Crane of Massachusetts. It was given a polite hearing, and sometime later John Gardner, a New Jersey Republican, introduced it in the House.

Actual passage of the bill—and even its emergence from committee —proved to be a long and difficult task. It was brought up each year, proving at least durable (in fact it would easily outlast the Roosevelt administration). Opposition came mainly from the same forces that opposed any regulation of child labor; the unearthing of facts about children and their needs was never a happy prospect for those who had a vested interest in preserving the status quo. Some claimed that it went too far, others that it did not go far enough. Some maintained that the proposal for a children's bureau was covered by existing agencies and statutes, others that the objective was good but ought to be reached in another way. Still others argued that it would be too costly and that the public could not afford the expense. Of course, there were always some who thought the proposed bureau would encroach upon the rights and duties of the states;[6] constitutionitis was a Washington disease which developed among several Congressmen whenever they did not have the nerve openly to oppose a good cause before the House. Few Congressmen wished to go on record against an agency designed merely to collect information about the nation's children, so the majority simply ignored the proposal.[7]

The NCLC continued to work for the bill through the years, reminding the public that creation of such a bureau would simply apply to human beings the government's traditional concern for plants and animals. While the U.S. Bureau of Animal Husbandry (a research agency) had a staff of more than one thousand and an annual budget of $1.5 million, the children's bureau bill called for a staff of only fourteen and an appropriation of a mere $50,000. The mortality rate for young domestic animals, the Committee noted, was considerably under that for young children. If the United States could assist in the conservation of livestock, why shouldn't it do the same for its future citizens?

The Committee waged a massive campaign at no small cost. Each year it sent form letters to interested individuals and groups throughout America urging that they write their Congressmen on behalf of the measure. Thousands of letters and pamphlets explaining the need for the proposal were broadcast into every state. Leading individuals in every walk of life were urged to support the bill.[8] The Committee's fifth annual conference, early in 1909, was devoted to this bill, and the three-day Chicago meeting ended with a resolution advocating passage.[9]

More significant, however, was the historic 1909 White House Conference on Dependent Children. This meeting of two hundred, organized and led by NCLC vice-chairman Homer Folks, adopted two resolutions (among others) that dealt with the proposed children's bureau: first, that Congress should enact the pending measure, and second, that President Roosevelt should deliver a special message to Congress urging such action.[10]

To comply with the request, the President sent Congress a special message, written by Alexander McKelway, calling for passage. "It is not only discreditable to us as a people," Roosevelt advised the nation's lawmakers on February 15, 1909, "that there is now no recognized and authoritative source of information upon . . . subjects related to child life, but in the absence of such information as should be supplied by the Federal Government many abuses have gone unchecked; public sentiment, with its great corrective power, can only be aroused by full knowledge of the facts." [11]

The well-publicized recommendations of the Chicago and Washington conferences, and Roosevelt's active support, forced Congress to act; it could no longer ignore the issue. Public hearings were finally scheduled, and the Committee lined up speakers to testify, including board members Folks, Lindsay, Wald, Devine, Addams, and Kelley. In addition, it continued to publicize the need for the bureau and brought considerable pressure to bear on Roosevelt's successor, President William Howard Taft, and other members of the new administration.

When by the fall of 1909 it became apparent that despite favorable public opinion Congress still would not act, the NCLC sent McKelway to Washington to direct a renewed campaign for the bill. After years of agitation, and five days of bitter floor debate, the Senate finally passed the measure on January 13, 1912, by a vote of 54 to 19. The House followed suit two months later, and President Taft signed the new law on April 9.[12]

The Committee meanwhile continued to work for effective child labor laws at the state level, especially in the South. Although thirty-four states had enacted new or had amended old laws since the Committee's inception, and though every Southern state now had some child labor law, improvement was slight. Field research in Alabama, North and South Carolina, and Georgia uncovered startling informa-

tion about school attendance and illiteracy. Among children in South
Carolina, for example, where school attendance was poor, about 50
per cent were illiterate, and similar situations existed in the other
states.[13]

As the result of legislative campaigns in these states, Alabama and
North Carolina raised their minimum working age from twelve to
thirteen years for children who had not attended school at least four
months during the preceding year. For others, Alabama fixed its age
limit at twelve, doing away with the exemptions that permitted ten-
year-old youngsters to work. In 1909 South Carolina adopted a system
of factory inspection.

At the same time, several bills aimed at improving Georgia's weak
law were defeated, and in North Carolina a compromise measure
agreed upon by the Committee and certain mill operators also failed,
due largely to bad faith on the part of the operators. By the end of
1909 only four Southern states (and the District of Columbia) had a
minimum working age of fourteen for factories. All the others, including the Carolinas—the two leading cotton textile-producing states
in the region—retained only a twelve-year age limit. Night work and
hours remained virtually unregulated, and enforcement of existing
laws was weak.[14]

While opposition to child labor regulation was entrenched in the
Southern textile states, a series of well-meant but inaccurate magazine
articles made matters worse for the NCLC. In 1905 the publicist Elbert
Hubbard, in "Slaughter of the Innocents," depicted child labor as
worse than slavery, and stated that children working in the mills lived
only about four years. Hubbard's indictment increased Southern hostility toward the Committee, as did Mrs. John Van Vorst's series of
inflammatory articles on mill conditions which appeared in the *Saturday Evening Post* in 1906. From the poet Edwin Markham came an
emotional portrayal, "Child at the Loom," in the *Cosmopolitan*. Although the great majority of children in the mills were employed as
spinners, doffers, or sweepers, Markham charged that "there must be
fifty thousand children at the southern looms." These and other errors
circulated by popular writers inevitably embarrassed a group so directly

concerned and so cautious in its investigations. The Committee was used to understatement, shunning exaggeration of any kind.[15]

The personal hostility of some Southern manufacturers and editors toward the genial but aggressive McKelway made matters worse. Although they stemmed from antagonisms he had aroused as a teacher, clergyman, and crusading editor before he joined the Committee, as well as from his more recent activities, the attacks on McKelway presaged greater antagonism toward the NCLC itself, especially in the Carolinas.[16]

McKelway's target, however, had not been the South or Southerners, but rather a few mill owners and their political agents. Far more than most, he argued that many of those who employed children were not essentially coldblooded profit-seekers but (with a few exceptions) victims of a pernicious system from which they would welcome relief. In speaking out, McKelway frequently made it clear—perhaps too clear for some of his colleagues—that in his opinion parents often were more responsible for child labor than the mill owners; greedy, lazy, or unaware of the debilitating effects of premature toil, they often urged and even insisted that their children go to work. He also emphasized that, historically, trade unions were not alone in calling for child labor reform; intelligent employers had done the same. As an example he cited the passage of England's first child labor law through the efforts of two large textile manufacturers, Sir Robert Peel and Robert Owen. McKelway urged compromise and cooperation with those "humane" and enlightened "Christian mill-owners" who "advocate our cause or bear with silent protest the reproaches that [some] . . . manufacturers . . . are bringing upon themselves through their opposition toward child labor reform." [17]

Yet as the attacks on McKelway continued, board members became seriously concerned about the Committee's future effectiveness in the South. The matter came to a head when the Committee received $5,000 from the Russell Sage Foundation to open a temporary branch office in Charlotte, North Carolina, and to extend its work in the Carolinas.[18] The board asked Lovejoy to determine whether McKelway's leadership was an embarrassment to the NCLC and whether the opposition he had created "stood as a barrier to further progress."

"One of the unsung heroes of social work," according to Clarke Chambers, Lovejoy was an excellent choice to conduct the investigation. Not only was he an effective speaker, having for many years traveled the Chautauqua circuit, but he had an unusual ability to discover the facts and interpret them, and thus his reports were noted for clarity and accuracy. His earnestness and zeal, his love of children and desire to help them, made Lovejoy entirely qualified to succeed Lindsay as the Committee's general secretary.

Lovejoy visited rural and urban manufacturing areas in North Carolina, interviewing mill men, school officials, physicians, clergymen, editors, lawyers, politicians, and others whose views seemed to him important. He discovered that, rather than a hindrance and a source of embarrassment, McKelway was an enormous asset; he had made far more friends than foes for the Committee and its cause. McKelway's chief detractors, Lovejoy discovered, were those manufacturers who opposed the regulation of child labor under any circumstances. With the facts in hand, Lovejoy recommended that the Committee continue its work in the Carolinas, but because of the tremendous opposition to outside or Northern influences, that it do so as quietly as possible.[19]

Although McKelway was easily vindicated by Lovejoy's report, which the board endorsed, he was to spend more and more of his time in Washington lobbying for the federal children's bureau bill, a matter to which he had already devoted some effort before the investigation.[20] His connection with reforms in the South thus became less important, and at his suggestion another field secretary, responsible to the central office but under McKelway's supervision, was hired to work in the Carolinas in cooperation with local groups, and no Charlotte office was established.

On the legislative front, the next two years were like those that had preceded them—a few minor successes but many failures, especially in Georgia and Alabama. The only important advances came in 1910 when North Carolina reduced its working hours for children from sixty-six to sixty per week, while South Carolina adopted a fixed twelve-year limit by abolishing the exemptions that applied to children of widows. The South Carolina legislature, however, refused to supply funds for inspectors who would enforce the statute.

The Committee's stubborn fight against child labor in the South forced it to knock down plausible defenses of the existing system whenever they appeared. For example, life in the mountain regions surrounding the mills seemed to provide a potent weapon for those who resisted far-reaching regulation. Disparaging contrasts between needy upland farmers and the mill operatives made the cotton textile industry appear "an actual blessing" for the poor.

The Committee had already demolished the arguments that very few children were employed, or that such employment provided a livelihood to needy youngsters and their families, or that it was the first rung on the ladder to success. (On the contrary, not many child laborers supported dependent parents, and their work hurt rather than helped their future.) Now it was argued that mill life at least provided good living conditions. In fact, as McKelway remarked, the mills were portrayed as a health resort, orphan asylum, juvenile reformatory, industrial school, and technical college all rolled into one.[21]

This argument had strong emotional appeal, for life could not help but be difficult on many poor farms. Thomas F. Parker, a South Carolina mill owner, spoke for many when he declared that the cotton mills were "the greatest and almost the only real friends that the poor whites of the South have. . . ." Their children were "infinitely better off in the cotton mills than on the soil-polluted, disease-breeding, one horse, privyless farms." Considering such "medieval conditions," he argued, "I view child-labor as an actual blessing when compared with the child misery which is found more particularly in the sand lands and in the Appalachian region." What was needed instead of "cheap criticism," he added, was "accurate knowledge of mill and mill-village conditions. . . ."[22]

Others agreed. A professor at Trinity College, in Durham, North Carolina, writing for the *South Atlantic Quarterly,* praised the social

service work at some South Carolina mills. As if replying to the adverse view of Southern factory conditions that had appeared in the
Saturday Evening Post, a writer for the *North American Review*
found elevating influences in mill life. A disgruntled investigator, who
had been relieved of his job with the federal group studying women
and child laborers in America, reiterated the same themes in *The
Child Who Toileth Not: The Story of a Government Investigation
Hitherto Suppressed,* which attacked both the NCLC and the Department of Labor.[23]

Also heard were Miss Gertrude Beeks and Mrs. J. Borden Harriman of the National Civic Federation, a business-oriented group
founded in 1900 allegedly to promote better labor-management relations. In an attempt to draw support away from the pending Beveridge
bill and any other movement for restrictive legislation, the Federation
had formed its own investigative committee, which had the support of
the National Association of Manufacturers. Denouncing "such radicals
as Miss Jane Addams and Mrs. Florence Kelley," it set out to refute
the "radical socialistic statements" of Beveridge and other advocates
of child labor regulation. Not surprisingly, its investigation of
Southern mills, according to Miss Beeks and Mrs. Harriman, revealed
that conditions in the South were nowhere as bad as the reformers
had portrayed. No real child labor problem existed; in fact, employers
were educating and in other ways helping their young workers. There
was, the ladies concluded, no serious child labor problem in the South
or in the nation.[24]

The Committee was surprised to encounter another stumbling block
in Dr. Charles W. Stiles of the Rockefeller Hookworm Commission.
For several years Stiles had been making a study of hookworm disease
and its effect on the people of the South's sandy soil regions. He
found that many of the cotton mill operatives, fresh from the farms,
brought the infection with them. One of his suggestions for remedying the situation was to put an end to all child labor legislation for
several years so as to encourage the movement of the poor farmer to
the mill towns where it would be easier to treat cases of hookworm.
Dr. Stiles said he "would rather place his ten-year-old daughter in the

spinning-room of a cotton mill than send her to the unsanitary sur-
roundings to be found on the average farm of some sections." [25]

In his writings Alexander McKelway had to confront such talk.
Having spent a good deal of time in the mountains acquiring an intimate knowledge of the people, he denied what he thought were exaggerated and even slanderous charges against the inhabitants of the
region. He questioned the theory that the best remedy for hookworm
was to remove the white farm population to the mills. Again in the
summer of 1910, this time in the company of Lovejoy, he traversed
the mountain regions of North Carolina to study further the condition
of the so-called poor whites whose only refuge, it was argued, was
the teeming cotton mill. The trip by carriage, saddle, and foot took
McKelway and Lovejoy over many miles of mountain roads where
they visited homes in the most backward areas.[26]

Thus equipped, McKelway and the NCLC were well prepared to
discuss the conditions of the mountain folk. It could be shown, of
course, that to cure them of hookworm it was not necessary for the
people to migrate to the mills, nor once there was it necessary to work
their immature children ten to twelve hours a day. Perhaps it was
true, McKelway conceded, that "mill pallor" was due to hookworm,
but that would indicate a greater—not less—need for regulation, for
diseased children required fresh open air and a chance to rebuild their
wasted bodies.

Responding to the alleged run-down and seedy condition of the
farm people, McKelway argued that, on the contrary, they were more
rugged and healthier than those he saw emerging from the cotton
mills. In fact, they were the sturdiest, most vigorous, and moral people
left in America, a sect multiplying in number without help from
immigrants. The fittest survive, McKelway claimed, and the only descendants of the pure, virile, sturdy scions of Colonial and Revolutionary times were the hardy white farmers of the South Atlantic
and Gulf regions. In these people lay the hope of the future.

As for the civilizing influences of the mill towns, McKelway
pointed out with tongue in cheek that there were not enough of them
to go around. Mississippi had only about twenty mills, and Louisiana

four—certainly not enough to save the rural white population from evil. In a more serious vein, he pointed to the illiteracy rate for mill children—it was three or four times greater than that for whites generally in the same states. The so-called welfare system of the mill villages (which McKelway claimed would be unnecessary if adults were paid a living wage) was a poor substitute for an education. In any case, whether or not the children were better off in the mills than on the farms was unimportant; the question was whether they were as well off in the mill villages as they had a right to be.[27]

Not content with this rebuttal, McKelway and the Committee hired a photographer, Lewis W. Hine, and sent him to the mills, including those owned by D. A. Tompkins, treasurer of the Civic Federation's child labor committee. Hine's contribution to the National Child Labor Committee was incalculable. A poor, shy, scrawny boy from the sawdust town of Oshkosh, Wisconsin, young Lewis had gone to work in a furniture factory when he was orphaned at fifteen. In winter, after walking a mile to work over a frozen river, he shivered in the cold drafty shop where for fifteen hours a day and $4 a week he had had to lift objects too heavy for his slender frame. He was helped in his schooling, however, and eventually obtained a Master's degree in education from the University of Chicago.

Hine's first job was as a nature teacher at the Ethical Culture School in New York City. In 1908, after several years as an amateur photographer, having taken pictures of immigrants, Bowery denizens, and Lower East Side slum children, he quit teaching to become one of America's first photographers interested in depicting the plight of the poor. After working for *The Survey* magazine, he was hired by the NCLC to do field studies and photograph conditions in the cotton mills, canneries, coal mines, glass-making factories, and tenement sweatshops. For the next twenty years, while serving as the Committee's official photographer, he developed thousands of vivid, appealing pictures of inestimable value in social work.[28]

Hine trained himself to be resourceful. Using any pretext he could get away with, he entered factories, sheds, mines, and homes by night or day, to photograph and interview working children. He secretly measured children's height according to the buttons on his coat, and scribbled notes while keeping his hands in his pockets. When he could not get into the factories and mines, he stayed outside until closing time and took pictures of the youngsters as they left work. He also persuaded suspicious mothers to let him photograph birth certificates and records from family bibles.

Lewis Hine's pictures of the human and inhumane element in industry—the pathetic faces of the working children and the conditions under which they toiled—aroused public sentiment against child labor in a way that no printed page or public lecture could. His pictures were obvious proof of shameful child labor practices, and no charge of fraud could be lodged against them. Printed in large numbers or made into stereopticon slides, they were widely circulated, exhibited, and used in illustrating lectures.[29]

Another asset for the NCLC at this time was the federal government's voluminous report on women and child wage-earners in America, as authorized by Congress in 1907. In some respects these findings were more valuable than anything the Committee itself had published. Because the Committee's testimony on child labor in the Southern cotton mills (and elsewhere, for that matter) revealed such flagrant conditions, the public tended to discredit it, coming as it did from an organization devoted to reform. The first volume in a government series which in time would total twenty, *The Cotton Textile Industry,* appeared in 1910. With more time and money at their disposal than the Committee's researchers, government officials painted an even darker picture of child labor in the mills. The whole dismal story was published in popular form and widely circulated. It was promptly condemned by industrial interests, who associated it with the NCLC.

The report detailed the now familiar story of child labor in Southern textile mills and the unhealthful and dangerous nature of much of the work. It revealed children's long hours, small wages, inadequate education, and bad moral tendencies, as evidenced by greater delinquency among working than among nonworking youngsters. As an example, one mill child under twelve was described as "an emaciated little elf 50 inches high and weighing perhaps 48 pounds who works from 6 at night till 6 in the morning and who is so tiny that she has to climb up on the spinning frame to reach the top row of spindles."[30]

Just how much remained to be done was made apparent by this survey of every leading industry, volume by volume. Also significant were the 1910 census returns, which showed that some two million children between the ages of ten and fifteen, or 18.4 per cent of the youngsters in that age group (compared with 18.2 per cent in 1900), were gainfully employed. The gap between the more progressive and the more backward states was growing wider.[31]

The Committee meanwhile had broadened the scope of its effort. While continuing its demands for reform in the cotton mills, in the mines, and in the glass-making factories, it began to pay attention to the canneries and the street trades.

The seafood canning industry was located chiefly in the South. Along the Gulf Coast from Louisiana eastward to Florida, and up the Atlantic Coast from Georgia to Maryland stretched a chain of oyster and shrimp canneries. Important fruit and vegetable canning states were Virginia, Maryland, Delaware, Indiana, New Jersey, and New York. The Committee surveyed the entire industry, North and South, and despite different problems according to product, it found conditions to be generally the same all over—miserable.

Each year labor agents or padrones secured an army of workers, usually Middle European or Italian immigrants who, with their families, from the oldest child to nursing babies, left their city flats in early June and remained in cannery labor camps until late fall. Some places the season lasted much longer; in the Maine sardine canneries, for example, it ran from April 15 to December 15. Families were herded together and shipped to the camps by train or by boat. Providing living quarters for the workers increased the canners' expenses, but wages were low and children were needed to help with the family's subsistence. While conditions in the labor camps varied, most were unfit to live in. All were poorly built and poorly furnished, without proper sanitation—if any—or adequate water supply. They usually were badly overcrowded; some even lacked partitions to separate the sexes. Disease was rampant in these dilapidated, filth-ridden, rat-infested hovels.[32]

The whistle to begin work blew at 3 or 4 A.M. The workers, including those who had just learned to toddle, snatched a piece of bread for breakfast and hurried to the sheds. Children who worked in the canneries were younger than those in the cotton mills or any other industrial establishment. Alexander McKelway and Lewis Hine, who visited many a cannery, found it not uncommon to see children three, four, or five years old at work in the sheds.

In seafood canneries reeking with steam and moisture-laden odors, the children split open rough, hard oyster shells, dropping the sharp pieces on the floor and the meat into pails. When filled, the pails were carried off to be weighed. For a pot that held four pounds of shelled oysters, the worker received five cents. The children usually filled one or two pots a day, their elders eight or nine.[33]

The sharp oyster shells were painful enough for tiny fingers, often causing them to bleed, but raw shrimp were far worse. They emitted a strong, viscous, alkaline liquid so corrosive that it ate holes in workers' leather shoes and even in the tin pails that were used. Each night the workers would soak their bleeding hands in a strong alum solution to harden the skin and help heal the wounds. Yet the plucking of shrimp and the shucking of oysters went on each day without a break even for meals, until the visible supply was disposed of, usually by late afternoon.[34]

In the fruit and vegetable canneries, where women and children did most of the work, conditions were equally bad. Here the hours were longer and more irrgeular. Since fruit and vegetables were highly perishable and could not be stored overnight on ice, as were oysters and shrimp, everything had to be canned within a few hours after being received. The length of the working day therefore depended entirely upon the size of the crops brought in and the time of arrival. As one canner put it: "The Lord ripens the crops." [35] By divine governance, therefore, the work usually began around 3 A.M. during the peak of the season, when eighteen-hour days and a work week of

90 to 110 hours were not uncommon. Perishable farm products took precedence over perishable children.

The children snipped off the ends of beans, hulled strawberries, stemmed currants, peeled apples and tomatoes, shelled peas, husked corn, and so forth. Sometimes sharp knives slipped out of the hands of tired or heedless young workers, cutting exposed flesh or perhaps slicing off a finger. Some children had to carry or drag filled containers to weighing stations—which seemed a long way off when a box full of beans weighed from nineteen to twenty-nine pounds, and corn crates from forty to sixty pounds.[36]

Since the working youngsters left home before summer vacation began and rarely returned until long after the fall term had started, they lagged far behind in their grades, if they attended school at all. Many did not and thus never learned English; they simply wandered about with their parents, following the seasons from strawberries and peaches in the North to oysters and shrimp in the South.

Where legal statutes applied, the NCLC learned, they were ignored by the employers, for most canneries were located in rural areas, making inspection difficult. And, as in the textile mills, children who served as "helpers" were not found on the payroll. Canners also avoided regulation by arguing that because they handled perishable foods the work was agricultural and thus not subject to factory or child labor legislation. To say the least, control was difficult.

When pressed, the canners argued that the season was short, that the summer work was performed in open sheds (whatever the elements), and that since the industry operated on a piecework basis, children worked only as long as they wished. Child labor in the canning industry was thus totally unregulated. Attempts to remedy the situation had failed year after year. Only in 1913, when New York State amended its child labor law to include canneries, did slow progress begin.[37]

The NCLC also turned its attention to street trading—selling newspapers, peddling, bootblacking, running errands, making deliveries, and carrying messages. While work of this sort—especially selling newspapers and shoe-shining—was done by adults in European countries, most street traders in America were children, many under ten years of age. Indulgent citizens often took it for granted that this working child was nobly helping to support a widowed mother or perhaps an ill parent. Factory or mine children might conjure up evil images, but it was easy to consider street traders, especially newsboys, who carried on their work in the "healthful open air," as rugged individuals starting on the road toward success.

Newsboys, peddlers, and bootblacks, sometimes known as "little merchants," were most difficult to regulate because they were self-employed. Unlike delivery children or messengers, who clearly worked for employers who might be held responsible for their welfare, "little merchants" were considered independent contractors. Newsboys, for example, received no salary or commission; they purchased the papers they delivered or sold, and their compensation was the difference between the cost of the papers and the amount of money they collected. Such business enterprise, however, placed on the child dealer burdens that even adult workers were not expected to bear. Newsboys carried the financial risk of collections; what they did not or could not collect was their loss. In no other industry were bad debts passed on to its delivery men.

Again, independent contractors were not covered by workmen's compensation legislation, which spread rapidly in the United States after 1911.[38] In most states, then, they had no protection in case of injury; in some states, in order to avoid any uncertainty, workmen's compensation laws were amended expressly to exclude them. Thus the newspaper publishers, the NCLC could argue, secured a double privilege at the cost of their young employees: they used younger children to distribute their goods than was permitted in almost any other industry, and, though they laid out the route, hours, and other conditions of employment, they escaped the responsibilities that all other industries were ordinarily obliged to assume.[39]

The need to regulate street trading arose less from its long hours or the inherent nature of the work than from the surrounding conditions, especially in large cities. Aside from being exposed to the physical dangers of the street—carriages, wagons, horse-cars, and automobiles—street traders lacked supervision by a parent or an employer. The city's noise and confusion made them nervous and excitable. Irregular eating and sleeping habits induced fatigue. As a result, they often ignored school or, if they attended, many became deficient. Frequently they resorted to cigarettes and liquor and turned to gambling during lulls in business or after hours. In sum, the occupation menaced a child's health, education, and morals. Frederick A. King of the University Settlement summed it up well: "The life of the street is at best a rough school of experience and at worst a free field in which the most evil and corrupting influences may work against the morals of the community." [40]

Yet, before 1900, with the exception of an 1892 Boston ordinance, there was no regulation of street trades in America. The first applicable state law was passed by New York in 1902–1903. Its modest provisions set the minimum working age for boys at ten years, permitting selling until 10 P.M., and neglected enforcement. Little progress followed. When in 1911 the NCLC began concentrating on the problem, only three states (New York, Massachusetts, and Wisconsin), the District of Columbia, and a few scattered cities regulated the street trades in any way.[41]

In cooperation with a group of doctors, teachers, and social workers, the Committee conducted studies which demonstrated the evil effects of the work. They showed that while a few successful men had started as newsboys, many others who began the same way ended as failures. Their lives had been marred by the lack of education, by physical hardship, and by unwholesome pleasures frequently associated with the street.

As the Committee's statistics indicated, and as the U.S. *Report* on the condition of women and child wage-earners in America further documented, a clear relationship existed between street work and crime. Despite the prevalent belief that idleness led to juvenile delinquency, working children in general and street traders in particular were more likely to become delinquents than nonworkers; an exceedingly large proportion of the prison and reform-school population had sold newspapers early in life. Finally, the Committee's investigations into the home lives of thousands of newsboys in widely scattered cities showed also that in most cases parents were not dependent upon their children's earnings; the poverty plea, in short, was highly exaggerated.[42]

The NCLC did not object to children delivering a small number of newspapers during daylight hours to subscribers in residential areas. It did oppose young children walking the streets at random during any hour of the day or night. All its attempts to draft street trades laws or improve existing ones, however, met with feverish opposition, especially from newspaper interests. And, as with the canneries, the Committee was unsuccessful for the most part in overcoming that opposition.[43] "Freedom of the press" had come to have a new meaning, and the newspapers did not intend to have that freedom curtailed by allowing authorities to regulate the ages and hours of newsboys.

So only a few state laws and municipal ordinances were passed, or slightly upgraded. And with three notable exceptions—in Milwaukee, Cincinnati, and Boston—even these, for the most part, were dead-letter laws; enforcement, as in the canning industry, was almost nil. On those rare occasions when a youngster was prosecuted for violating a newsboy law, the courts did not punish the offender. An employer of child labor in a factory could be made to pay a fine, but the self-employed newsboy stood alone before the judge. And since public sympathy was with the newsboy working his way to the top, violators usually were let off with, at most, a warning.[44]

The night messenger service was an exception to the rule, for the evils of this form of street trading were spectacular. Once the facts were known, it took little argument to convince most people that this occupation should be reserved for adults.[45] In 1909 and 1910 the Committee investigated the night messenger service in twenty-seven cities in nine states. With slight variation, it discovered everywhere that there was much more to the night messenger service than simply delivering telegrams, actually a minor part of the job. For the most part, uniformed night messenger boys spent their time helping prostitutes, pimps, gamblers, and other habitués of the underworld. They answered calls from whorehouses, carried notes to and from patrons, bought opium, cocaine, and other narcotics for the prostitutes and their customers, purchased liquor during unlawful hours, showed visiting firemen the red-light districts, and did various other jobs for those engaged in night-life vice.[46] These people, in return, provided certain services as well as sizable tips, as the following conversation between an NCLC agent and a seventeen-year-old night messenger indicates:

AGENT: How do you know they are whore houses?
MESSENGER: Don't I get called to them with messages?
AGENT: How can they call?
MESSENGER: Well, they all have call boxes. We go in all of 'em. We see some great sights there. Last week I got a call in the ———— Hotel on 13th Street, and when I answered the woman let me in her room where she was all naked, except for a little shirt she had on, and that could cover very little of her. . . . She sent me to get her something to eat and when I came back she was laying flat on the bed.
AGENT: Did you trip over her?
MESSENGER: I could hardly get next to her, but I get mine alright.
AGENT: What do you mean?
MESSENGER: Well, a lot of girls like to stay with us messengers. We have whores come to our office too. We have a table there and do the trick on it. We get a lot of coats and lay them over the table and in that way make a soft spot.
AGENT: I wish I could get a look in on that. . . . I would like to just walk in and send a telegram when that trick happens again.
MESSENGER: You wouldn't see a thing if you did, because we do it all down the cellar.
AGENT: Does your manager know what goes on?
MESSENGER: I should say he does. He sends us out after the whores, and then he takes his whack first.[47]

Such employment, the NCLC contended, subjected children to more bad influences than any other occupation at which they worked. Besides the chance of disease, the children were almost certain candidates for the ranks of the unskilled and eventually the unemployed. The night messenger service, Lovejoy maintained, "is an industrial blind alley. Instead of being an avenue to higher . . . opportunities, the

work leaves the boy at the end of one or five years as undeveloped
. . . as when he began. Meanwhile his years have been absorbed, his
energy sapped, his sensibilities blunted, and his ideals shattered." [48]

With the facts at hand, the Committee in 1910 vigorously cam-
paigned for legislation that would set a twenty-one-year minimum age
for employment in the occupation. The general managers of the leading messenger companies—Western Union and Postal Telegraph—
expressed surprise at the disclosures of practice but were reluctant to
accept corrective measures to stop them. Company officials, however,
could hardly defend any presumed right of young boys to visit whorehouses during hours of employment, since aside from other considerations it was illegal. They belatedly offered to work with the NCLC to
secure restrictive legislation but insisted on an eighteen-year minimum
age. Working with the New York State Child Labor Committee, the
NCLC soon won a statute that barred all those under twenty-one years
of age from engaging in messenger work between the hours of 10
P.M and 5 A.M.[49]

In an effort to get similar laws elsewhere, the Committee dispatched
agents to numerous cities and states. That same year, Ohio passed a
law limiting night messenger service to those over eighteen, and
Maryland set sixteen as a minimum age. Bills identical to New York's
failed in Massachusetts and New Jersey but were passed the following year. In 1911 the Committee helped to pass similar statutes in five
other states—Wisconsin, Michigan, Tennessee, California, and New
Hampshire. Maryland soon raised its age limit to eighteen years. By
the spring of 1913, seven states limited employment in the night
messenger service to those over twenty-one, and ten others had an
eighteen-year minimum age.[50]

Despite failures of sorts, the NCLC continued to grow. Beginning
in 1904 with less than fifty people and an income of about $13,500,
by 1912 it had a contributing membership of over 6,400 and an
annual budget of nearly $60,000. The printed material it issued had
increased from about two to six million pages a year. Besides its
twenty-seven affiliated state and local committees, the NCLC cooperated with educators, medical experts, jurists, reform agencies, relief

societies, trade unions, churches, and other agencies working for the protection of child life. In the eight years of its existence the Committee had succeeded in arousing public opinion and helping, in part at least, thirty-nine states to pass new child labor laws or amend existing statutes.[51]

Yet a survey of the situation in 1912 was not encouraging. A reduction in hours here, a twelve-year limit there, or an inspection law somewhere else, invaluable as they were, did not appear very significant in comparison with what remained to be done. (The Committee spent almost as much time fighting deleterious legislation as it spent promoting good statutes.) Too, the life of NCLC investigators during these years was, to say the least, strenuous. They were run out of hotels, forbidden to enter factories, or, when they did get in, children were hidden from them. Some mill towns even posted signs at the outskirts that no one could enter without permission.[52]

What did the Committee have to show for its efforts? In 1910 it had drafted a Uniform Child Labor Law which, in the following year, the American Bar Association adopted and recommended for passage by all state legislatures. The law's standards were minimal and based upon what had already been achieved in one or more states. In 1912 not a single state reached all those standards. Indeed, only nine had attained those encompassed in the Committee's 1904 model law, namely a fourteen-year minimum age for employment in manufacturing, sixteen for mining, a maximum work day of eight hours for children between the ages of fourteen and sixteen, the prohibition of night work for those under sixteen, and documentary proof of age. In 1912,

twenty-two states (including the four leading southern textile-producing ones) still permitted children under fourteen to work in factories;

thirty states still allowed boys under sixteen to work in mines;

thirty-one states still authorized children under sixteen to work more than eight hours a day;

twenty-eight states still let children under sixteen work at night;

twenty-three states still did not require adequate documentary proof of age.

The employment of children in the street trades—with the exception of the night messenger service—in the canneries, and in tenement sweatshops was still virtually unregulated. Child labor on the nation's farms had eluded legislation altogether.[53]

And what about implementation? The passage of laws, even good ones, could never insure their effectiveness. Voluntary compliance was visionary; strict supervision and control were essential. Without the proper machinery to enforce child labor statutes, they were valueless. In many places factory inspection, where it existed at all, was weak and inefficient. In most states inspectors were political appointees. In other states very little money or none at all was appropriated to enforce the law. As the NCLC confessed, it had expended most of its money and energy in efforts to secure new laws or improve old ones; it had not followed through on enforcement and administration.[54]

None of the members of the Committee thought of giving up in the face of this situation. Vague hope, primitive fighting instinct, firm belief in human nature, and, above all, deep conviction about the justness of the cause combined to sustain them. In fact, an incredible sense of optimism continued to pervade their activities.[55] To most of them, the past was to learn from, not to lament about. Certainly, despite the disappointing results, no one could deny that public apathy was waning and that regulation was winning acceptance, however slowly and grudgingly.

By 1912, however, there was a perceptible shift in attitude among the Committee members: most were beginning to feel that the slow, uneven process of state regulation was an inadequate way to solve the problem. They were coming around to the position that only a handful had taken six years earlier—that federal child labor legislation was essential to curtail the injustice.

V

Federal Child Labor Legislation

A turning point in the child labor reform movement came in 1912. On April 9, after six years of concerted effort by the National Child Labor Committee and by others, the United States Children's Bureau became a reality. In recognition of Alexander McKelway's leadership in the fight to create the Bureau, President Taft, upon signing the measure into law, cheerfully gave him the pen.[1]

In the meantime, the Committee had considered prospective candidates to head the Bureau, and the President agreed not to act until he had the Committee's recommendation. When Jane Addams, Lillian Wald, and Samuel McCune Lindsay each refused the post, the Committee unanimously decided on Julia Lathrop, who had assured the board that she would accept. On April 15, Miss Wald, Edward T. Devine, Paul Warburg, Owen Lovejoy, and Judge Julian Mack, a leader in the children's court movement, met with President Taft and submitted Miss Lathrop's name; two days later she was named to head the Bureau.[2]

While not as well known as some of her colleagues, Miss Lathrop was highly qualified for the position. A licensed attorney, a long-time Hull-House resident, and a member of the Illinois State Board of

Charities, she was a recognized leader in the field of child welfare. In addition to her known executive ability, she was considered far-sighted, logical, charming, and, importantly, a woman who could lead others to get things done. In Lillian Wald's words, Julia Lathrop was "the best qualified person in the country . . . for the job." [3] The agency would remain in her capable hands until 1921.

Given a modest appropriation of $25,640 and placed in the Department of Commerce and Labor (from where it was transferred the following year to the newly created Department of Labor), the Children's Bureau had no administrative power. Rather it was a research and propaganda agency directed to "investigate and report upon all matters pertaining to the welfare of children and child life among all our classes of people." It was to establish the facts, bring together widely scattered material, and acquaint the public with conditions affecting the lives of American children. [4] This clearing house would prove of enormous help to the NCLC. Much of the energy and money the Committee had expended investigating child labor could now be released for the fight for better legislation and enforcement.

That the public attitude toward child labor in America was shifting was indicated by the creation of the Children's Bureau, by the enactment of the District of Columbia child labor law, by the federal investigation into the working conditions of women and children, and by the American Bar Association's adoption of a Uniform Child Labor Law. Clearly, more and more citizens and elected officials were becoming aware of child labor conditions and of the need for action. Thus the nation was edging toward acceptance of a single child labor standard, something that only the federal government could effect.

The 1912 presidential campaign furthered this development. Quite aware of the changing popular attitude, Theodore Roosevelt dramatically shifted his position to support Senator Beveridge's pleas for national child labor legislation. TR ran on a platform that called for federal measures for industrial and social justice, including the abolition of child labor. [5]

Interestingly, the Progressive party platform on which Roosevelt ran had originated at a committee meeting of social workers appointed in 1909 at the National Conference of Charities and Correction. This Committee on Occupational Standards (which later changed its name to the Committee on Standards of Living and Labor), headed by Paul Kellogg, social reformer, long-time editor of *The Survey,* and close friend of the anti–child labor forces, made a systematic study of "certain minimum requirements of well-being" in an industrial society. Three years later, with Owen Lovejoy as its chairman, the committee decided to summarize its work and formulate a program of minimum standards to help "direct public thought and secure official action."

Lovejoy's committee drafted a platform of minimum "Social Standards for Industry," which the delegates to the 1912 National Conference adopted. Among other things, the program called for an eight-hour day and a six-day work week, the abolition of tenement homework, and the prohibition of child labor.[6] Owen Lovejoy, Homer Folks, Samuel McCune Lindsay, and Jane Addams of the NCLC, along with Paul Kellogg and others, then helped get all this into the Progressive party platform—the most advanced major party platform presented to the American people up to that time.[7]

But Roosevelt did not win the 1912 election, and a brighter future for America's working children would rest with Woodrow Wilson, the President-elect. Committee members soon found out where the new President stood when shortly after the election he met informally with a group of social workers. During the meeting, characterized by *The Survey* as "something in the nature of a hearing on the state of the country," spokesmen for several reform groups cited the needs in their respective fields. Owen Lovejoy, representing the NCLC, outlined for Wilson the scope and purpose of the newly created Children's Bureau, emphasizing the need to collect more adequate information and to put an end to child labor. While expressing sympathy for the cause, the President replied that, in his opinion, the government was "not so much an initiating agency as a responsive one, depending on the vigorous action of its citizens."[8]

More specifically, Wilson held that federal child labor regulation was illegal. His position had not changed since 1908 when, as a political scientist, referring to the Beveridge bill, he had written:

The proposed federal legislation . . . affords a striking example of a tendency to carry Congressional power over interstate commerce beyond the utmost boundaries of reasonable and honest inference. If the power to regulate commerce between the states can be stretched to include regulation of labor in mills and factories, it can be made to embrace every particular of the industrial organization and action of the country.[9]

Some years later, Wilson, born a Southerner, reminded those about him that the Democratic party, which controlled Congress, "represents a very strong states' rights feeling. It is very plain that you have to go much further than most interpretations of the Constitution would allow if you were to give the [federal] government general control over child labor throughout the country." [10]

A number of Congressmen from the North and West felt differently. In their opinion, the public wanted an end to child labor, and the only way to get it was through the establishment of a uniform national standard. Thus Senator Ira Copley of Illinois and Representative Miles Poindexter of Washington, Roosevelt supporters in 1912, introduced a federal child labor bill which was similar to the Beveridge proposal except in its enforcement features. It sought to use federal power to prohibit the employment of children under fourteen years of age in any mill, factory, cannery, workshop, manufacturing, or mechanical establishment, or of children under sixteen in any mine, quarry, or other dangerous or immoral occupation. At the request of the International Child Welfare League, Senator William Kenyon of Iowa introduced a similar measure, except that it applied only to children fourteen years of age or under.[11]

More and more, social workers were turning to the federal government for help in solving the problem. The United States *Report,* the 1910 census figures, the reluctance of many states to act and the wide disparity of measures among those that did (which brought competitive advantages to the more backward states and thus tended to retard further progress) and, above all, the inability or unwillingness of the states to enforce their laws—all made it increasingly apparent that uniform national legislation was necessary.[12] Without endorsing a specific proposal, the delegates to the National Conference of Charities and Correction in July 1913 went on record in favor of federal child labor legislation.

Lindsay, Folks, Jane Addams, and Florence Kelley, always staunch advocates of federal legislation, meanwhile continued to urge the NCLC to work for a national child labor law of some kind. McKelway by now was more convinced than ever that "the only answer lay with 'Uncle Sam.'" Even Felix Adler, who earlier had voted negatively with the majority, concluded that federal help was necessary.[13]

As a result, in April and May of 1913 the Committee began to review its policy on federal child labor legislation; if it did nothing else, it would have to take a stand on the issue when the pending bills came up in Congress. In December a special committee—Folks, Mrs. Kelley, Devine, and Lovejoy—was appointed to analyze and compare the bills, but it concluded that neither was satisfactory. By excluding fifteen- and sixteen-year-olds, Senator Kenyon's bill fell short of the Committee's minimum standards, and by stating that law violators must do so "knowingly," the Copley bill contained weak enforcement provisions. The group decided to submit its own measure, one that would be both legally sound and effective.

Lovejoy was named to draft the new bill. Over a period of months he consulted with lawyers, state officials, spokesmen for interested reform groups, liberal Congressmen, and several federal officials, including Miss Lathrop of the Children's Bureau and two members of the President's Cabinet. Chiefly responsible for the form and substance of the measure as drawn up were William Draper Lewis, dean of the University of Pennsylvania Law School, and Charles P. Neill, former commissioner of the Bureau of Labor. Neill had supervised the federal investigation of women and child laborers in America and had become a trustee of NCLC, as would Dean Lewis some years later. In 1912 Lewis had headed the platform committee at the Progressive party convention.

While based on the same principle as the Beveridge and the two pending child labor bills—that the power of Congress to regulate interstate commerce included the power to prohibit child labor—the special committee's bill "To Prevent Interstate Commerce in the Products of Child Labor and for Other Purposes" differed from the others in several respects. It was, first of all, more extensive, for it not only banned the employment of children under fourteen in factories, workshops, and canneries, and children under sixteen in mines and quarries, but it also prohibited all children under sixteen from working more than eight hours a day, and between the hours of 7 P.M. and 7 A.M. By applying restrictions to "older" children and by dealing with hours as well, the bill marked an important advance over the others. Also, unlike all other measures, the Committee's proposal dealt with the actual offender, the employer of child labor, and not the carrier of child-made goods. Thus it was more direct. It was not a drastic bill, however, for it merely embodied the four principal standards of the Uniform Child Labor Law, standards the American people already tolerated in whole or in part in many of the states. In fact, several states already had more advanced laws than that now proposed.[14]

With some minor revision, the NCLC's board of trustees endorsed the bill and resolved that "the officers of the Committee be authorized to take measures to secure its enactment," including the designation of a Senator and Representative to introduce it in Congress. The federal bill, it was decided, should be pushed even at the cost of the Committee's other work.[15]

A new committee—Lovejoy, Folks, Kelley, Adler, Devine, and Dr. Stephen S. Wise, rabbi of New York City's Free Synagogue and a newly appointed trustee—was charged with carrying out the board's action. The members immediately requested an appointment with President Wilson and asked Representative A. Mitchell Palmer, a young, reform-minded Democrat from Pennsylvania who later became U.S. Attorney General, to introduce the bill in the House. Robert L. Owen of Oklahoma, a progressive Democrat, agreed to sponsor the measure in the Senate.

Wilson met with Adler, McKelway, and Lovejoy on February 2, 1914. Speaking for the group, Adler reviewed for the President the slow steps by which the Committee had arrived at the decision to seek federal legislation. Referring to Wilson's earlier statement that federal child labor legislation would likely be unconstitutional, Adler asked the President to read a memo the Committee had prepared on this very point. He then pleaded with the President to withhold adverse comment until the Committee had a chance to initiate an educational campaign. Wilson, though he reiterated his view that such legislation could not be upheld and, if passed, would open the door to unlimited federal regulation, promised to give the matter careful consideration and say nothing to impede the progress of the campaign.[16]

With the guarantee of at least presidential neutrality, the legislative battle began. The so-called Palmer-Owen bill was introduced in Congress and Senator Kenyon withdrew his measure. Public hearings were scheduled and, as usual, the Committee set in motion all its machinery to push for acceptance. Pamphlets, public addresses, posters, and letters urged people to write their Congressmen, arrange meetings, make speeches, and obtain newspaper publicity for the bill. The measure was endorsed and supported by state and local child labor committees and a wide variety of other organizations, including the U.S. Children's Bureau, the National Consumers' League, the American Federation of Labor, the American Medical Association, the Farmers' Educational and Cooperative Union of America, the International Child Welfare League, women's clubs, church conferences, temperance unions, and health associations.[17]

There was little overt opposition to the measure. As the Committee had assumed, public sentiment supported federal control of child labor. The only opponents to appear at public hearings were three South Carolina mill men. Lewis K. Parker, president of the Parker Cotton Mills, acted as spokesman for the owners. Even he disavowed any interest in perpetuating child labor, stating that he was pleased to see that conditions in the South were improving. He and his colleagues opposed the measure on legal grounds. (Since the NCLC and the federal government had previously discredited the mill owners' defense of child labor, there was little else they could do.) They hoped to convince Congress that the bill was invalid.[18]

The most vigorous attack on the Palmer-Owen bill came from David Clark, editor of the *Southern Textile Bulletin* of Charlotte, North Carolina. Clark argued that not a single child's health had been harmed by work in the mills. The South, he charged, was being maligned by the NCLC, a "New England Organization using sensationalist publicity." The interstate shipment of whiskey, he declared, was more harmful than child labor; why didn't Northerners raise the moral climate of their own states before telling Southerners how to run theirs?

Clark organized a militant Southern drive against the proposed bill. At his initiative, seven prominent mill owners "selected for their fighting qualities" met at Greenville, South Carolina, to form the Executive Committee of Southern Cotton Manufacturers, an organization that raised a large sum to protect the interests of the owners. Clark was elected secretary and treasurer of the group, and former North Carolina Governor W. W. Kitchin, brother of Claude Kitchin, floor leader of the U.S. House, would represent it in Washington.[19]

Nearly nine months after congressional hearings were concluded, the Committee on Labor's unanimous report was finally submitted to the House. Two days later, on February 15, 1915, the Palmer-Owen bill came up for a vote and, after little discussion, it was passed by the wide margin of 233 to 43. The outcome plainly depicted the sectional character of the political struggle. Of the forty-three votes cast against the bill, thirty-five were from six Southern states—the South Atlantic states in which textile manufacturing and canning were centered. From only four states—North Carolina, South Carolina, Georgia, and Mississippi—did a majority oppose the bill. Congressman Palmer was quite right when, during the floor debate, he had asserted that the nation-at-large decisively favored the bill: "The Republican Party, and the Progressive Party, and the Democratic Party, and the Nation," he had stated, "have declared for this kind of legislation. The country is for it, as it is for very few things in either branch of Congress today." [20]

Two weeks after House action, the Senate Committee on Interstate and Foreign Commerce reported it favorably. Because the session was coming to a close and the calendar was crowded, managers of the bill sought to bring it directly to the floor. Unanimous consent, however, was needed, and while President Wilson remained silent, Senator Lee Overman of North Carolina, a state extremely deficient in its child labor laws, and the only one without any factory inspection, objected. Three days later, March 4, 1915, Congress adjourned.[21] Disappointed but undaunted, the NCLC prepared for another campaign.

At the next session, Representative Edward Keating, a young Colorado Democrat with labor union ties, sponsored the measure in the House, and Robert Owen again introduced it in the Senate. As in the past, widespread support was evident. Lawyers, businessmen, political and labor leaders, government officials, physicians, educators, social workers, clergymen, authors, and journalists went on record in favor of the measure. So did the press. In at least thirty-two states leading newspapers published editorials in favor of the bill. The *Chicago Tribune,* the *Memphis Commercial Appeal,* the *Boston Evening Transcript,* the *Philadelphia Ledger,* the *New York Tribune,* the *New Orleans Times-Picayune,* the *Kansas City Post* and the *San Francisco Call* actively supported it.[22]

On January 5, 1916, the Keating-Owen bill was referred to the House Committee on Labor. At public hearings a week later Lovejoy and McKelway urged passage of the measure. They were joined by Thomas I. Parkinson, director of the Columbia University Legislative Drafting Bureau, an agency specializing in legal research that had been retained by the NCLC to prepare reports to meet the legal criticisms leveled at the bill.

Again, opposition to the measure at the three days of open hearings came almost exclusively from a small group of Southern textile men. They were joined this time by James A. Emery, chief attorney for the National Association of Manufacturers who, after admitting that his appearance had not been authorized by the association, nevertheless claimed that he spoke for its more than four thousand members.[23] Legal counsel for the textile people at the hearings was W. W. Kitchin.

Opposition to the proposed measure rested on all the old arguments: the absence of compulsory education to absorb the energies of the liberated child workers; the necessity of work to prevent the moral perversion of young children; the importance of acquiring, while young, the necessary skills for future work in the textile factories; the robbing of widowed mothers of their livelihood; the abridgement of the inherent personal right to work; and the illegal invasion of states' rights.[24]

Despite more vociferous opposition than in the previous year, the House Labor Committee on January 15, 1916, recommended passage of the bill and placed it on the order of the day for the 26th. Opposition on the floor availed little, and the House passed the Keating-Owen bill 343 to 46 in a vote that crossed party lines.[25] Again, the votes against the measure came almost entirely from the South Atlantic states. All those from North and South Carolina strove to defeat it, as did most of the representatives from Georgia and Mississippi. But, as one observer has pointed out, from the "southern states where manufacturing was not so firmly entrenched but where the states' rights appeal was presumably strong, there was no such united opposition." In six of those states, solid delegations supported the bill, and in the other five the majority did. Of 150 Southern Congressmen, 105, or more than two out of three, voted for the child labor bill. Only one Congressman from outside the South, a Republican from New Jersey, cast a negative vote.[26]

As was feared, action in the Senate would not be as prompt. There the opposing arguments were pretty much the same, but, as a *Survey* editor acidly noted: "The same undertakers who officiated so successfully last year [at the burial of the Palmer-Owen bill] are again proceeding with the funeral arrangements." [27]

In April the Senate Committee on Interstate and Foreign Commerce recommended passage of a slightly amended version of the bill, one which the NCLC and its legal counsel, Thomas I. Parkinson, found acceptable. Republican minority leader Jacob H. Gallinger of New Hampshire reported that his party stood solidly behind the measure, and it was believed that a majority of Democrats also favored its enactment.

Once more, however, Senator Lee Overman controlled the fate of the bill. When on June 3 it came before the Committee of the Whole, he again objected in a situation that required unanimous consent in order to get the measure onto the calendar for the day and thus bring it to the Senate floor. As a result, the bill was set aside for a second time—perhaps indefinitely, for later that day Congress recessed for the national political conventions.[28]

Behind-the-scenes politics would now play a sizable role in the measure's future. The political situation for Wilson and the Democrats was precarious: Theodore Roosevelt was back in the Republican fold, and many Progressives had been alienated by Wilson's neglect of social reform. As Democratic leaders considered planks for the party's 1916 platform, it was clear that bold, vigorous action was needed. In the hope of attracting Progressives to the party, Senator Owen, co-sponsor of the bill, suggested that Democrats adopt the social justice plank of the Progressive party's 1912 platform. Wilson squelched the idea, saying that most of the programs in that plank existed "merely in thesis, because they affected matters controlled by the state and not by the national government." [29]

At the President's request for a memorandum outlining issues "we could all agree upon," Owen drew up a general plank that endorsed all the popular social justice proposals and at the same time managed to evade the states' rights issue. Among its provisions was a pledge for "the harmonious exercise of the public authority of State and Nation in . . . the prohibition of child labor." This rather vague proposal, which Wilson agreed to support, was later replaced in the Democratic platform (adopted on June 16) by a definite commitment to federal legislation. It read: "We favor the speedy enactment of an effective Federal Child Labor Law." The Republicans also adopted a plank favoring the enactment of such legislation.[30]

Despite the pledge, when the Senate reconvened after the party conventions that nominated Charles Evans Hughes and renominated Wilson, intransigent Southern opponents of the Keating-Owen bill planned to prevent the measure from reaching a vote. When the Democratic Caucus met they threatened to filibuster the child labor bill if it came up for discussion. Fearful that such action would preclude the passage of other important legislation, party leaders yielded and struck the Keating-Owen bill from the list of measures to be enacted before adjournment.

Alexander McKelway, who was in Washington to lobby for the bill, was a long-time friend of Wilson's and a solid Democrat. Naturally, to McKelway the bill was of unquestioned merit. But he also viewed it as a political issue, one on which Progressives would judge the Wilson regime and the party's "genuine interest in humane measures opposed by commercial interests." He lost no time warning the President that failure to enact it would cost him and the party a great deal of support in the coming election. He reminded Wilson that Republicans in Congress would support the measure and that Wilson's opponent, former Chief Justice Hughes, was expected to endorse their action.[31]

The President had said nothing in support of the bill, nor had he opposed it. Now, aware of public pressure for immediate enactment, he concluded that, as McKelway saw it, victory at the polls could be achieved only by convincing Progressives that the Democratic party was the party of reform. To rally support for the bill would be a sound political move.

Wilson therefore decided to postpone acceptance of his renomination until he received assurance from Democratic legislators that the Keating-Owen bill would be enacted during the current session. That promise came on July 18 when party leaders, to their surprise, were summoned to the President's room at the Capitol; Wilson had come to the Hill to urge them to reconsider the bill in light of the political realities of the situation.

Apparently the broad political view convinced the lawmakers—as indeed it had convinced Wilson—"of the utmost importance that the child labor bill . . . be passed at this session." "I am encouraged to believe that the situation has changed considerably," the President wrote to McKelway just after his visit to Capitol Hill. Indeed it had; one week later the Democratic Caucus placed the bill on its list of priority legislation.[32]

On August 3, 1916, Senator Joseph T. Robinson, an Arkansas Democrat, rose on the Senate floor and moved for consideration of the Keating-Owen bill. Supporting and opposing arguments followed —without a filibuster. Opposition centered mainly on states' rights and the question of constitutionality.[33] Proponents of the measure rested their case largely on recent Supreme Court decisions, particularly those which upheld the so-called Lottery and White Slave Acts, which they felt lent legal support to the bill.[34] On August 8, when the bill came to a vote, a last-minute attempt by Senator Overman to weaken it by adding an amendment that would have delayed its implementation for three years was rejected. The final roll call showed that fifty-two Senators voted for the bill and twelve opposed it; the remaining thirty-two abstained. Ten Southern Democrats and the two Republican Senators from Pennsylvania—a state that had more child laborers than all the Southern states combined—had voted against the measure.[35]

On September 1, 1916, President Wilson signed the Keating-Owen bill into law. "I want to say with what real emotion I sign this bill," he remarked to a group of interested on-lookers, "because I know how long the struggle has been to secure legislation of this sort and what it is going to mean to the health and to the vigor of the country, and also to the happiness of those whom it affects. . . . It is with genuine pride that I play my part in completing this legislation. I congratulate the country and felicitate myself." The next day Wilson formally accepted his party's renomination for the presidency, declaring that he stood squarely on his record of achievement, a portion of which comprised "the emancipation of the children of the nation by releasing them from hurtful labor." [36]

The NCLC was more inclined to credit the victory to McKelway than to Wilson. For his part, McKelway felt that Albert Beveridge deserved much of the credit, and the former Indiana Senator agreed: "When I see the cartoons in the [N. Y.] *World* giving Wilson credit for the national child labor law . . . my emotions are aroused. This reform is mine," he confided to a friend.[37]

Wilson nonetheless reaped most of the rewards. "If President

Wilson was seeking political credit when he insisted on the passage of this measure, he is entitled to it now," conceded the Republican *New York Tribune,* usually an administration critic. "While he was merely taking up near its end the campaign carried on by reformers for years, he gave aid when it was much needed and he took his stand regardless of offending wealthy Southerners whose political support he may need."

Or, as Judge Ben B. Lindsey, the noted juvenile court reformer, wrote the President: "Your splendid attitude on this question and willingness to change from your former position with the states' rights Democrats to Federal or National control when it became clearly apparent that it is the best method to put an end to certain evils or advance certain rights should be sufficient proof to wavering Progressives that the Democratic Party is as willing as the Republican Party in proper cases to put the National Welfare above state considerations." [38]

Apparently it was, for although the peace issue no doubt helped Wilson achieve his narrow victory in 1916, he would not have recaptured the White House had it not been for the fact that the child labor law (and other social justice measures) won for him the support of many Progressives, liberal Republicans, and independents who had followed Theodore Roosevelt in 1912.[39]

NCLC members were overjoyed with the passage of the law, calling it "the greatest single accomplishment" in the Committee's history. Yet they realized that it would not end child labor in America. They knew that the statute would free only those 150,000 youngsters working in mines, quarries, canneries, mills, factories, and other enterprises engaged in interstate commerce. The great majority of working children, some 1,850,000 who toiled at home, in the fields, in the streets, and elsewhere, would be unaffected by the law. But by obtaining a uniform minimum standard of protection in the forty-eight states, plus the machinery and methods of enforcement, and by putting federal authority behind the principle of child labor control, Committee members felt that the law would have a marked effect upon the universal problem. It was reasonable to expect the states to revise their own laws according to the federal standard, for an industry doing business in low-standard states would naturally be the object of special vigilance by federal inspectors. Furthermore, with children either eliminated from industry or barred from entering it, it was hoped that many states would somehow improve their school systems and compulsory attendance laws.[40]

Enactment of the federal law thus inspired NCLC members to carry on their battle. At the same time it prescribed their course of action— campaigns for state laws to protect children working on farms and in streets, homes, offices, stores, restaurants, service stations, bowling alleys, and so forth. If it was wrong for a thirteen-year-old to work in a mill, it was wrong for a nine- or ten-year-old child to miss five months of school each year while he worked in a Colorado beet field.[41]

Meanwhile, procedures had to be worked out for implementing the federal law which was to go into effect on September 1, 1917. The Department of Labor was to administer the law, and Secretary William B. Williams assigned the task of enforcement to the Children's Bureau, which created a Child Labor Division for the purpose. Grace Abbott, a member of Chicago's Hull-House social work circle who had been active in the Illinois child labor movement, was appointed director of the new division.[42]

The NCLC was to aid the Children's Bureau and an advisory board, created under the provisions of the act, in establishing operating procedures. But a coolness soon developed between the Committee and the Bureau—between McKelway and Julia Lathrop in particular— over work permits and factory inspection. In essence, the Children's Bureau was more willing to cooperate with state factory inspectors than was the National Committee. And Miss Lathrop apparently thought it would be unwise for the Bureau to become too closely associated with the controversial private organization.

The breach opened wider when Miss Lathrop turned down a suggestion that McKelway considered important. He complained to Owen Lovejoy that the best way to get an idea discarded was to suggest it to the Bureau, while to Miss Lathrop he wrote an indignant letter reminding her that had it not been for the NCLC there would have been no Children's Bureau, nor would she be its chief. Unorthodox diplomacy aside, the Committee redrafted the advisory board's regulations and, through a subcommittee stationed in Washington, performed a number of other valuable services. The Committee was also instrumental in securing more funds for the Bureau to enforce the law.[43]

With the nation's entrance into World War I in the spring of 1917, a new phase of activity began. Opponents of the child labor law began to argue that enforcement should be postponed until after the conflict, so as not to aggravate a growing labor shortage. The NCLC worked to prevent the suspension or relaxation of child labor or compulsory school attendance laws on the pretext of wartime necessity. Committee members pointed to the English and French experience, which revealed that hiring children and lengthening their hours lowered efficiency, raised illness rates, and, in the end, reduced output. Employing "young children for long hours was dangerous to the future welfare of the country and clearly not the way to promote sustained maximum production," the Committee stated.[44]

Another obstacle to smooth enforcement arose in the summer of 1917. Following passage of the Keating-Owen Act, David Clark had announced in the *Southern Textile Bulletin* that the Executive Committee of Southern Cotton Manufacturers would test its validity in court. In mid-August, shortly before the law was to become operative, certain cotton mill owners brought proceedings against it.

In a highly contrived case prepared by Clark and the executive committee, Roland Dagenhart, acting as complainant, sought an injunction to bar application of the statute. The Federal Court of the Western Judicial District of North Carolina was asked to restrain any interference with the employment of Dagenhart's two children at the Fidelity Cotton Mills in Charlotte. The plaintiff would show that his thirteen-year-old son John was to be discharged because of his age. The other, Reuben, fifteen, was to be fired because, under the law, he could not work more than eight hours a day, whereas the usual work day in North Carolina mills was eleven hours. The suit as drawn illustrated perfectly the contrast between the federal and the North Carolina statutes, or for that matter those of other states.[45]

The court was presided over by Judge James E. Boyd, a crusty character whose opposition to child labor laws was well known. In preparing for the case, still more friction developed between the Children's Bureau and McKelway, this time over the choice of government counsel to assist District Attorney William C. Hammer in the proceedings. McKelway wanted Thomas I. Parkinson, a legal draftsman associated with the Committee, to be assigned to the case. Without consulting Children's Bureau officials, or even other NCLC members, he arranged with someone in the U.S. Attorney General's office to have Parkinson defend the statute. Julia Lathrop, who naturally was incensed over McKelway's "lack of consideration and respect" for the Bureau, sought to have Dean Roscoe Pound of the Harvard Law School, a noted trial lawyer and authority on the Constitution who had volunteered his services, assist the Justice Department's defense. In the end, Parkinson was given priority in the case, but Dean Pound also pleaded before the redoubtable Judge Boyd.[46]

It mattered little who led the defense, for Boyd had probably made up his mind long before the case was heard. On August 31, after three days of hearings, he granted a permanent injunction, holding that the law was unconstitutional. Boyd never committed his reasons to writing, which meant, among other things, that he was not required to cite applicable precedents. But his judgment and subsequent orders to the defendants made it plain that his decision was based largely on the grounds that Congress did not have the power to regulate local labor conditions and that the measure violated the due process clause of the Fifth Amendment because it deprived a father of the right to his children's earnings until they were twenty-one years of age. The decision aroused the interest of several legal critics and historians, one of whom pungently commented that "Judge Boyd's decision cannot stand as law. It is a displaced fossil from a bygone epoch of constitutionalism and as such merits a place in the cabinet of legal curiosities, but it deserves no weight whatever in the choice of current legislative programs to meet the needs of the day." Another critic recently referred to it as a bunch of "pure absurdities" and "a severe breach of judicial canons." [47]

Although the law remained operative throughout the rest of the country, Attorney General Thomas Gregory promptly gave notice that the Justice Department would appeal the case to the United States Supreme Court. The motion to appeal was wholeheartedly supported by the NCLC and the Children's Bureau. The Committee preoccupied itself with assembling the most effective defense, an unusually important matter because of the friction that had developed over the proceedings in the district court. Solicitor General John W. Davis asked the Committee to prepare material bearing on the reasonableness of the law in helping him to construct the government's brief.[48] Because of previous Supreme Court decisions and a wartime crisis that would seem to favor sustaining national legislative authority, friends of reform were confident that the statute would be upheld.

The appeal was heard by the Court in the middle of April, and on June 3, 1918, nine months after the act had taken effect, the decision was handed down. In a 5 to 4 decision the Court ruled that the Keating-Owen Law was unconstitutional. The *Hammer v. Dagenhart* case came down to this: the federal child labor law was an unwarranted exercise of the commerce power and, in effect, an invasion of states' rights; the measure regulated local labor conditions in manufacturing, not interstate commerce. "If Congress can thus regulate matters entrusted to local authorities by prohibition of the movement of commodities in interstate commerce," the majority declared, "all freedom of commerce will be at an end, and the power of the States over local matters may be eliminated, and thus our system of government be practically destroyed." Oliver Wendell Holmes wrote a vigorous minority opinion for the four dissenting justices, in which he rebuked the majority for being more concerned with the technical rights of Congress than with the human rights of children: "If there is any matter upon which civilized countries have agreed . . . it is the evil of premature and excessive child labor," he argued.

The Court, however, did not hold that child labor should not be regulated; nor did it maintain that it could not be regulated through federal legislation. It merely said that it could not be regulated through the interstate commerce clause.[49] One form of federal control had been annulled, but another might offer a way to overcome the judicial veto.

Alexander McKelway, who had devoted fourteen years of his life to the abolition of child labor, had died of a heart attack in April and thus was spared the crushing disappointment of the decision, but many others were shocked. Leaders in and out of Congress, students of the Constitution, American journalists, and most newspapers criticized the ruling. Committee members who had been so confident that the Court would uphold the law, had given no thought to an alternative plan.[50]

In the Southern textile districts the decision brought cheers and rejoicing. An Alabama newspaper quoted the Cotton Manufacturers' Association president: "As a member of the Executive Committee . . . having charge of the fight against the federal child labor law, I can only say that I think to the southern industry is due the thanks and gratitude of the nation because they fought alone in the face of blind prejudice aroused by paid agitators all over the country." A South Carolina newspaper reported that children's hours in the mills, reduced to eight when the federal law went into effect, were being raised to eleven again.[51]

Not only in South Carolina but throughout the South—with the exception of North Carolina—factory inspectors assigned by the Children's Bureau to enforce the new statute had impressed upon mill managers the need to comply with the federal statute. Most managers had done so; they had rearranged their operations to conform to the law, dismissing those children who were ineligible to work under its provisions.

In addition, as had been hoped, a movement to raise state legislative standards had occurred. Southerners realized that if state laws were made to conform to national standards and proper enforcement machinery provided, there would be little federal interference in such state affairs. Only North Carolina mill men, who had initiated the test case, were not ready to yield even to state inspection, which might remain binding even if the national law was invalidated.[52]

The effect of the improved state legislation and of the federal statute, during the nine months it had been in operation, was indeed beneficent; the number of employed children throughout the South and the nation rapidly diminished. But with the federal restrictions removed, the trend quickly reversed itself. Child labor increased as age limits were lowered, hours were extended, and violations of state laws were ignored.[53]

The evidence of a sharp rise in child labor, and the narrow margin of the Supreme Court ruling (along with Justice Holmes's dissent), provoked an outpouring of popular demands for new federal child labor legislation. Interested members of Congress, sympathetic federal and state officials, reform organizations, and prominent citizens all joined in the movement. Several constitutional amendments and new child labor bills were introduced in Congress.[54]

The NCLC appointed a Special Committee on Federal Legislation that was instructed to consult with experts and outline a course of action, including possible use of the federal taxing power to curtail child labor. But time was needed to study the various alternatives, including the proposals already introduced in Congress.[55]

Meanwhile, the war emergency, the labor shortage, and high wages continued to draw an increasing number of young people into industry. In July 1918 Felix Frankfurter, an attorney and social reformer who was serving as head of the War Labor Policies Board, inserted a clause in all federal contracts which made the standards of the Keating-Owen Act mandatory for all companies engaged in government work.[56] Child laborers not covered by this order were still without federal protection; something had to be done to help them.

With President Wilson's approval and the help of the American Federation of Labor, the Committee drafted a bill that embodied the same standards as the Keating-Owen Act but was based on the emergency wartime powers of Congress. Considered a war measure "for the purpose of conserving the manpower of the Nation and thereby more effectively providing for the national security and defense," if passed it would be effective until six months after the end of the war. Thus there would be enough time for careful consideration of a permanent measure.

The bill was introduced in the House on August 15 by Congressman Edward Keating. Despite the President's endorsement, supporters of the bill could not get prompt action. While there was some concern about the vagueness of the war powers, the real barrier was timing. Late summer sessions were infrequent, especially since the coming fall elections kept most Congressmen away from Washington. And with the end of the war—November 11, 1918—the question became academic. It was no longer possible to cite the military crisis to justify federal regulation of child labor.[57]

Meanwhile, the Committee's conferences with its legal advisers and with the Children's Bureau had convinced it that the use of the federal taxing power would be the quickest and best method of securing permanent federal child labor standards. An excise tax would be levied on articles or commodities made in whole or in part by child labor; ostensibly it would be a way of raising revenue, but in fact the tax would be pegged so high that it would deprive employers of their profits, so that such work could be eliminated.[58]

The war was drawing to a close when a special drafting committee —Thomas Parkinson, Roscoe Pound, and Henry M. Bates, dean of the University of Michigan Law School—drew up a tax measure which the NCLC intended to have introduced in Congress as an amendment to the 1918 Revenue Bill.

To the Committee's surprise, however, on November 15 Senator Atlee Pomerene, a liberal Democrat from Ohio, introduced a bill similar to the Committee's (except in its enforcement provisions), one that he had worked out with the help of two colleagues, Senators William S. Kenyon of Iowa and Irvine L. Lenroot, a Wisconsin Republican. The Pomerene Amendment, like the NCLC measure, provided for the employment standards of the Keating-Owen Act; it placed a 10 per cent tax on the net profits of all canneries, mills, factories, or other manufacturing establishments that employed children under fourteen years of age, on all mines and quarries that employed children under sixteen, or on any concern that employed children under sixteen for more than eight hours a day, six days a week, or at night. The measure was a frank attempt to tax out of existence an injustice which, under the Supreme Court's ruling, could not be directly abolished.[59]

The NCLC was forced to choose between supporting its own draft or the Pomerene Amendment. After consulting with the AFL, Children's Bureau officials, and several Congressmen, Secretary Lovejoy advised the board to endorse the amendment and work for its passage; it was, in his opinion, the only bill with a chance of being enacted. At their December 17 meeting the trustees took his advice, and other friendly groups fell into line.[60]

The next day, after little debate, the Pomerene Amendment to the Revenue Act passed the Senate by a vote of 50 to 12—a vote strikingly similar to that on the Keating-Owen bill. Realizing that the measure would surely get through Congress, Southern mill men had decided it would be a waste of time and money to fight its passage.

In early February 1919 the "Tax on Employment of Child Labor" was approved in the House by a 310 to 11 margin. President Wilson signed it into law on February 24; it was to become effective in sixty days.[61] Quite obviously, neither the American people nor their elected officials had changed their attitude toward federal regulation as a result of the Keating-Owen Act. On the contrary, that experience seemed to confirm the popular will in respect to a national standard and federal enforcement.

David Clark, perennial champion of the economic interests of the Southern cotton textile group, promptly declared that the new law would be challenged. He again raised funds for the litigation and reemployed the same attorneys who had successfully handled the first case. After weighing several alternatives, the complainants decided to use a man named Eugene W. Johnson who was asked to seek a permanent injunction to restrain the Atherton Mills of North Carolina from discharging his son John, age fifteen, or curtailing his employment to eight hours a day.

Again the case was heard by Judge James E. Boyd. When the court convened on May 2, 1919, it was expected that, as in the Dagenhart proceedings, arguments of the suit would take several days. Counsel for the plaintiff, however, had barely opened the case when Judge Boyd broke in to say that he had already made up his mind, that the statute in his view was unconstitutional, and that no further argument was necessary. Boyd's indictment of the child labor tax rested on the same opinions he had expressed in the first case, namely that Congress had sought to accomplish by indirection what it could not do by direct prohibition, and that the statute invaded states' rights.[62] Again, as before, although the law remained in force throughout the rest of the country, the Justice Department gave notice that it would appeal the ruling to the Supreme Court.

Boyd's decision provoked a storm of reaction that ranged from violent denunciation to mild disapproval. There was some talk of amending the Constitution, although it was generally felt that the high court would this time uphold the law. Senator Kenyon, a supporter and one of the draftsmen of the measure, spoke for many when he said: "I have absolute faith that the Supreme Court will sustain the law. We studied every phase of the case when we drafted the section, including the point raised by Judge Boyd, that it was an invasion of the rights of state. I do not believe that the Supreme Court will rule against it. If it does it will have to go back on every one of its own decisions regarding the taxing power of the United States." [63]

Even most employers of child labor agreed with the Senator from Iowa. Assuming that the law would be permanent, they began adjusting their operations to meet its provisions. Again, many states enacted improved child labor and compulsory school attendance laws, and another sharp reduction in child labor resulted.[64]

In December 1919, seven months after Boyd's ruling, the Johnson case was argued before the Supreme Court. For various reasons, including the appointment of a new Chief Justice, the need to reargue the case, and its consolidation with two other suits that challenged the validity of the child labor tax, a decision was not rendered until May 15, 1922. By that time the national mood differed greatly from what it had been at the time the law was enacted.

In *Bailey v. Drexel Furniture Company* the Supreme Court, in an 8 to 1 decision, declared the second federal child labor law unconstitutional. (Justice John Clarke, the lone dissenter, wrote no minority decision.) Speaking for the majority, Chief Justice William Howard Taft held that the case "cannot be distinguished from that of *Hammer v. Dagenhart.*" The second federal child labor law, like its predecessor, regulated local labor conditions and was thus an invasion of states' rights. In the first measure the commerce power had been abused; in the second the taxing power.

Again, the Court was not unfriendly to the cause, indicating, in fact, that child labor was a disgrace and a menace to the nation's public health, and that a way should be found to control it. It merely ruled, for the second time, that the wrong way had been chosen, that it was impossible under the Constitution for Congress or the federal government to correct the injustice.[65]

VI

Tenements, Farms, and Schools

M ANY citizens resented the Court's action in striking down the child labor tax.[1] Most advocates of reform were bitterly disappointed once again. On the whole, however, while the NCLC viewed the ruling with due seriousness, it was not completely pessimistic. Indeed, some members of the Committee looked upon the adverse ruling as a blessing in disguise. In their opinion the injustice of child labor was so momentous that direct, not indirect, control was required. The federal statutes had moreover been restricted in their coverage, excluding from their provisions the very areas that contained the overwhelming majority of child laborers—tenement homework, agriculture, the street trades, and so forth.[2]

Convinced that the American people supported federal regulation of child labor, the NCLC turned to the practical question of finding a way to abolish it. If legal or judicial barriers to federal legislation could not be overcome, the only remaining course seemed to be an amendment to the Constitution, one that gave Congress the express right to regulate the evil. We value our traditions, Committee members said, but traditions sometimes need to be changed: "It is not more important to maintain a sacred political tradition than to protect little children exposed to industrial exploitation." [3]

One of the more pitiful forms of such exploitation still in need of regulation was industrial homework. Child labor in the tenements combined the evils of long hours, low wages, and monotonous work in filthy, badly ventilated, and overcrowded rooms, with the degradation of neglected education and shattered health; few other kinds of labor sapped the strength and spirits of children quite so pervasively. The factory child at least went home to a different environment after work; the young tenement worker had no place to go but the street.

The exact number of children employed in the nation's tenements was never accurately determined; the census did not record such figures. But the total must have been large. In 1910, after extensive investigations of tenement homework, federal agents concluded that "all children of a household where homework is done are drafted into this work with more or less regularity, after school, at night, and on Sunday." In 1911 there were thirteen thousand tenement buildings (structures housing three or more families who lived independently of one another) in New York City alone in which homework was legally carried on; no one knew how many others among the city's eighty thousand tenement buildings contained illegal workshops. And nearly every large city had its share.[4]

Almost any commodity small enough to be carried and not requiring the use of elaborate machinery or highly skilled labor could be manufactured or finished at home. The work varied from pulling bastings—usually the task of the youngest ones—to sewing on buttons, putting linings in coats, making artificial flowers, stringing beads, embroidering lace, or making cigarettes, hair brushes, powder puffs, and other small items.

Manufacturers eulogized homework as a cure for juvenile delinquency and female promiscuity. It allegedly gave children an opportunity to help support their families or earn spending money. Rhetoric aside, employers sought homeworkers because they saved the cost of more factory space, including rent, heat, light, and machinery; because they worked more cheaply than inside help; and, most importantly, because their homes were away from the watchful eyes of inspectors and the public, and thus their work could go on unregulated.[5]

Children in households that did homework had little chance of receiving a decent education. Because most of the work could be done by unskilled labor, parents frequently kept their children out of school to help them. Those children who did attend school would work at home before or after classes, often into the early morning hours, making it virtually impossible for them to keep up with their lessons; thus they would fall behind and then drop out. If they were of pre-school age—and studies showed that many were—so much the better, for they could work all day without being bothered about school.

Intense family labor in the tenements also presented serious risks to the consumer: tuberculosis and other contagious diseases were frequent among homework families. In 1912 Dr. Annie S. Daniel found that of the 182 homeworking families she had investigated, seventy-nine had contagious diseases ranging from scarlet fever to polio. In Chicago, inspectors found some smallpox patients lying on piles of unfinished clothes, and others concealed under them. In the six congested wards below Fourteenth Street in New York City (those with the greatest density of licensed tenement houses), Board of Health records for one year showed 232 cases of typhoid, 2,443 cases of measles, 1,344 cases of scarlet fever, 2,065 cases of diphtheria and croup, and 3,025 cases of pulmonary tuberculosis. A manager of one of New York City's finest clothing houses, whose goods were finished in the tenements, admitted that "if the people knew under what conditions their clothes were made . . . they would not buy . . . or wear them. . . ."[6]

Industrial homework had been a target of reformers for many years, going back to the nineteenth century, but the obvious arguments against the practice had been cited to little or no avail.[7] There were few legislative barriers to homework. Because of the belief in the sanctity of the home, it was difficult to pass laws regulating the practice. What legislation did exist was futile. Some cities required individuals to obtain permits for the home manufacture of certain articles, or to obtain a license for each workroom or tenement house used to produce articles at home. None of these measures, however, had any effect on child labor.

Violations were almost impossible to prove or prosecute. Parents could not be arraigned, for they were not legally the employer of the child. The employer was the owner of the goods, but to convict him inspectors had to prove conclusively that he knew illegal child labor would be used on his goods. It would take thousands of inspectors to visit all the homes engaged in the practice. Even when an inspector showed up, child employment could be easily concealed. What was to stop a parent from saying that his youngster was just "playing"? How many children went back to work after the inspector left? Who could tell whether a home that was clean one day would be filthy the next, or whether a homeworker who was well one day would quickly develop an infectious disease? What was the use of forbidding one tenement family from taking in work when another in the same building was allowed to work at home?

In short, homework defied regulation; no system of licensing or inspection had been devised that could effectively reach all the homes in which it was carried on. As a result, it flourished as much in 1922 as in 1904. After many investigations, Committee members (and most reformers) were convinced that the only way to end the pernicious practice was to abolish homework altogether.[8] Work on all marketed goods had to be brought into the shop and placed under factory laws that regulated working conditions. Perhaps a federal child labor amendment would lead to that result.

In some ways, of all child labor the hardest to control would be that in fields and on farms. For years the public had recognized that child labor in mines, factories, and mills was a serious problem; as laws on the statute books testified, every state in the Union had made at least some attempt to improve the situation in those areas. Now the public was awakening to the child labor problem on the nation's streets and in its tenements. While the protection afforded children working in these areas certainly was inadequate, at least the evils connected with the work were being acknowledged. Not so in agriculture, where the statute books were blank. In agriculture any child could work at any age under any conditions for any number of hours a day or week.

Child labor on the farm was shrouded with even more prejudices and misconceptions than child labor on the street. For decades the joys of farm life and the superior morality of the rural environment had been celebrated by so many American writers and publicists, including Thomas Jefferson, that it had become a kind of mass creed. Most people assumed that children's work on the farm was entirely wholesome, that they worked outdoors in the fresh air with their parents, learning valuable lessons in family association and useful skills in farming; such work ought to be encouraged.

A United States Census report, based on material collected in 1900, reflected the popular attitude when it mentioned "one broad class of occupations in which child labor is not open to most of the objections ordinarily urged against it." The report went on to say: "These are the occupations connected with agriculture. The work of the child on the farm is essentially not injurious to health or morals, and does not necessarily interfere with opportunities for schooling." [9] In discussing his national child labor bill in Congress in 1907, Senator Albert Beveridge pointed out that it did "not strike at the employment of children engaged in agriculture. I do not for a moment pretend," the Senator declared, "that working children on the farm is bad for them." [10]

There were other difficulties involved in controlling the practice. Farmers or their rural representatives held the balance of power in badly proportioned state legislatures; securing legislation to regulate agricultural child labor was thus extremely difficult. And farm production was so widely scattered that even if laws were passed they would be enormously difficult to enforce.

Local school authorities, who could keep the children in school and thus out of the fields, were the only ones who might control the situation. Often, however, they were unwilling to support the movement; they frequently kept their own children out of school to work on the crops, or they allowed children to stay out of school because they did not want to incur the ill feelings of their neighbors. Particularly in the case of migrants, many of whom were Negroes or members of other minority groups (some of whom did not speak English), school officials were not anxious to bring the children into their schools for financial or for other reasons; the few who were allowed to attend school seldom stayed long enough to profit from the instruction.

Finally, as in canning, much of the work was highly seasonal and had to be done immediately, especially harvesting. And as one woman who owned a New Jersey cranberry bog testified at a hearing on a proposed child labor law: "If man-made laws about when children must attend school are in conflict with God-made laws about when the crops shall ripen, then the laws of God must be obeyed." [11]

As a result of such formidable barriers, and with the rapid growth of large-scale farming (stimulated by the development of commercialized canning and the refrigerator car), by the early twentieth century work on the crops was in many ways the most serious child labor problem in America. For every child working in another occupation, more than two worked on a farm. Well over a million boys and girls, sometimes on their parents' farms but often on others', either alone or in migrant groups, labored under conditions as undesirable as in any factory or mine. In the open air, under the hot sun or chilling rain, they worked at backbreaking, dreary, repetitive tasks for long hours under unsuitable and often hazardous living and working conditions that precluded school attendance.

The rapid mechanization of farm work reduced the demand for handwork and, in general, the usefuless of children in farming. Yet in the sugar beet fields of Michigan and Colorado, the onion fields of Ohio, the tobacco fields of Connecticut, Massachusetts, Kentucky, and Virginia, the cotton fields of Arkansas and Texas, the truck farms of Maryland, New York, New Jersey, and California, the cranberry bogs of New Jersey and Wisconsin, the fruit farms of California, Oregon, Washington, and elsewhere, hand workers were still very much in demand, and large numbers of children of all ages flocked to the fields each year.[12]

The highly specialized farm, with its single crop and whole acres ripening at once, demanded a great many workers for a short time. To meet the demand there came an army of migrants, often family labor since most of the work could be done by women and children. Some migratory workers spent the year going from crop to crop; they seldom were in the same place for two successive months. Others resided in cities during the winter and traveled to the fields in spring and summer. There they lived in makeshift shacks under unbelievably indecent and unsanitary conditions. Families of five to eight persons lived in rooms only six by eight feet, with no sanitary provisions and without screens to keep out swarming bugs and insects. Barracks measuring eighteen by thirty feet housed sixty to seventy-five people.[13] Drinking water often was distant and unsafe; dysentery and other diseases were rife. Local health and welfare services were denied the workers because they were transients.

In the fields the children, some only three or four years old, worked from sunup to sundown in order to supplement the family's meager income. In the cotton fields it was chiefly a story of bending and picking under the relentlessly hot sun. The motions were simple—pick, pick, pick, drop into the bag and step forward—it was a question of endurance and speed for six days a week, several months a year. Aside from heat exhaustion, most children working at stoop labor, so-called, whether in the cotton fields or on some other product, developed serious back injuries.

In some cases, as in pulling and topping sugar beets, the work involved great physical strain. Ten-year-old girls (using large, sharp knives) topped five tons of beets a day; allowing for the weight of the beets when they were pulled, the children handled some twelve to fifteen tons of beets a day. One Children's Bureau report indicated that 70 per cent of the children working in Colorado beet fields were physically malformed "apparently due to strain." Whatever the crop, the children had to carry their own boxes or bushels, often weighing from twenty to forty pounds, to weighing stations, sometimes several hundred feet away.

Cranberry bogs featured damp earth, swarms of mosquitoes, exposure to late autumn weather, and the physical brutality of the padrones. It was not unusual to see young children still pulling and topping beets in mid-November when ice was in the furrows and cold winds howled; insufficiently clothed and with badly chapped hands, they worked early and late by lantern light, and when a heavy frost was expected or feared the work continued through Sunday.

Most children who worked in the fields did not return to the classroom until mid-November or December, exhausted from months of toil; they then returned to the grind in early spring. This late arrival and early departure frequently resulted in retarded minds and permanent withdrawal from school; ignorance and illiteracy were widespread among those who worked on the crops.

The NCLC's concern for agricultural child labor dated back to its founding. Early in 1905 Committee agents were instructed to look into child abuse on farms.[14] The Committee published its first full-scale report on rural child labor in 1909, and its first study of migrant workers appeared five years later. It made numerous studies of all phases of the problem, from coast to coast, and they all pointed to the same conclusion—that the farm child or migrant agricultural laborer usually worked too long and too hard, received too little proper care and education, and too often turned out to be a mere drudge, a liability rather than an asset to his community. The facts proved that not only the children but the entire nation suffered from agricultural child labor.[15]

The national emergency created by America's entrance into World War I made the situation worse. Opponents of reform who used the war as an excuse for returning children to the labor force were especially eager for their employment in agriculture. As more and more men were called into service at a time when the nation's food needs increased, states permitted the practical suspension or relaxation of their compulsory school attendance laws, the only weapon that stood between the children and exploitation in the fields.

The NCLC did all it could to prevent the states from lowering their standards. When such efforts proved futile, the Committee concentrated on insuring the safety and welfare of those excused from school to work on the crops, and on protecting farmers from an influx of child labor. The Committee formulated and circulated among school authorities, local, state, and federal officials, and other interested persons a widely heralded plan that called for the limited use of high school juniors and seniors under careful regulation and supervision.[16]

The number and percentage of child workers in agriculture had gone from about 1,000,000 and 66 per cent in 1900 to 1,500,000 and 75 per cent in 1910. Improved state laws and the federal child labor statute, which reduced the openings for children in industry, seemed to drive more boys and girls into unregulated agriculture. And thousands of children who left school during the war to work in the fields remained there when the conflict came to an end.[17]

As a result, after the war, in addition to initiating a massive back-to-school movement, the Committee decided that its next great task was the regulation of agricultural child labor. When, in the summer of 1921, Felix Adler resigned as chairman of the Committee's board of trustees after seventeen years in office, he was replaced by David F. Houston. An economist and educator, Houston was also an authority on country life, especially its social and economic problems; he had been Secretary of Agriculture during President Wilson's two terms. None who heard Houston's inaugural remarks could doubt that the Committee's greatest concern would be the problem of rural child labor: "There is more to be done . . . to end child labor in factories and cities," he declared, yet the immediate task was "to give our assiduous attention to child labor in agriculture." [18]

Between 1919 and 1924 the Committee made numerous investigations of rural child labor, reports of which were widely circulated in an effort to dispel false notions about the benefits of farm work. Yet it was unable to break down the aura of romantic charm that attended child labor in the fields. All the facts about loss of schooling and recreational needs, retardation, excessively long working hours, physical strain, and miserable living conditions fell on deaf ears; five years of intensive work failed to achieve anything more than confirmation of already known facts to which nobody listened. As farming became more commercialized and children and their parents followed the crops over wider areas, the situation worsened.[19]

The Committee greatly broadened its activities during the postwar years to include the whole field of human conservation. Its members had never looked upon child labor reform as a negative movement; rather, it was a means to an end—the making of useful and happy lives. Committee people knew they could never abolish the injustice merely by securing child labor laws—state or federal—however advanced and flawless they were. To keep the child from going to work they had to follow him into the school, the street, and the home; they could not be indifferent to the problems of education and vocational guidance, recreation and public health, mothers' pensions and minimum wages, workmen's compensation and unemployment insurance, indeed, all aspects of child and family welfare.[20]

When children were being exploited in mines and factories, and the public was, for the most part, uneducated or unconcerned about the problem, there was no point in proliferating the Committee's activities in search of various constructive measures for human welfare. Now, with an aroused public, more money, and state and federal legislation that, with a few exceptions, regulated child labor's most glaring abuses, the Committee could concern itself with these other matters.

World War I and military conscription had highlighted the need for such constructive work. Approximately 31 per cent of all Americans between the ages of twenty-one and thirty-one drafted for service were rejected because they were physically unfit. The draft also revealed an appalling amount of illiteracy in the United States. Of approximately 1,500,000 men who were tested, over 300,000, or 20 per cent, were unable to read or write—one of the highest illiteracy rates of all the advanced countries in the world. The average level of education among the draftees was sixth grade.[21]

Clearly, the United States had been providing neither the necessary physical nor educational opportunities for a large number of its citizens, and it was having its effect on the national strength. Elimination of the most obnoxious forms of child labor was essential, but was not in itself enough. Nothing less than concern for the whole field of child welfare and social deprivation would suffice.

Owen Lovejoy struck this note in 1919. Programs in every field of health, recreation, and education, he declared, were essential for "the development of all the children of the nation into healthy, intelligent, moral, efficient men and women—competent as American citizens." Raymond Fuller, a Committee staff member, called the shift in policy a move from "social melioration" toward "social construction." [22]

In the spring of 1919 the Committee changed the name of its official publication from the *Child Labor Bulletin* to the *American Child,* a quarterly subtitled "A Bulletin of General Child Welfare." In the belief that "no problem can be isolated, but that all matters affecting human welfare are related," the journal, its editor explained, would be devoted to the "whole child"; it would contain "up-to-date news and discussion by experts on education, child labor, juvenile delinquency, probation, recreation, and [various] . . . laws affecting children." [23]

Meanwhile, the Committee had been enlarging its staff to include specialists in all fields of child welfare. And at the request of public officials or groups of local residents, it had begun to make some broad state surveys. Dr. Edward N. Clopper, an educator who had joined the Committee in 1908 and who since 1913 had been a field secretary, directed the first such intensive study in Oklahoma in 1917. A year later requests for similar studies came from North Carolina and Alabama, states that had bitterly opposed the Committee's child labor investigations and legislative campaigns. Later surveys would be conducted in Michigan, Tennessee, Kentucky, and West Virginia.

Aimed at ultimately coordinating all the child welfare laws and agencies of each state, the studies covered all aspects of child welfare. Their results confirmed the Committee's contention that child labor was inseparably linked with other areas of social welfare, and that good health, adequate education, and sufficient family income, among other things, were essential in order to secure for children what the

Committee's charter referred to as "an opportunity for . . . education and physical development sufficient for the demands of citizenship and the requirements of industrial efficiency."

Eventually the studies were responsible for improved child labor standards and compulsory school attendance laws, the appointment of children's code commissions, the creation of juvenile courts and boards of child welfare, and the licensing and state supervision of maternity hospitals.[24] In 1918 the Committee helped to create, and then affiliated with, the National Child Health Organization, headed by Dr. L. Emmett Holt, an authority on children's diseases. The NCLC gave office space and clerical help to the organization which, in cooperation with the U.S. Bureau of Education, conducted several successful nation-wide campaigns to raise the health standards of American schoolchildren.[25]

The field of education, perhaps even more than health, was so closely related to child labor that from the outset it interested the Committee. Since children barred from or forced out of work could not be left uneducated on the streets—indeed, one of the main reasons the Committee labored to free children from industrial bondage was to give them a better educational opportunity—and conversely, children at school could not be at work, education was the positive side of child labor reform. Committee members therefore saw it as their duty to promote education; they considered every step forward in schooling a victory for their own program.[26]

Children needed schools to receive them and teachers to instruct them. But they also had to have a curriculum adapted to their needs and their interests—vocational, recreational, and social. As many others at the time realized, Latin, Greek, and the prevailing academic curriculum, a relic from a bygone era, rarely met the needs, interests, and intellectual capacities of thousands of schoolchildren, especially those not going on to college. Indeed, the lack of relevance and appeal of the public school curriculum was one of the principal causes of early school-leaving and child labor.

Committee members were in the vanguard of the so-called progressive education movement, which sought to make the public schools more responsive to the needs of the child who was not intended for college. They encouraged such educational reforms as special un-graded schools for the mentally retarded, technical schools or pro-grams for training in skilled crafts and trades, vocational guidance programs, commercial courses, public health and personal hygiene instruction, and school-directed athletic and recreation programs. In short, they sought to expand the school curriculum to satisfy the needs and aptitudes of all children, and to relate the school to surrounding family and neighborhood life.[27]

Many school systems (especially rural ones) and states lacked the resources to revise and extend their educational programs and facili-ties. In the belief that just as child labor was a national matter, the country had a duty to educate all its citizens, as early as 1908 the Committee took part in several attempts to secure federal aid to edu-cation, especially in developing agricultural and industrial training within primary schools.[28] All were unsuccessful, but the NCLC con-tinued the fight, devoting the first issue of the *Child Labor Bulletin* (June 1912) to "Child Labor and Education." In 1917 the Commit-tee cooperated in a successful effort to pass the Smith-Hughes Act, which made $1,000,000 available to the states annually, on a match-ing basis, to improve their public secondary schools through estab-lishing vocational and continuing education programs—programs that most directly offered constructive alternatives to child labor.[29]

The betterment of rural schools was an important element in pro-moting rural school attendance, which in turn would keep children out of the fields. Thus in February 1918, at the request of the Com-mittee on National Aid to Education headed by John Dewey (and founded two years earlier by McKelway, Lovejoy, and others), the NCLC inaugurated a campaign for federal aid to elementary education, hoping the funds would be used largely to improve rural education, especially in the South. Several months later it cooperated with the National Education Association in drafting a bill, introduced in Congress by Senator Hoke Smith, that provided for the creation of a federal Department of Education and $1,000,000 annually to be divided among the states for improving rural education, teacher training, physical education, and health instruction.[30]

This increasing involvement in a broad spectrum of activities created some serious problems for the Committee. Among other things, in the spring of 1918 the question of a change in name arose. Some members felt the Committee's name no longer revealed the true nature and scope of its work, and the board created a special four-man committee to consider the issue.[31]

A month later, the committee recommended changing the organization's name to the National Child Conservation Board. A heated discussion followed, during which Florence Kelley, upset with the Committee over its recent skirmishes with the Children's Bureau and distressed by the spread of its activities, adamantly opposed the name change, declaring that she deplored the tendency "to spread the work of the Committee thin over an immeasurable area instead of continuing to strive to achieve the abolition of child labor evil." Lovejoy spoke for the proposal, saying that it "does not indicate any change in policy, but rather a description of the policy already adopted." The Committee's chief aim, he assured Mrs. Kelley, was to continue the fight against child labor, but to do so effectively it must support a wide range of child welfare activities. Action was deferred, but Mrs. Kelley remained dissatisfied; she would soon resign from the Committee.[32]

The matter dragged on. Many meetings were held over the next two years and more than six hundred committee members were polled on the question. While most of them favored a name change, there was no real agreement on a substitute. Some members conceded that the present name was too limited, but for one reason or another, sentimental, legal, or tactical, they thought it should be retained. And Owen Lovejoy, the influential Committee secretary, changed his mind.

It became increasingly clear that some members, especially the staff, wanted to change the Committee's policy and goals as well. Rather than merely cooperating with other local agencies and national bodies working for child welfare while continuing to stress the elimination of child labor, they wished to reverse the priorities. In fact, they even suggested disbanding the Committee or merging with other related groups, and they hoped to use a change in name as an entering wedge for their cause.[33]

The issue came to a head in December 1920, when field secretary Edward Clopper recommended splitting the office in two, placing the Committee's real work—field studies, legislative campaigns, and so forth—under his direction in Cincinnati, leaving Lovejoy in New York to care for fund raising and little else. When the board, including its new chairman, David Houston, sided with Lovejoy and decided that the Committee's main field of work would be "child labor in industry and agriculture" and "not that of general child welfare" ("although the problems it seeks to solve are complex and cannot be separated from those of general welfare"), Clopper and several other staff members resigned.[34] The original name was retained.

The 1920 census returns offered comfort to both sides in the dispute. On the surface it appeared that child labor was vanishing. According to the figures, in 1920 the number of working children between the ages of ten and fifteen was slightly over one million, compared with two million in 1910, a decrease of nearly 50 per cent. During the same period the total population of that age group had increased by 15.5 per cent; thus the percentage of working children had actually declined from 18.4 in 1910 to 8.5 a decade later.[35]

Clearly, conditions were improving. Better child labor and school attendance laws in the states were having their effect. More important, practical experience under the first and second federal statutes had convinced many skeptical employers that child labor was unnecessary and that its elimination would not hurt them competitively. New machines which needed skilled workers to operate them were making child labor increasingly uneconomic. Too, the development of scientific management, the growth of organized labor, and the change in parental attitudes as more people abandoned their rural work habits (which made the family the natural working unit) all affected the situation.[36]

Yet not all the injustice had been rooted out. One of every twelve children between the ages of ten and fifteen, over a million in all, still labored under adverse conditions. Even this figure was misleading. There were, of course, the usual shortcomings of the census returns, which did not include thousands of working children less than ten years old, nor numerous others who worked in streets and tenements or on farms before or after school. And while the 1910 census had been taken in April, during the planting season, the 1920 census was taken in January, when agriculture was at a standstill. Thus the many children engaged in this harmful form of labor were not recorded. The 1920 figures also reflected the sharp decline in child labor that resulted from enactment of the two federal child labor laws, the second of which, in 1922, had just been nullified. While nobody knew what would follow the Court decision, history had demonstrated that reformers should prepare for the worst.[37]

Thus there was much less cause for discouragement than a decade earlier, yet a great deal remained to be done. The question was how to do it? More and more people were turning to a constitutional amendment.

VII

The Proposed Federal Child Labor Amendment

THE campaign to amend the Constitution to permit federal regulation of child labor had begun soon after the Supreme Court, on May 15, 1922, for a second time invalidated a child labor law passed by Congress. As the Court had denied reformers the use of the two most important federal powers for achieving their goal—interstate commerce and taxing—many citizens felt that constitutional reform was the only alternative.

As early as May 17, Representative Roy G. Fitzgerald of Ohio introduced a resolution for an amendment that would empower Congress to regulate the employment of persons under eighteen; two days later Senator Hiram Johnson of California did the same in the Senate.[1] But while outside pressure grew, Congress adjourned without acting.

Samuel Gompers, a lifelong opponent of child labor, now asked numerous national social, civic, religious, and labor groups to send delegates to the American Federation of Labor headquarters in Washington for a conference on the situation. Besides Gompers, others present on June 1 included Reverend E. O. Watson, executive secretary of the Federal Council of Churches of Christ in America; Father John A. Ryan of Catholic University and the National Catholic Welfare Council; Florence Kelley, general secretary of the National Consumers' League; and Matilda Lindsay of the National Women's Trade Union League.[2] Out of this gathering emerged the Permanent Conference for the Abolition of Child Labor, representing some twenty-five national groups with a variety of political and social views. The Conference decided that the only way to eliminate child labor was by amending the Constitution.[3]

The National Child Labor Committee agreed. Unlike the *Dagenhart* decision, the Supreme Court's *Bailey* ruling did not come as a great surprise to the Committee. Most members, indeed, had expected the child labor tax to be invalidated. Only a day after the adverse decision, the board of trustees created a special subcommittee to study the situation and recommend a course of action.

At its next meeting, on May 31, the board resolved to work for some kind of federal action to eliminate child labor, and Owen Lovejoy was asked to participate in the conference called by Gompers, to be held the next day. The trustees also affirmed their desire to continue working to revise state laws that were below the standards encompassed in the recently nullified federal statute. Several days later, however, the board concluded that there was "no opportunity to secure legislation regulating child labor by the federal authorities under the present Constitution," and it endorsed a resolution favoring an active campaign for amendment. Lovejoy then reported that he had accepted an offer to serve on a committee of ten chosen by the Permanent Conference to draft a child labor amendment.[4]

In preparing the draft the special committee consulted several noted constitutional lawyers, including Roscoe Pound, former Secretary of War Newton D. Baker, Professor Ernst Freund of the University of Chicago Law School, and Joseph P. Chamberlain of Columbia University Law School. The final version, written by Edward P. Costigan, a member of the United States Tariff Commission (later U.S. Senator from Colorado) would be introduced in the Senate on July 26 by Medill McCormick of Illinois and in the House by Israel M. Foster of Ohio.[5]

Not only reform organizations were now interested in constitutional amendment to control child labor; support was widespread and diverse. Herbert Hoover, for example, was concerned with the problem. Shortly after the *Bailey* case he publicly endorsed a child labor amendment in order to end "a blight . . . more deplorable than war." Other prominent supporters included Senator Henry Cabot Lodge and President Harding,[6] neither of whom was known for his reform activities.

The purpose of the amendment—federal regulation of child labor —certainly was not novel, even to conservative Congressmen. It had been tried twice before, and it had worked. The need for federal control could still be demonstrated. Grace Abbott, new chief of the Children's Bureau, reported in January 1923 that in only thirteen states did laws measure up to the standards set by the earlier federal statutes. Some states, in fact, had lowered their standards since the *Bailey* decision. Many state labor officials favored federal action; in reply to a questionnaire, a large majority of those responding testified that the federal laws had been helpful in enforcing state statutes.

As feared, all available evidence indicated that since the federal statute had been declared unconstitutional, there had been a widespread increase in child labor. Not only had many children returned to work, but in those states that lacked the eight-hour standard they worked long hours. Finally, one of the most important effects of the Supreme Court's adverse ruling was to stimulate, once again, the movement of certain industries into states with lax child labor laws. Massachusetts cotton textile plants, for example, were preparing to move South (or were expanding their Southern mills) in order to take advantage of low child labor standards.[7]

When Congress reconvened late in the fall of 1922, the Senate acted first. A subcommittee of the Judiciary Committee held hearings in January 1923 on a number of resolutions for a child labor amendment. A parade of witnesses representing organizations sent by the Permanent Conference for the Abolition of Child Labor testified on behalf of the McCormick-Foster measure. Opposition, chiefly from Southerners, was mild. On February 19, 1923, the Judiciary Committee reported favorably a slightly different amendment, one submitted

at the last minute by Lovejoy and the National Child Labor Committee, which granted Congress power "concurrent with the several
states, to limit or prohibit the labor of persons under the age of 18
years." But again Congress adjourned before it could agree on the
form of the measure.[8]

While members of the Permanent Conference were pleased with
the Judiciary Committee's favorable recommendation, they were incensed because Lovejoy and the NCLC had suggested last-minute
changes in wording which, in effect, created a schism in the ranks
of the reformers. But the NCLC wanted nothing in the amendment
that might be interpreted as limiting the power of the states to regulate or prohibit child labor, especially as some states might wish to
exceed federal standards. As used, the term "concurrent" had been
interpreted by the Supreme Court in the past to mean precisely what
the Committee wanted.

A lengthy debate, particularly between Grace Abbott and Florence
Kelley on the one hand and Owen Lovejoy on the other, attracted
partisans on either side. By the time Congress reconvened in December 1923, substantial agreement had been reached; those in favor of
an amendment worked together in support of a new measure introduced early in the session by Congressman Israel Foster of Ohio and
Senator Samuel Shortlidge of California.[9] From February 7 to March 8,
1924, the House held hearings on various proposals, but as interest
grew the opponents of reform took a more determined stand than
they had shown a year earlier.

The opposition was led by David Clark and James A. Emery, general counsel of the National Association of Manufacturers, both of
whom had previously appeared at the Capitol to oppose measures for
social justice. They were joined by other organizations, some created
solely to fight the proposed amendment and others organized to oppose other social or reform legislation.

Chief among them were the so-called Sentinels of the Republic
and the *Woman Patriot,* a biweekly published in Washington, D.C.
The Sentinels was started in 1922 by Louis A. Coolidge of Boston,
treasurer of the United Shoe Machinery Company. Its chief object, in

theory, was to oppose increasing centralization of power in the federal government; in practice, its chief object was to oppose the child labor amendment and other reform measures. Its official program decried woman suffrage, the federal Maternity and Infancy (Sheppard-Towner) Act, and federal aid to education. It took a strong stand against federal child labor legislation as "the surest means of safeguarding our institutions from the assaults of communism." Financed largely by business and industry, the group flaunted the motto: "Every citizen a Sentinel! Every home a sentry box." [10]

The *Woman Patriot* once had been the organ of the Anti-Suffrage Association, a body devoted to "the defense of the family and the state against feminism and socialism." The anti-suffragists also actively opposed the Children's Bureau and various welfare measures. Speaking of this group and other patriots of the right who opposed the fight against child labor, the editor of *The American Child* observed: "If a cause is known by the enemies it makes, the proposed Amendment is to be congratulated." [11]

A spirited debate over the issue occurred on the House floor. Nearly one hundred members of the lower chamber spoke out on the measure, with most of the discussion centering about the old issues of states' rights and whether child labor conditions made federal control desirable. Apparently most members felt that the national government should be the supervising authority: on April 26, 1924, the House voted favorably on a resolution for an amendment by the overwhelming vote of 297 to 69.[12]

The Senate debated the matter toward the end of May. Eventually, more than one hundred pages of the *Congressional Record* were filled with speeches, discussions, and evidence relating to the bill. Its opponents dwelt at length on the presumed subversive intent of the proponents of the measure. Few Senators, however, were influenced by this argument, and at 10 P.M. on June 2 the resolution was approved by a vote of 61 to 23, or five more than the necessary two-thirds.[13]

The amendment finally approved was the one jointly drawn by the NCLC and the Permanent Conference. At the request of the Senate

Judiciary Committee, however, it had undergone some changes. The final draft was primarily the work of two members of the Senate who were considered authorities on the Constitution—George Wharton Pepper of Pennsylvania, a stalwart Republican and a Protestant, and Thomas J. Walsh of Montana, a Democrat and a Catholic.

The wording of the amendment received careful attention. It was felt that since the amendment was an enabling act, a grant of power allowing Congress to enact child labor legislation and not a specific law or prohibition, it should be broad and inclusive. The specific provisions of restrictive legislation would be left to Congress to determine from time to time in light of changing conditions.

Congress was given the power to regulate labor up to age *eighteen* rather than sixteen, not because the framers wanted to prohibit all employment up to that age, but to make it possible for Congress to regulate the work of sixteen- and seventeen-year-olds in hazardous occupations.

The word *child* was omitted from the amendment because the term had been defined in different ways in previous court cases, and its use might therefore cause uncertainty at a later date.

The word *labor* was used rather than *employment* in order to avoid evasions possible under the latter term; "little merchants" and children "helping" their parents in canneries or in industrial homework, for example, were not technically employed.[14] So the proposed amendment read:

Section 1. The Congress shall have power to limit, regulate, and prohibit the labor of persons under eighteen years of age.
Section 2. The power of the several States is unimpaired by this article except that the operation of State laws shall be suspended to the extent necessary to give effect to legislation enacted by the Congress.[15]

The amendment, then, gave to Congress the right to fix national standards while at the same time allowing the states to enact and enforce higher standards if they so desired.

The battle now shifted from Congress to the states, where three-fourths, or thirty-six of them, had to pass the amendment for it to become effective. The NCLC board met to discuss strategy and set in motion the machinery for organizing ratification campaigns throughout the country. Although they knew that a strenuous fight lay ahead, Committee members and most proponents of the amendment were encouraged by the size of the favorable vote in Congress and by friendly press reaction. The opposition itself believed the country to be behind the amendment. Senator James A. Reed of Missouri, an opponent of the measure, declared on the Senate floor that it "would not receive a vote in this body were there not so many individuals looking over their shoulders toward the ballot boxes of November." [16]

A favorable vote for ratification by Arkansas at the end of June, only a few weeks after Congress had approved the measure, was another encouraging sign. So too was the support of the three major political parties—Republican, Democratic, and Progressive—and their respective presidential candidates, Calvin Coolidge, John W. Davis, and Robert M. LaFollette.[17]

The optimism proved to be short-lived. During the summer of 1924 the country was swept with a bitter propaganda campaign which misrepresented the amendment's history, its authors and supporters, its terms and objectives. The opposition used newspaper and magazine articles, editorials and advertisements, printed leaflets, radio speeches, and public meetings. The strength of the opposition and the speed with which it developed seemed amazing. As the friendly *New Republic* described the situation: "The friends of the amendment were totally unprepared to combat the flood of distorted propaganda which let loose upon them. They had been accustomed to argue their case before reasonable and attentive human beings. They suddenly found themselves compelled to discuss a matter of public policy with a monstrous jazz band." [18]

Soon the ratification campaign suffered a number of reverses and lost its early momentum. Prospects for Southern support faded with a near unanimous rejection by the Louisiana House in late June and by Georgia's total rejection in early July. The North Carolina Senate then rejected the measure. In all three Southern states extravagant charges were lodged against the supporters of the amendment, who were denounced in Georgia as "long-haired agitatists." Arguments of this sort would be repeated again and again throughout the nation over the next few months—and years.[19] While some were thoughtful and based on sincere conviction, most were exaggerated and even hysterical in their bias and distortion of fact. Briefly stated, the most common charges were: [20]

(1) The amendment was unnecessary. Despite evidence to the contrary, especially since nullification of the second federal child labor law, critics insisted that state regulations were adequate and that child labor was declining.

(2) The wording of the amendment was too broad. Opponents particularly attacked the use of the word "labor" rather than "employment," and inclusion of an eighteen- rather than a sixteen-year minimum age. Despite the reasonableness of the first two federal child labor laws and the establishment of minimum standards, the opposition asserted that Congress could never be trusted to use such a grant of authority wisely, that it would pass a variety of extreme laws.

(3) The amendment endangered states' rights. Despite the fact that the measure in no way impaired the rights of the states to enact their own labor legislation, and that the states already had and retained even broader power to regulate child labor than Congress would have under the proposed amendment, critics argued that it would restrict state government.

(4) The amendment would mean an ominous increase of federal power, and an extensive bureaucracy would arise to enforce the laws that would be enacted. Experience, of course, had shown that a federal child labor law could be successfully administered without duplicating the work of the states or creating a cumbersome bureaucracy.

(5) Parental control of children would be surrendered to the federal government. While few practices did more to lower the wage scale (and the standard of living), create insecurity, and break up the home than child labor, and while the term "labor" had always

been construed by the courts to mean gainful employment (labor for hire), opponents charged that under the amendment Congress would have the power to prohibit the work of children at home or on the family farm.

(6) The amendment was a communist-inspired plot. Despite the fact that the measure was drafted by leaders of the United States Senate in conjunction with eminent legal authorities, and was supported by such national leaders as Warren G. Harding and Calvin Coolidge, its opponents charged that it was a radical plot to subvert American institutions.

Aside from the intrinsic merits of these charges, they were particularly effective in the political and social climate of the mid-1920's. During and after World War I the people's doubt over the efficacy of government—especially at the federal level—had broadened, even among some liberals who were disturbed by the growth of big government during the war. The spread of bureaucracy and coercive power, and the restraints imposed publicly and privately upon freedom of ideas all had their effect on many sensitive people who now questioned the further extension of the federal authority.[21]

Related, too, was the prohibition amendment. Although the child labor amendment was merely an enabling act and in no sense prohibitory, and although it had nothing in common with prohibition, opponents were able to use the prohibition issue to their advantage. The prohibition (and, to some extent, the woman suffrage) amendment altered the views of many regarding sumptuary legislation and left widespread antagonism toward reformers and constitutional change. As one legislator, the father of five, put it: "They have taken our women away from us by constitutional amendment; they have taken our liquor away from us; and now they want to take our children." [22]

The early 1920's also saw a move in some parts of the nation to retard sectarian education; in some states bills were introduced that would require the attendance of all children in public schools. These developments aroused fears among certain religious groups, chiefly Roman Catholics and some Lutherans, that federal control of education and the abolition of parochial schools would follow passage of the child labor amendment, especially since the dictionary definition of labor was "physical or mental toil" (i.e., classroom work).[23]

Finally, the amendment ran into the legacy of the so-called Red Scare of 1919–1920. Although the nationalistic drive for conformity and the rooting out of real or imagined foreign influences from American life had largely abated by 1924, fear of communism still persisted. Opponents of child labor reform deliberately aroused these feelings, stigmatizing the amendment as a subversive movement spawned by the Russian Revolution, thus adding another dimension to the arguments against it.[24]

This insidious charge was set forth in detail for the first time at the House hearings on March 1, 1924, by Mary G. Kilbreth, president of the Woman Patriot Publishing Company. Federal child labor regulation, she asserted, was basically a socialist and communist idea to acquire state control of the children. She condemned the advocates of the amendment, especially Florence Kelley, as Reds.[25] Senator Thomas F. Bayard of Delaware then introduced a petition that was being circulated by Miss Kilbreth. It contained a scurrilous attack upon the amendment's supporters. "This benign-looking amendment," the document read, "drawn and promoted principally by an American Socialist leader (Mrs. Florence Kelley, translator of Karl Marx and friend of Frederick Engels, who instructed her how to introduce socialism into the flesh and blood of Americans), is a straight Socialist measure. It is also promoted under direct orders from Moscow." [26]

While not all opponents were as ready as the *Woman Patriot* to charge that child labor reform was hatched in Moscow, the efforts to play upon fears of communism were obvious. Respected and responsible citizens also criticized the amendment in terms that suggested the Red Menace, perhaps more subtly. President Nicholas Murray Butler of Columbia University, for example, asserted that the amendment would make possible "a more far-reaching series of changes in our family, social, economic and political life than have heretofore been dreamed of by the most ardent revolutionary." [27]

Soon it became obvious that business interests were in the forefront of the opposition. The editor of the *Manufacturers' Record,* a leading trade journal, wrote:

The proposed amendment is fathered by Socialists, Communists, and Bolshevists. They are the active workers in its favor. They look forward to its adoption as giving them the power to nationalize the children of the land and bring about in this country the exact conditions which prevail in Russia.

If adopted, this amendment would be the greatest thing ever done in America in behalf of the activities of Hell. It would make millions of young people under 18 years of age idlers in brain and body, and thus make them the devil's best workshop. It would destroy the initiative and self-reliance and manhood and womanhood of all the coming generations.[28]

The National Association of Manufacturers made defeat of the amendment its major item of business for 1924, and its influence was considerable. It set up a National Committee for Rejection of the 20th Amendment, headed by Millard D. Brown, president of Continental Mills in Philadelphia. Housed in the same Washington, D.C., building with James A. Emery, NAM general counsel, the committee distributed pamphlets and urged state legislatures to vote against ratification.[29]

While this routine opposition by the NAM was not surprising, its zealous effort to stimulate resistance from the farm community was unforeseen and difficult to combat. For example, the *Manufacturers' Record* warned that the amendment "takes entirely from the parents the right to have their children, sons or daughters, do any work of any kind, so long as they are under 18 years of age," including "driving the cows to pasture, or hoeing the vegetables, or doing any work of that character, even for their own parents. Under that bill the mother would have no right to teach her daughter to do any housework whatsoever, whether it be the sweeping of floors or the washing of dishes." [30]

David Clark was especially active in circulating propaganda among farmers. In July 1924 he quietly organized the Farmers' States' Rights

League, a prime example of the propaganda methods used by opponents of the child labor amendment. This organization soon flooded Western states and their newspapers with anti-amendment messages and cartoons. This agrarian front was actually headed by the cashier of a cotton mill bank in North Carolina; its vice-president was an employee of a cotton mill store; its chief agent, the man who wrote the advertisements for farm papers, was an employee of the Clark Publishing Company, owned by editor David Clark of the *Southern Textile Bulletin.*[31]

The revelation, early in 1925, that Southern cotton mill interests were directing the campaign to influence the farm community had little effect on the amendment's fate. Agrarian hostility to the child labor amendment was already deep-seated and troublesome. At the House hearings in March 1924, American Farm Bureau Federation agents openly opposed the amendment, the first time members of a farm organization had ever appeared before a congressional committee to take such action. (Later the Farm Bureau distributed a leaflet, signed by a little-known Chicago lawyer, entitled *National Child Labor Law or Socialistic Bureaucratic Control Supplanting Parental Control of Children, Plain Politics for Parents.*) Several state Granges went on record against the amendment, as did the national organization at its annual convention in 1924. With few exceptions, farm journals also opposed the measure.[32]

Meanwhile, the NCLC joined with some twenty other national organizations to create the Organizations Associated for Ratification of the Child Labor Amendment, which served as a clearing house for information and activity in behalf of the measure. Mrs. Arthur C. Watkins of the Parent-Teachers Association was named chairman, Julia Lathrop vice-chairman, and Marguerite Owen, of the League of Women Voters, secretary-treasurer of the group. Owen Lovejoy and his assistant, Wiley Swift, were on the steering committee.[33]

On its own, the Committee prepared and distributed leaflets, furnished public speakers, prepared special articles, explained the issues and answered questions, and engaged well-known artists to paint child labor posters for national distribution. It supplied daily and weekly news summaries to child labor committees and other interested organizations around the country, replied to hundreds of unfriendly editorials, utilized every national news agency available, and provided a semi-weekly news service to eight hundred friendly newspapers. Between June and December 1924 the Committee printed and distributed almost a half-million pieces of literature.[34]

Yet the forces for ratification continued to suffer defeats. Especially bitter was the unexpected reaction of voters in Massachusetts, the home of several reform groups. The state's child labor laws were among the best in America; its industrialists therefore (save those who owned mills in the South) had everything to gain by regulations that would tend to equalize their competitive position. The Massachusetts legislature had moreover adopted a resolution in February 1924 petitioning Congress to propose a child labor amendment. Republican Senator Henry Cabot Lodge and Democratic Congressman William P. Connery, Jr., had both introduced resolutions for a child labor amendment, and several other Massachusetts Congressmen had testified in favor of such a measure at the House hearings. All candidates for major political office, including the governor and lieutenant-governor, favored it.[35]

The campaign against the amendment in Massachusetts was, to one observer, "distinguished by misrepresentation, ignorance and deceit." The legislature decided to hold a referendum on the amendment in November 1924, so the opposition had several months in which to propagandize. The NAM and the Sentinels of the Republic leaped into the fray with the cry that the child labor amendment was communist-inspired. The Associated Industries of Massachusetts, headed by Clifford S. Anderson of the Norton Company in Worcester and a member of the NAM's National Committee for Rejection of the 20th Amendment, formed the Citizens' Committee to Protect Our Homes and Children, many of whose members also belonged to the Sentinels. This group disseminated most of the anti-amendment propaganda, which had as its main theme the threat to the family and the communist menace.[36]

Industrialists formed the hard core of the opposition in Massachusetts, but they were joined by other prominent citizens such as attorney Moorfield Storey, Harvard University President A. Lawrence Lowell, Boston's Mayor James M. Curley, and, most important, the influential Cardinal William O'Connell.[37] Some Roman Catholic groups, such as the National Catholic Welfare Council and the National Council of Catholic Women, supported the amendment, as did a few prominent Catholic leaders, including Father James A. Ryan of Catholic University in Washington, D.C. But the main body of the Church hierarchy and most laymen opposed it, especially in Massachusetts and New York. It was argued that enlarging the federal power posed a severe threat to the privacy of the home and parental rights as well as to the Church's prerogatives, especially in the field of education.

On October 4, 1924, *The Pilot,* official organ of the Archdiocese of Boston, declared that "for parental control over children [the amendment] . . . would substitute the will of Congress and the dictate of a centralized bureaucracy more in keeping with Soviet Russia than with the fundamental principles of American Government." Cardinal O'Connell instructed every pastor in the diocese to warn his parishioners of "the dangers hidden in the proposed Child Labor Amendment and the necessity of their . . . voting on election day to protect the interests of their children." [38]

The opposition of the Catholic Church in Massachusetts was a telling blow. On November 4 the voters rejected the amendment by a margin of nearly three to one. The one-sided defeat suggested that reformers had badly misjudged popular sentiment on the issue. In this first and only direct test, the defeat undermined their contention that most people had favored the amendment. In any event, Massachusetts lawmakers decided not to ignore the advisory referendum. In contrast to their earlier stand, all but a few members of the legislature voted against ratification in mid-February 1925.[39] The issue was dead in Massachusetts.

Elsewhere the failure of the referendum had been noted with interest. By January 1925 six states had rejected the amendment—Georgia, Kansas, North Carolina, South Carolina, Oklahoma, and Texas. Only three had affirmed it—Arkansas, Arizona, and California; thirty-six were needed for ratification. New York, the nation's leader in population and industry, was crucial. If it ratified the amendment, perhaps the tide would shift and others would fall in line. Reform forces prepared for what they saw as the decisive campaign. Many of the same organizations that had actively opposed the measure in Massachusetts, including the NAM, the Sentinels of the Republic, the American Farm Bureau Federation, and the Citizens Committee to Protect Our Homes and Children, prepared for the fight in New York. Reform troops assumed that they would have the support of Governor Alfred E. Smith, a vigorous opponent of child labor who had an outstanding record in the field of social legislation.

After the proposed amendment was defeated in the Massachusetts referendum, stories began circulating that although Governor Smith favored ratification, he was committed to a similar test of popular will in New York State. When proponents of the measure, including Florence Kelley, talked with him they found it to be true. Smith already had planned to insert a recommendation for a referendum in his annual message to the legislature, which he did on January 7, 1925.[40]

Supporters of the amendment felt that Smith, America's foremost Roman Catholic layman, had been influenced by a strong and well-organized Church: most members of the hierarchy, including New York City's Cardinal Hayes, actively opposed the measure. Whatever the reason, Florence Kelley voiced her bitter disappointment in remarking that Smith had "gone over to the enemy." [41] "Deeply do I rue the day," she lamented, "when I signed an appeal with many other social workers, addressed to all other social workers, begging them to vote for Governor Smith because of his excellent record in behalf of social measures in the past. That record is, alas, wiped out by this dreadful act." [42]

Fearful of a repetition of the Massachusetts debacle, the pro-amendment forces in the state naturally opposed a referendum. Publicly they asserted that such a test would be meaningless because the legislature would have to act on the matter anyway. Privately, how-

ever, they admitted that they did not have the resources to compete
with the opposition: "Whoever has the most money to buy the most
space on the front page of the newspapers and the most time of the
most expensive radio stations, wins the referendum." [43] Consequently,
sometime in February 1925 the proponents of ratification agreed with
Governor Smith to table the amendment in the 1925 legislative
session and not submit it for a vote to either the people or the lawmakers. In this manner the amendment became a dead issue in New
York State, and for the next ten years all bills to ratify it died in
committee.[44]

Elsewhere, one state after another voted against the amendment.
By early spring, when twelve states had rejected and only four (including Wisconsin) had ratified it, failure seemed certain; only a handful
of supporters, especially Florence Kelley and Grace Abbott, refused
to admit defeat. Apparently more in tune with the majority was
Herbert Croly, who, as editor of the liberal *New Republic,* was a
staunch backer of the proposal. "I consider your article on the Child
Labor Amendment as extraordinarily able and persuasive piece of
writing," he wrote an author, but he was returning it because he felt
the amendment was clearly beaten. "The only aspect of it which is
worth discussing now is what the effect of the defeat will be and
what the causes of it were." [45]

The ratification forces had proved no match for their well-organized
and well-heeled opponents who had managed to entwine self-interest
with the blessing of the Church and the myths of the agrarian past.
Playing on the popular fears and sensitive issues of the 1920's, the
opposition had used every means to discredit and distort the clear
intent of the amendment. Emotional appeals rather than cold logic
seemed to have carried the day.[46]

Yet it would be too simple to place the entire blame on reactionary
religious elements and the rural and business interests that misrepresented the issue. The eighteen-year minimum age, and the power
that would have been given to Congress to "limit, regulate and prohibit" labor, seriously alarmed many people, even some who had

opposed child labor and had supported the original federal statutes. The reformers, in short, had misjudged the public mind; they believed that Congress would not exploit the grant of power, but the people did not. Public distrust of the federal government as an instrument of reform was far deeper in the 1920's than the reformers had anticipated.[47] Although some of them would continue the fight for ratification, by the end of 1925 most proponents of the amendment had abandoned the fray.[48]

In the spring of 1925, a growing number of NCLC members had argued that while the Committee should continue to cooperate with other groups seeking ratification, its major effort should again be devoted to persuading the individual states to raise their legal standards. This strategy would smoke out all those who had gone on record in favor of state action as opposed to federal. "The plan is vital," testified Samuel McCune Lindsay, "for it forces the opposition to prove their willingness to take care of their own problem or else acknowledge the need of a national standard. Our devotion is always to cure the patient," he concluded, "not to specify the remedy." [49]

Owen Lovejoy felt the same way: "Now is the opportunity to test the sufficiency of state legislation and state administration," he said. Discussion of the amendment throughout the country had "been invaluable in bringing the evils of child labor to the attention of the public. It ought to stimulate increased and more effective state regulation. . . . It ought to mean that the refusal of state legislatures to confer this power on the Federal Government is also their pledge to end the evil without delay." [50] On May 20, 1925, the board resolved that "it is the sense of this Committee that while adhering to its advocacy of the Federal Child Labor Amendment, it cannot ignore the fact that it is impracticable to get favorable legislative action in the near future, and accordingly the emphasis of its work will be placed as heretofore upon State legislation." [51]

Florence Kelley, recalling the long struggle for the woman suffrage amendment, was deeply disappointed with the Committee's decision. It was, to Mrs. Kelley, further evidence of "rabbit-hearted" leadership.[52] But the Committee was not as gloomy, and it settled down for a long, hard campaign. It continued to cooperate with state groups in making general studies, so as to improve and coordinate their child welfare laws. It pressed the states to revive their child labor laws and adopt a high uniform standard. And, having halted sometime earlier its studies of child labor in agriculture so as not to prejudice rural communities against the amendment, the Committee now began some of its most intensive studies of child labor on the farms.

Yet with the exception of one or two minor advances in the more backward states, little was accomplished during the late 1920's. Instead of "ending the evil without delay," as Owen Lovejoy had hoped, the Committee found itself busy trying to hold the line on existing regulations. In fact, fewer states took steps to measure up to the NCLC's minimum standards in the five years from 1925 to 1929 than in any other five-year period since the Committee's founding. If anything, there was some increase in child labor.[53]

In the midst of these discouraging years, Owen Lovejoy announced his retirement in February 1926, after nearly twenty-two years of service. The Committee's dynamic general secretary had come to be regarded as a permanent friend of working children; few others had equaled his record of achievement on behalf of America's exploited youth. Lovejoy's chief contribution to the Committee had been in education and persuasion. Operating largely through personal contacts, he had traveled extensively, often into unfriendly areas, to bring the challenge of the underprivileged working child directly to the American people. His effectiveness as a platform speaker had helped the NCLC enormously during the period of its greatest achievement. But now that the Committee was subordinating his kind of work to research and the technical details of law and administration, it was time, he believed, to step down and devote more time to his family and personal matters.[54]

The board asked Wiley Swift, Lovejoy's assistant, to fill the vacancy for the time being. Born and educated in the South, Swift was allied with the Committee's conservative wing.[55] His first action was to cut back on field work and research which, he felt, rested with the state committees and with other private and public agencies and well-financed foundations. The crusading phase of the Committee's work had passed; the organization, in Swift's opinion, should be largely a clearing house in matters of child labor.[56]

This approach created further dissension within the NCLC and opposition from without. Not only Florence Kelley but Lillian Wald, Grace Abbott, Maud Wood Park, and others expressed their concern about the Committee's future.[57] In an attempt to restore confidence, a militant worker, Gertrude Folks Zimand, the daughter of the crusading Homer Folks, was named Swift's assistant. The board also instructed Lindsay to confer with Mrs. Park and Miss Abbott to discover what could be done to effect closer cooperation between the Committee and other organizations interested in child welfare and in the child labor amendment. Soon Lillian Wald began spreading the "confidential" news that Swift was resigning and that the Committee was looking for a suitable successor.[58] Actually this would not occur for some time.

The Committee now found itself interested in a project of the National Association of Manufacturers. After playing a major role in blocking the child labor amendment, the NAM appointed a Junior Education and Employment Committee "to study and make known the facts" and, allegedly, to secure adequate state legislation to protect school-age children.[59] Part One of the NAM's National Education and Employment Program appeared in October 1926. Suggesting that there were many mentally inferior children in the public schools who could not profit by further education, and so should go to work, the document in effect was an attack on the requirement for sixteen years of compulsory schooling, wherever it existed. The report urged a uniform limit of fourteen years of school and a sixth-grade minimum for work permits instead of the eighth-grade minimum favored by the NCLC.

Raymond Fuller, an able and experienced polemicist, replied directly to the NAM's argument in *Fourteen Is Too Early,* an effective portrayal of the problem. Fuller eloquently discussed the need to develop practical courses that would interest many normal children who were being labeled mentally inferior by the NAM. In any case, Fuller wrote, mental inferiority hardly justified the transfer of such children from school to child labor. Backward children needed more education and guidance, not less, than their more gifted schoolmates.[60]

The NAM thereupon mystified both its friends and its critics when some months later it published more of its findings and proposed that children under the age of fourteen *not* be gainfully employed. Those beyond that age should have completed the sixth grade in school and, until age sixteen, should attend continuation school for at least four hours a week. The work week should not consist of more than forty-eight hours, while work between the hours of 9 P.M. and 7 A.M. and in dangerous occupations ought to be prohibited.

All this amounted to something of a concession, for it was the first time the NAM had ever supported the idea that working children between the ages of fourteen and sixteen should be subject to regulation. Whatever its shortcomings, the NAM's proposals, if effected, would raise legal standards in many of the more backward states. Although the program fell short of the NCLC's minimum standards in several respects,[61] some of the Committee's members, especially Wiley Swift, appeared jubilant. In Swift's opinion, the NAM was to be congratulated; its position was "a distinct step forward in the history of child labor" which could be interpreted as "one of the most important events" in years.

When Swift went even further and recommended cooperation with the NAM, he ran into a storm of protest.[62] Rabbi Stephen S. Wise, Lillian Wald, and other board members questioned his judgment and openly doubted the sagacity of his statement, which was widely quoted. National Education Association leaders spoke out against the NAM plan and those who supported it. Swift was denounced by the *Union Teacher,* the New York State teachers' union journal, which urged the NCLC to repudiate his statement.

Florence Kelley seized upon the incident as further evidence that the NCLC's executive staff had sold out to the manufacturers. "The treason of the National Child Labor Committee to the cause of the wage-earning children has had a continuing paralyzing effect upon me," and Wiley Swift was but "a public nuisance and an infinite injury to the children of today and a long time to come," she declared privately. Openly, she wrote in *The Survey* in October 1927, "Any persons who . . . believe that this new program is a benevolent undertaking . . . or who try to cooperate in it, [are] . . . naive souls unacquainted with the continuous record of the national manufacturers' association, and ill-informed as to the extraordinarily valuable safeguards which are to be undermined by carrying out its program. Or they will be shepherds deserting their lambs." [63]

Mrs. Kelley and the National Consumers' League attacked the program in their own way. They urged educators across the country to speak out against it, held public meetings, and organized a Committee of Fifty to undermine Swift's proposal. The NCLC, on the other hand, never officially condemned the program or repudiated Swift's statements. Rather, it decided to test NAM intentions by waiting to see what it would do during the next legislative year, when forty-four state legislatures would be in session.[64] Some 123 bills of concern to the NCLC were introduced in thirty-seven state legislatures during 1929. The final accounting, however, showed few gains. Again, the chief accomplishment seemed nothing more than holding the line for existing standards. The NAM did not openly support or oppose a single bill; its educational program would not be heard of again.[65]

On December 16 and 17, 1929, the National Child Labor Committee celebrated its twenty-fifth anniversary. To the gala event at New York's Hotel Roosevelt came local and state dignitaries and federal officials. Governor Franklin D. Roosevelt, the principal speaker, discussed "The Function of Government in Child Protection," chastising businessmen who objected to what they termed the high cost of social and labor legislation. New York State, he declared, would not curtail its program in this field in order to retain those industries that threatened to migrate to less progressive states. Public opinion, Roosevelt said, would force universally high standards and fugitive industries would return to the Empire State.[66]

Apart from such rhetoric, the NCLC could take satisfaction in reviewing its work and deeds over a quarter of a century:

> In 1904 only 17 states attempted to keep children under fourteen out of factories; by 1929 every state had some kind of fourteen-year limit, and in 39 states no child under fourteen could work in a factory under any circumstances.
>
> In 1904 only 5 states prohibited the employment of children under sixteen years of age in factories at night; by 1929 the number was 36.
>
> In 1904 only 2 states had established an eight-hour day for children under sixteen in factories; by 1929 the number had risen to 36.[67]

While substantial progress had been made in the one type of employment most generally condemned as unsuitable for children—in mine, mill and factory—in fact by 1929 it had less use for them because of mechanical progress. Even in these industries, child labor had not been eliminated entirely. And industrial standards had to be extended to all gainful employment—to work in stores, offices, laundries, restaurants, and bowling alleys, for example, as well to the tenements, the streets, and the fields. In those areas where children had not been replaced by machines, they were either exempt from legislation or not covered by it.[68] Much remained to be done.

In the fall of 1930 Wiley Swift stepped down as acting secretary and was replaced by Courtenay Dinwiddie, a more militant and aggressive worker who came to the Committee from the New York City Department of Health. A quiet yet forceful man of wide and varied experience in health and child welfare work throughout the country, Dinwiddie by temperament, training, and commitment was deeply concerned about the welfare of children and well qualified to direct the NCLC's work through the complicated and chaotic years ahead.[69] His presence eliminated much of the dissension on the Committee that had been caused by Swift.

Few people at the time realized that the depression would be as prolonged and severe as it was, or that one of the end results would be higher child labor standards. At first, as economic conditions worsened and unemployment spread, the number of young workers naturally declined.[70] Yet, in some ways, child labor matters also deteriorated. Children who continued to work or who left school to work for wages could find little better than blind-alley jobs with no educational value and little chance for promotion. The number of children working in unregulated occupations, such as industrial homework and the street trades, increased as well. A new and alarming problem was idleness among children who had left school for work but who, either unable to find a job or dismissed from one, did not return to school.

By late 1932, however, in the depths of the depression, the pressure on retail prices led employers to hire young boys and girls who would work for lower wages and longer hours than experienced adults. By spring 1933 the employment of children under sweatshop conditions was again widespread, especially in the garment centers of the industrial East. In April a series of children's strikes in western Pennsylvania shirt factories called national attention to this trend. Ruth Scandrett, former chief factory inspector in Alabama who was studying child labor conditions in the Lehigh Valley for the NCLC when the strikes began, reported: "I have become hardened by my years in the South to child labor and substandard conditions, but never have I seen so many children work for so little or under such conditions as exist in Pennsylvania." [71]

The Committee tried desperately to reverse the trend—to keep more children in school so as to reduce both child labor and adult unemployment. It pointed to the absurdity of allowing more than a million immature children to interrupt their schooling and compete in the labor market when over ten million adults had no jobs. It fostered stay-in-school campaigns and tried to prevent cuts in school budgets; it sought to raise the school-leaving age, strengthen vocational education and guidance programs, and get communities to establish special classes for young unemployed workers.[72]

Faced with the ruin of industries because of sweatshop competition, with the spreading contagion of unemployment and soaring relief expenditures, and with the realization that the labor of immature children was sapping the foundation of the nation's welfare, politicians and legislators sensed the need to act. Taking the NCLC completely by surprise,[73] they began to react favorably to the child labor amendment.

VIII

Depression Decade: Successes and Setbacks

A̲FTER the election of 1932 a group of interested associations and citizens answered a call from the Children's Bureau to discuss the child labor situation and its prospects for the future. At the meeting it was decided that although national regulation was still essential, it would be wiser to press for a sixteen-year minimum-age law in all the states rather than ratification of the amendment. The NCLC had reached the same conclusion.[1] It was a misjudgment of public opinion.

By 1933 the spreading contagion of child labor had found every weakness and loophole in state labor legislation. Sweatshops and fly-by-night plants were exploiting children for little or no pay, moving at will across state lines to take advantage of laws of nearby states. The individual states were unable to halt these abuses which had far-reaching effects, including the complete breakdown of wage scales. Everywhere people were looking to Washington for help and direction.

One federal measure on which fairly prompt action was possible was the child labor amendment; in some states it still languished in committee, while in others it had already been defeated. Between February 1 and July 15, 1933, nine state legislatures ratified the measure. President Roosevelt and his Cabinet urged that other states take similar action. The halfway mark was passed by December, when five more states voted approval in special sessions, bringing the total to twenty.[2] It now seemed possible that sixteen more states would approve the measure and that the amendment would become a reality. The NCLC and its friends responded to this turnabout by renewing their active support of the measure.[3]

The revival of interest in the amendment was reinforced by the National Recovery Administration, established under the provisions of the National Industrial Recovery Act. Passed in June 1933 to meet the crisis in unemployment and industry, the NIRA sought to end cutthroat competition by promoting cooperative action among trade groups, to raise prices by limiting production, and to guarantee labor a reasonable work week and decent wages. It hoped to accomplish these ends through the adoption of codes of fair competition for all branches of business and industry. The codes were to remain in effect for the emergency period, which by law was two years, or less should the President declare the emergency at an end. Committees representing management, labor, and the public were to draw up the codes and submit them to the President for approval and promulgation; in the event of irreconcilable disagreement in the drafting process, Roosevelt could intervene and impose a code of his own. To provide for the interim period before specific standards could be formulated and accepted, FDR proposed a blanket code, and the NRA was established to implement it. Under General Hugh S. Johnson, who was named Administrator, the work soon began.[4]

Because of its close relationship to adult unemployment and low wages, child labor became one of the main targets of the NRA. The industrial codes presented a unique means of dealing directly and uniformly with child labor throughout entire industries, and the NCLC took advantage of the opportunity.

Early in the course of code-drafting the Committee submitted to the NRA a statement of general principles which it felt should govern the child labor provisions of all the codes, those issued separately for each industry or for industry as a whole. Most important, the Committee urged adoption of a sixteen-year minimum age for all work except where unemployment was acute or the job was hazardous, in which case it proposed an eighteen-year minimum.[5]

Working closely with the Children's Bureau, the NCLC maintained agents in Washington throughout the summer and fall of 1933 to assist in the intensive work necessary to insure adequate child labor provisions in the codes. Specific suggestions for individual codes were submitted to the NRA, and Committee members appeared at all code hearings. As proposed codes were made public, the Committee submitted briefs regarding their clauses on child labor, apprenticeship, and industrial homework. No code that affected child labor was neglected, although major attention was given to those industries involving the gravest and most long-standing abuses. Up to October 1, 1933, the work included briefs on forty-five codes and an immense amount of personal work with NRA representatives and others in positions of influence, as well as a constant stream of publicity to secure public support for advanced child labor provisions.[6]

The first code to be proposed, the one for the cotton textile industry, set no minimum working age and contained no reference at all to child labor. The NCLC protested and urged other groups and individuals to wire General Johnson asking for a ban on child labor. The press responded with vigorous editorial endorsement of the Committee's stand and, after a night-long conference (on July 9, 1933), the industry capitulated by accepting a clause forbidding the employment of children under sixteen in cotton textile mills.[7]

The Code of Fair Competition adopted by the cotton textile industry, effective July 17, was especially welcome. Not only had the mills traditionally been a stronghold of child labor, but as the first one adopted this code set the standard for other industries. Less than two weeks later, President Roosevelt promulgated a blanket code, operative until December 31. The first section of the decree specified a sixteen-year minimum working age, except for nonmanufacturing or nonmining industries where fourteen- to sixteen-year-old children could work three hours a day, between 7 A.M. and 7 P.M., when school was not in session. Thus a national minimum for which the Committee had been working for years, one that existed in only a few states, had been enacted by a stroke of the pen.[8]

This emergency method of shaping uniform national child labor standards met with wide support and surprisingly little opposition. Since the national character of the provisions relieved employers of the fear of being undercut by manufacturers in other sections who previously had depended on child labor, the codes were welcomed by employers as well as by adult workers and parents. Codes with sixteen-year minimum working ages came rapidly. By December 1933, when the blanket code expired, 119 separate industrial agreements had been approved and adopted, and of these only two contained exemptions allowing for the employment of children under sixteen years of age; the motion picture industry and the legitimate theater were permitted to employ children at any age, subject to state laws, and fourteen- to sixteen-year-olds could work in the retail trades three hours a day (or one eight-hour day a week), between 7 A.M. and 7 P.M. when school was not in session. Sixty-one codes established sixteen years as the minimum age for all employment, while the remaining fifty-six provided a higher minimum age, usually eighteen, for work regarded as hazardous or detrimental to health.[9]

In the short time between July 1933, when the first code was adopted, and December, a new and dramatic chapter in the history of child labor control was written—over 100,000 children under sixteen were removed from industry and some thirty thousand to fifty thousand others between sixteen and eighteen were taken out of hazardous occupations, such as mining, logging, and sawmill operations. For the first time in American industrial history, child labor declined sharply in the face of improving business and employment.

During the four-month period ending December 31, 1933, not a single work permit was issued to a child under sixteen in the entire state of Alabama, or in such Northern industrial cities as Fall River and Bedford, Massachusetts; Jersey City, Hoboken, and Camden, New Jersey; Buffalo, New York; or Allentown, Pennsylvania,

where only a few months earlier hundreds of young shirt-workers had
gone out on strike. These situations were typical.[10]

"We have done more to eliminate child labor in the last three or
four months than we were able to do in the preceding ten years,"
wrote Courtenay Dinwiddie, NCLC general secretary, in November
1933. The "removal of children from the major industries during
the emergency, even though its permanence is not assured," he added
thoughtfully, "will always be a credit to the Administration, and the
universal endorsement which this action met throughout the country
is a credit to the American people." [11]

While the exemptions from the sixteen-year minimum age were
hardly of major importance, there was one notable exception—newsboys. The newspaper and periodical publishers, determined to have
no interference with their child workers, took a recalcitrant stand. Of
all the codes that were eventually approved, none approached the
newspaper pact for laxity. The nation's press had been among the
most enthusiastic supporters of the child labor provisions of other
industrial codes. Hardly a paper had failed to applaud the removal
of children from mills, mines, factories or stores. But when it came
to selling papers, the publishers, who employed some half a million
minors, had their own song to sing. As originally drafted by the
American Newspaper Publishers' Association in August 1933, the
code contained no age or hours restrictions whatsoever; it permitted
any child, of any age, to sell or deliver newspapers at any hour of the
day or night provided that such work did not interfere with school
attendance.[12]

The NCLC had asked for a sixteen-year minimum for boys and
eighteen for girls who sold or delivered newspapers at night, and a
fourteen-year minimum (for boys, sixteen for girls) for such work
between the hours of 7 A.M. and 7 P.M. At a public hearing on the
proposed code the Committee insisted that the following clause be
inserted:

That the publishers shall not employ or permit to be employed directly or through any distributing agent any persons under age 16

years except boys 14-16 years to deliver or sell newspapers between 7 A.M. and 7 P.M. where such work does not interfere with hours of day school.[13]

A Hearst Publishing Company circulation manager, protesting the NCLC's recommendations, admitted that the two newspapers he represented used "somewhere in the neighborhood" of one thousand boys under twelve years old and four hundred under ten. But in defense of the practice, H. W. Stodghill, president and circulation manager of the *Louisville Courier-Journal* and chairman of the welfare committee of the International Circulation Managers' Association, argued that there was "a question as to whether the work of the newspaper boy is child labor or play. . . ." He and his colleagues thought it was play, and the newsboys earned money in the bargain.

Lewis E. Lawes, warden of Sing Sing Prison, felt differently. A census conducted at the prison, he testified, showed that 69 per cent of the inmates had sold newspapers in their youth. Yet E. E. Keevin, editor of *Newsboy World,* a trade journal, maintained in his turn that to take away routes from young newsboys "would constitute a national menace and drive them into the Devil's Workshop." [14]

Some of the most damaging attacks on the rather smug attitude of the publishers came from their own ranks. An editorial in *Editor and Publisher,* an industry organ, maintained that the "fourteen-year limit that is now proposed against which the circulation departments are crusading, is a sensible and fair proposal. . . . Joining hands with the exploiters of child labor in this country . . . is not the way out for the American press." And the *New York Daily News* said bluntly: "When our fellow publishers talk of freedom of the press they mean freedom to hire children to deliver newspapers before light on winter mornings because children are cheaper." [15] The *Milwaukee Journal,* the *St. Louis Post-Dispatch* and a few other independent newspapers argued in a like manner.

As it was finally agreed upon in February 1934, the newspaper code set a fourteen-year minimum age for street sellers in cities over fifty thousand population, a twelve-year minimum in cities with fifty thousand or fewer people, and a twelve-year limit for carriers, with an exemption for ten-year-old boys already employed in cities of fifty thousand people or under. Carriers were allowed to begin work at 5 A.M.; night work was prohibited only to those under sixteen engaged in selling.[16] Thus the newspapers, which had applauded sixteen-year limits for day and night work in other industries, gained the most favored provisions for themselves. (Even these standards were hardly tested, for the Supreme Court was to find the NRA unconstitutional shortly after the code became operative.) [17]

By the fall of 1934 most of American industry, including a majority of the child-employers, was operating under codes that set the minimum age for employment at sixteen. Of more than five hundred agreements, only thirteen contained exemptions allowing children under sixteen to work under certain conditions.[18] The employment of children under sixteen in nonagricultural occupations, and of children under eighteen in hazardous occupations, reached an all-time low.[19] Industrial homework was also substantially curtailed by the NRA, for it was prohibited entirely in many industries where it had been used extensively, including most of the major garment industries—a course that had been recommended by the NCLC for more than twenty years. The practice never again flourished.[20]

The NCLC, of course, never believed that the industrial codes would be a permanent solution to the regulation of child labor. Some 500,-000 working children, including many of the most grievously exploited—those laboring in agriculture and in domestic service, for example—were not touched by the codes, and, as many people failed to realize, they were only temporary. Unless their child labor provisions were made permanent through ratification of the child labor amendment and passage of federal legislation, all the gains might be lost when the codes expired—the very thing that happened when the federal child labor laws were declared illegal.

But an attitude of complacent optimism developed as a result of the success with the codes, and it became a source of difficulty for the Committee and ammunition for those who still opposed regulation. Even the well informed assumed that the codes had solved the problem, and that there was no need for further activity. President

Roosevelt himself demonstrated this false sense of security when, in his annual message to Congress in January 1934, he stated that "child labor is abolished." [21]

Sixteen more states were needed for ratification of the amendment, but which of the remaining twenty-eight were the most likely to adopt the measure could not be predicted. Active campaigns had to be conducted in all these states, and repeated many times in some. Thus the Committee engaged in one of the most extensive oprations in its history—the campaign to make the gains of the NRA permanent through adoption of the amendment, first during the 1935 legislative year, and again in 1937.[22]

Every avenue for organizing public opinion was utilized. Local groups were reactivated and provided with printed materials or with more direct aid, including money and personnel. The NCLC helped create a Non-Partisan Committee for Ratification of the Child Labor Amendment under the chairmanship of C. C. Burlingham, prominent lawyer and one-time president of the New York Bar Association. Composed of well-known lawyers, businessmen, educators, clergymen, and civic leaders, the group added prestige to the ratification forces and helped to answer the assorted arguments of the opposition.[23]

A Catholic Citizens Committee for Ratification was organized, presumably by its chairman, Frank P. Walsh, lawyer, prominent public servant, and since 1931 chairman of the New York State Power Authority. "No man can speak for me as a Catholic against the Child Labor Amendment," Walsh declared in announcing creation of the committee. "I have a right to speak as a member of the Catholic Church and I wish to stand here and resent publicly the hypocritical misrepresentation given the Church by some of its so-called leaders." Composed of priests, lawyers, educators, industrialists, labor union leaders, and spokesmen for civic groups, Walsh's committee sought to organize Catholic sentiment in favor of the amendment in those states which had not yet ratified, especially New York. The group was severely criticized by the clergy and by most Catholic papers and accomplished little. Yet it was useful in publicizing the fact that a number of prominent Catholics favored the amendment.[24]

The temporary success of the codes had not necessarily destroyed opposition to the amendment among traditional interest groups, and when the NCLC began anew its campaign for ratification, old opponents rose to offer old arguments. Men like Nicholas Murray Butler, Elihu Root, and A. Lawrence Lowell opposed the amendment because they felt it violated states' rights. The old bogey of communism was raised again, but some of the steam was taken out of this argument when the American Legion went on record as favoring the amendment.[25] Farmers again contended that the amendment would prevent their children from milking the family cow or washing the dinner dishes, and spokesmen for several religious groups warned the faithful that the federal government would assume complete authority over their children and their education. A new assertion was that the amendment would Hitlerize children. And one widely circulated handout informed the public that the amendment "which Jewish Governor [Herbert] Lehman tried to railroad through the New York State Legislature . . . following previous action by Illinois under Jewish Governor Horner" was a plot "to sabotage the U.S. Constitution." [26]

Chief spokesman for the opposition this time was a group called the National Committee for the Protection of Child, Family, School, and Church. This high-flown outfit was set up in January 1934 by Sterling E. Edmunds, a St. Louis attorney and executive committee member of the Sentinels of the Republic. Its basic idea was nothing more than defeat of the amendment.[27] Financed by big business, the group comprised members of the Sentinels, the Woman Patriot Publishing Company, and others actively opposed to the amendment. Working out of its St. Louis headquarters, it flooded state legislatures with lobbyists and literature which claimed the amendment would lead to the nationalization of youth, compulsory military training in the schools, and a swarm of federal snoopers in every home. The Edmunds committee distributed newspaper propaganda, sponsored radio talks, lined up powerful interests to block the measure, and offered its services to help defeat the amendment in any state where it was being considered.[28]

The opposition would not have been as strong as it was without the active support of the press which, with a few notable exceptions, did about all it could to defeat the amendment. Most of the newspaper opposition developed late in 1933 after the NCLC had attempted to secure reasonable provisions for the newspaper code under the NRA; before that time most of the press, in rural and metropolitan areas alike, had favored ratification. Then the American Newspaper Publishers' Association and the International Circulation Managers' Association linked the code and the amendment, portraying both as an attempt to prevent all children under eighteen from engaging in any form of work, including the sale and delivery of newspapers. Some seventy of the nation's leading newspapers, including the *New York Sun*, the *New York Herald Tribune*, and the *St. Louis Post-Dispatch*, which earlier had favored the amendment, suddenly turned against it. Even the *Chicago Tribune*, a consistent supporter of the amendment ever since one of its chief owners, Medill McCormick, had introduced it in the Senate in 1923, now opposed the measure.[29]

Attacks by the press took a variety of forms, including resolutions by various managers' associations; a barrage of editorial criticism, cartoons, and unfavorable articles; marked bias in the handling of news items; misleading (and sometimes even absurd) interpretation of the NCLC's position; suppression of favorable news items, including President Roosevelt's endorsement of the measure; full-page advertisements; and feature articles lauding the newsboy and lamenting his demise if the measure were ratified. Rarely, if ever, have opinions on a social issue been as full of false statements and bias dictated by self-interest as those published by newspapers intent on killing the amendment. So vicious was the newspaper campaign that William Allen White, owner-editor of the *Emporia* (Kansas) *Gazette* and one of America's most respected journalists, sounded a telling rebuke: "The newspapers should stop their fight on the Child Labor Amendment. It is discrediting the newspaper profession and weakening our just position on other matters." [30]

The Committee used every available channel to counteract the press. It urged newspapers in favor of the amendment to intensify their support, and it quoted widely the *Editor and Publisher* editorial deprecating the attack. The Committee also arranged for many favorable magazine articles and radio broadcasts, and distributed numerous leaflets in an effort to get the facts to the public.[31]

Proponents of reform also had to contend with a hostile American Bar Association. At its annual meeting in 1933 the association went on record opposing the amendment after its president, Clarence E. Martin, maintained in his opening address that it was "a communistic effort to nationalize children, making them primarily responsible to the government instead of to their parents. It strikes at the home. It appears to be a definite positive plan to destroy the Republic and substitute a social democracy." As one member of the group plainly admitted: "A lawyer's first duty is to his client, and lawyers' clients are not children who work for a living." [32]

Some months later the American Bar Association appointed a Special Committee to Oppose Ratification of the Proposed Child Labor Amendment, headed by William D. Guthrie of New York.[33] The committee's report, published in the *American Bar Association Journal* for January 1935, presented the one anti-amendment argument that was new in the 1930's—that the amendment already was dead and could not therefore be ratified. The lawyers held that since the amendment had been before the states for ten years it had failed of ratification within a "reasonable" time, and that once a state legislature rejects an amendment it loses the power subsequently to ratify it. As more than one-fourth of the states had rejected the amendment, its ratification was no longer possible.[34]

As a substitute, the Bar Association suggested its Uniform Child Labor Law, a measure with much lower standards than those in force throughout the country under the industrial codes. In effect, then, it advocated a lowering of child labor standards when the emergency of the depression ended.

To counter the American Bar Association, the NCLC marshaled the opinions of some of the nation's most prominent lawyers, including George W. Alger, C. C. Burlingham, Nicholas Kelley, George Z. Medalie, Franklin Chase Hoyt, William Church Osborn, Newton

Baker, Roscoe Pound, and Samuel Seabury, who argued that the amendment was legal and still open for ratification.[35] But the ABA's position weighed heavily when added to the formidable opposition of religious groups, well-financed business organizations, and a powerful press. As the economy began to recover, there was less concern about child labor as a cause of adult unemployment. More important, the rise of dictatorships and extreme nationalism in Europe and the Far East, together with the oppression of religious groups, were ugly realities that aroused fears in the minds of many: strong central governments became suspect. Opponents contended that the rash of New Deal "alphabet agencies" were but a taste of the federal control in store for the country should the amendment be adopted. In any event, only four states—Idaho, Indiana, Utah, and Wyoming—ratified the amendment in 1934–1935; twelve more were still needed.[36]

Again the Supreme Court was to prove decisive in the issue. In May 1935 the Court held that the NRA, based on Congress' right to regulate interstate commerce, was unconstitutional. In *Schechter Poultry Corporation v. United States,* the Court unanimously found the act null and void on two counts: first, that Congress had improperly delegated legislative powers to the President; and second, that the provisions of the poultry code (and hence others) were a regulation of intrastate, not interstate, commerce.[37] The New Deal's far-reaching plan for industry, and the NCLC's efforts on behalf of exploited children, lay in fragments.

As when the two federal child labor laws were declared illegal, the child employment curve shot upward again. Children's Bureau and state reports on the issuance of work permits indicated that with the revival of business in 1936 came a marked increase in the number of working children. The number of work permits issued to fourteen- and fifteen-year-olds in ten states, the District of Columbia, and ninety-eight cities rose by 150 per cent during the first five months of the year as compared with the same period in 1935.[38] Clearly, workers over sixteen years of age were being replaced by young children who worked for lower wages.

The rapid return of child labor after the *Schechter* decision, and the failure of state legislatures to raise their standards to a level with those in the codes, pointed again to the need for ratification of the amendment, which the Committee hoped to achieve in 1937.[39] There were some hopeful signs. In December 1935 the American Farm Bureau Federation, long a foe of the measure, had approved the amendment and had recommended that its state federations do the same. Thirty-six national organizations with a membership of more than forty million included ratification in their programs for immediate action.[40] And a Gallup poll published in May 1936 showed that 61 per cent of the American people favored the amendment. "If the Child Labor Amendment were officially submitted to the people for ratification," stated Dr. George Gallup, director of the American Institute of Public Opinion, "forty-five states would probably vote 'yes' and only three [South Dakota, Kansas, and Maryland] vote 'no.'"[41]

Some important newspapers reversed their position and came out in support of the amendment; evidence of public sentiment probably caused the change of heart, or head. On January 8, 1937, President Roosevelt sent a letter to the governors and governors-elect of the nineteen states which had not yet ratified the amendment and whose legislatures were scheduled to meet that year, urging favorable action. Two days later, former President Herbert Hoover, in his first public statement since the election of 1936, said: "The President is right. The Child Labor Constitutional Amendment should be ratified."[42]

Apparently the public had been well educated about the true purposes of the amendment, despite local setbacks and some farfetched arguments in opposition. State legislatures, however, did not respond to the wishes of the majority; rather, they continued to listen to powerful minority interests. Resolutions for ratification continued to die, often in committee without a vote. Even in Nevada, where the Gallup poll showed that 69 per cent of the people favored the amendment, it was turned down.

In February 1937 another Gallup poll resulted in an even more sweeping straw vote for the amendment. In less than a year since the previous poll, public support had increased from 61 per cent to 76. Every state in the Union reported a majority of voters in favor of ratification.[43] In the face of this evidence and despite heroic efforts by the NCLC and other national and local organizations to make state legislatures respond to the will of the people, only four states—Kansas, Kentucky, New Mexico, and Nevada—took favorable action in 1937. Eight more were needed for ratification.

In the key state of New York the amendment was killed by the Assembly (after favorable action by the Senate) despite the fact that, according to the Gallup poll, 83 per cent of the residents favored it, and it had the active support of President Roosevelt, Governor Herbert Lehman, and New York City's Mayor Fiorello H. LaGuardia. In Rhode Island, where 88 per cent of the people were found to favor the amendment, it also failed of ratification.[44]

Defeats like these were enough to discourage the most stouthearted advocates of the amendment, but defeat was an old story for NCLC members. While preparing to renew their drive, hoping for success in 1939, sudden events in Washington aroused interest in a new federal child labor bill. Favorable Supreme Court decisions on the legality of the National Labor Relations Act, a measure aimed at protecting the right of employees to organize labor unions and to bargain collectively, and the Ashurst-Sumners Act, a federal statute barring the shipment of prison-made goods into states that had laws against the sale of such goods, had broadened the interpretation of interstate commerce and opened the door wider for successful enactment of a federal child labor law outside of the amendment.[45]

The NCLC preferred an amendment, of course, feeling that even the best federal law would be limited. Children employed in industries that shipped goods in interstate commerce comprised only about one-fourth of those working. The rest worked either in intrastate industries or in occupations not classified as interstate commerce, such as industrial homework, street trading, or agriculture. But the chances of getting a federal law appeared good, and no one could know whether eight more states would ratify the amendment at their next legislative sessions. If they did, so much the better; if not, at least the children in interstate industries could be protected if a good federal statute were passed.[46]

Of the fifty or more bills introduced in the 75th Congress (1937–1938), most were based on the principle of prison-made goods, which held that articles could not be shipped into states that forbade the practices under which they had been produced.[47] The NCLC opposed this tactic for the regulation of child labor. To be effective, such statutes required enabling legislation by each state, something proven impossible to secure. Moreover, such legislation would not establish national standards. And to prohibit the "sale of goods made by children" (rather than regulating the employment of minors) necessitated proving that children had worked on specific goods, an extremely difficult task. For these reasons the NCLC preferred the more direct method of the first federal child labor law as the soundest and best way of regulating the practice. Thus the Committee directed its efforts toward securing a child labor bill based on the interstate commerce clause, one that established a minimum working age of sixteen except for a few occupations to be specified as especially hazardous—they would have an eighteen-year minimum.[48]

While President Roosevelt favored regulation of child labor, he also sought to enact minimum-wage and maximum-hours legislation. Possibly in the belief that he could get such a measure through Congress more easily if it were made more attractive by integrating it with child labor, FDR sought to combine the two into a single measure. As one lawmaker observed, the child-labor sweetener was put in the bill "because it was desired to say to Senators, 'When you vote against this bill you are also voting against the prohibition of child labor.' "[49]

The NCLC and the Children's Bureau naturally favored a separate child labor bill, but eventually they capitulated to administration pressure and rallied behind the Black-Connery Wages and Hours (or Fair Labor Standards) bill. The measure, which among other things would prohibit the interstate transportation of goods from any place where children had been employed, had emerged from a meeting held in April 1937 by Katharine Lenroot, chief of the Children's Bureau since November 1934, and Benjamin Cohen, a close presidential adviser. Also present were Grace Abbott, former head of the Bureau,

Homer Folks, who had become NCLC board chairman in 1935, Courtenay Dinwiddie, NCLC general secretary, former Congressman Edward Keating, and Lucy R. Mason of the National Consumers' League.[50]

Another bill, introduced in March 1937 by Senator Burton K. Wheeler and Congressman Edwin C. Johnson, would make the products of child labor "subject to the laws of the State into which they were shipped," and prohibit the transportation of goods made by child labor into states where the practice was outlawed.[51]

The NCLC's activities on behalf of the Black-Connery bill were limited to the child labor provisions of the measure. It worked closely with the Children's Bureau to get the strongest and most enforceable provisions written into the proposed legislation. Specifically, the Committee wanted a direct approach instead of the prison-made goods formula favored by some, and it opposed an exemption in the bill that permitted children of any age and in any occupation to be employed by their parents. While designed to permit light work around the home, such a loophole would actually permit the unrestricted employment of children in industrial homework and even in hazardous occupations. The Committee also wanted the Children's Bureau to administer the act, rather than a separate board as originally proposed.[52]

As finally passed in June 1938, the child labor provisions of the Fair Labor Standards Act showed the results of the NCLC's efforts. Denounced by the Cotton Textile Institute as not "indigenous to America" and by the NAM as "a step in the direction of Communism, bolshevism, and Naziism," [53] the measure closely followed the legislative principle on which the first child labor law was based, as advocated by the Committee. It prohibited the shipment in interstate commerce of goods made wherever child labor had been employed within thirty days prior to shipment. The act defined child labor as the employment of children under sixteen, or the employment of children under eighteen in occupations designated as hazardous by the Children's Bureau. (The first and second federal child labor laws had established fourteen-year minimum ages, and sixteen for hazardous occupations. When the Fair Labor Standards Act was passed, only eleven states had a sixteen-year standard.)

The Children's Bureau could exempt fourteen- and fifteen-year-old children for work (other than in manufacturing and mining) that did not interfere with their schooling, health, or well-being. Although the exemption for children "employed by their parents" could not be eliminated entirely, it too was made inapplicable to manufacturing and mining. Thus children working in canneries and industrial home-work, for example, were brought under the provisions of the law. (Homework had always flourished chiefly by virtue of its low wages; but the new law carried with it a minimum-wage provision, which applied equally to adults and children, so that employers' incentive to rely on the practice was gone.) Finally, administration of the act was placed in the hands of the Children's Bureau.[54]

The law had some weaknesses. Children who worked in agriculture were exempt "while not legally required to attend school." This opened the door for some control over the employment of children in industrial agriculture while schools were in session, but it left the peak employment period during the summer months beyond the law's reach. If the legal school year in a state was only six or seven months, as was the case in some places in order to permit children to work on farms, or if a state allowed children to miss school for farm work, as was also common practice, nothing could be done about it. Nor could anything be done to protect very young pre-school children. More important, the law provided no protection for migratory child workers, for in most states such children were not permanent residents and thus were not subject to compulsory school attendance laws.

Another weakness in the statute was the provision prohibiting not child labor but "the shipment in interstate commerce of goods" made in establishments that used children. Several child-employing services that handled but did not produce goods, such as the transportation industry, thus escaped the law. Or the communications industry, which employed young boys to carry telegrams. According to a Supreme Court ruling, telegrams were goods, but they were not produced or shipped in interstate commerce and thus the messengers were not covered by the statute. Newsboys, too, escaped, because they worked on the street and not in the plants where the papers were produced.

Finally, the "thirty days prior to shipment" clause permitted evasion by employers whose business was such that prompt shipment did not have to follow production of goods.[55]

Despite these weaknesses, the child labor provisions of the Fair Labor Standards Act were important steps in the right direction. If sustained by the courts, they would virtually end child labor in any industry that produced and shipped goods in interstate commerce, including most mines and factories.

The Children's Bureau sought and won compacts with most of the state labor departments, which agreed to act in its behalf in carrying out much of the inspection and enforcement work. Most states also cooperated readily in revising their certificate requirements and procedures. Within a year, state work permits were accepted as evidence of age under the federal act in forty-three states and the District of Columbia. The joint federal-state administration that was so simple, successful, and economical (and helpful in enforcing state statutes) in the first federal child labor law was renewed.

The exemption to the sixteen-year minimum age authorized the employment of fourteen- and fifteen-year-old children under conditions and in occupations (other than manufacturing and mining) which would not interfere with their education, health, or well-being. Night work rules prohibited employment between 7 P.M. and 6 A.M. in the excluded occupations. Hours of work were limited to three a day and eighteen a week when school was in session, and to eight a day and forty a week when it was not.

In cooperation with the NCLC, which furnished the data, the Children's Bureau focused upon those especially dangerous occupations for which a working age of eighteen should be the minimum. It promulgated hazardous work orders as rapidly as studies could be made and hearings held; employment in the production of explosives, in the operation of motor vehicles, and in coal mining were the first occupations for which an eighteen-year minimum was established.[56]

The Committee had always been opportunistic in the sense that it lost no chance to improve legislative safeguards for children, even though the standards fell short of desired goals. Never was the wisdom of that policy more clearly illustrated than in the years following enactment of the Wages and Hours Act; little did the Committee know in 1937 and 1938, when it decided that a federal law was worth pursuing while continuing to work for the amendment, how useful the measure would become. The act proved to be an invaluable protective measure in the impending war-produced employment boom.[57]

Yet it was not a substitute for the child labor amendment. In 1938 about 850,000 children under sixteen were gainfully employed; only some thirty thousand to fifty thousand, or less than 6 per cent of the total (25 per cent of those working in nonagricultural occupations), would be affected by the act. The great majority of child laborers, those employed in commercial agriculture, intrastate industries, the street trades, mercantile establishments, the messenger and delivery service, hotels, restaurants, beauty parlors, bowling alleys, garages, and so forth, were not reached by the law.[58] Broader federal legislation (as well as higher state standards) was still essential.

The Committee hoped to accomplish through the amendment what it did not win through the Fair Labor Standards Act. It took pains to avoid repetition of the overconfident aftermath of the NRA codes, persuading the President to state publicly the *limitations* as well as the anticipated results of the Wages and Hours Act. "I realize that with reference to the elimination of oppressive child labor," Roosevelt declared immediately after enactment of the measure, "our task will be only partially completed with the passage of this bill. This legislation will not prohibit oppressive employment of minors and children in industries which are purely local in character and have no relation to interstate commerce, as such employment is believed to be beyond the reach of federal authority. Such abuses will have to be dealt with either by the respective states or await the action of the federal government after the pending child labor amendment to the Constitution . . . has been ratified. But until the elimination of oppressive child labor has been fully achieved, we must not relax our efforts." [59]

By January 1938 twenty-eight states ratified the amendment. All were Northern states except Kentucky, whose favorable action in

January 1937 was challenged in the state supreme court. In October 1937 the court held that the state, having rejected the amendent in 1926, could not reverse its action. It further ruled that since the amendment had not been ratified within a reasonable period of time after its submission to the states by Congress, it was no longer pending—precisely the position the American Bar Association had taken almost three years earlier. One month earlier, however, the Kansas supreme court had taken the opposite view on the same question. The Kansas case was appealed to the United States Supreme Court, where it was argued in the autumn of 1938.[60]

On June 5, 1939, the Court handed down a 5 to 4 opinion for which reformers had been hopefully waiting. It held that the question was a political one and therefore not justiciable; only Congress (not state courts) could determine the fate of the amendment. And since Congress had not repealed the amendment, it was still open for ratification despite the lapse of time since 1924. The Court ruled furthermore that states could reverse their previous action either for or against the amendment; thus the fact that more than one-fourth of the states had rejected the amendment had no bearing on its future.[61] The Supreme Court's decision, however, had no effect on the six states with legislatures still in session that year which had not ratified the amendment. In fact, no other state ever ratified the measure.[62]

Less than two years later the Court handed down another ruling that vindicated NCLC efforts. On February 3, 1941, it unanimously upheld the legality of the Fair Labor Standards Act, specifically overruling the 1918 decision that had invalidated the Keating-Owen law. "The conclusion is inescapable," stated Justice Harlan Stone, "that *Hammer v. Dagenhart* was a departure in the interpretation of the commerce clause before and since the decision and that such vitality, as a precedent, as it then had has long since been exhausted. It should be and now is overruled." [63]

It was a momentous victory. Thereafter no mill, mine, factory, or cannery that shipped goods out of state was permitted to compete with schooling for children under sixteen years of age; fourteen- and fifteen-year-olds could work in suitable jobs for limited periods outside of school hours, and minors under eighteen were protected against employment that imperiled their health or safety.

This epoch-making decision, together with other Supreme Court rulings, especially those involving the National Labor Relations Act, clearly established Congress' power to protect children employed in industries engaged in interstate commerce and suggested that other areas of child labor, such as industrial agriculture, could be brought under federal regulation without amending the Constitution. The NCLC at once halted its active campaign for the amendment and laid plans to extend the child labor provisions of the Fair Labor Standards Act to children in occupations that were interstate in character but did not fall within the law.

The one attempt at national regulation of some of the more than half a million children working in industrial agriculture was through federal payments in the sugar beet industry. The NRA's industrial codes did not apply to agricultural occupations, but the Agricultural Adjustment Act of May 1933 did. The AAA was the administration's attempt to raise farm prices and income by cutting back production. In return for cooperation, the Agricultural Adjustment Administration was authorized to pay farmers subsidies for acreage withdrawn from production, or for certain labor or marketing practices. At first the act applied only to growers of specified crops; later it was extended to other basic commodities as defined by the Secretary of Agriculture.[64]

Thus the first federal law affecting children in agriculture was the Jones-Costigan (Sugar Stabilization) Act passed in November 1934. It defined sugar beets and sugar cane as basic commodities under the AAA and gave the Secretary of Agriculture power to fix minimum-wage and child labor standards as a prerequisite to the payment of benefits to growers. After extensive public hearings at which the NCLC, long familiar with the exploitation of children in the sugar beet fields, provided most of the testimony, the government and the growers entered into production control contracts for the 1935–1936 seasons. The agreements provided that no child under fourteen would be employed and that children under sixteen would not be permitted to work more than eight hours a day; children of growers on home farms were exempt from these regulations.[65]

On January 6, 1936, the Supreme Court found the AAA unconstitutional,[66] thus invalidating the production control agreements. They were replaced, however, by the Beet Sugar Act of 1937 which specified nearly the same child labor standards as those in the former contracts.

Interestingly, NCLC and Children's Bureau studies found that the first sugar act worked well. During 1935, when it was in force, child labor in the beet fields was sharply reduced. Later, between the time it was invalidated and passage of the 1937 act, children under fourteen returned to the fields in large numbers.[67] Thus the sugar legislation served as another illustration of a fact that had long become abundantly clear to the NCLC and its allies, namely, that the only effective way of stopping the exploitation of laboring children was through federal legislation.

The Committee sought to extend federal protection to all children under sixteen who worked on the crops. In November 1941, when only nine states had child labor laws that applied to agriculture, and only four of those covered employment outside school hours, the Committee drafted and had introduced in Congress a bill to bring industrial agriculture under the child labor provisions of the Fair Labor Standards Act. When, a month later, America entered World War II the bill was buried under an avalanche of war measures.[68] Since it was never acted upon, agricultural child labor as a whole remained unregulated.

The war also had an adverse effect on those agricultural child laborers most in need—migrants. For two decades and more the NCLC had continued doggedly to educate the public about the economic and social conditions of families who followed the crops.[69] It received unexpected support when their plight became a matter of popular discussion and national concern in the mid-thirties. Dislocations from both technological and natural causes—drought, soil erosion, dust storms (as well as some administration farm policies) [70]— sharply raised the number of families on the road looking for work.

In 1939 John Steinbeck's best-seller, *The Grapes of Wrath,* placed the migrant in the national spotlight. A year later, when the number of migrants reached an estimated four million, the migrant became the subject of congressional concern and, because he could not qualify for local assistance, various proposals for federal aid.[71]

For two years the NCLC had urged that a special congressional committee probe the causes of migrancy. Now, in 1940, the House set up the Committee to Investigate Interstate Migration under John Tolan of California. The NCLC gathered reports and information for the Tolan Committee, which published a complete report early in 1941. But there was little action.[72] As a preventive measure to forestall unnecessary migration, the Tolan Committee emphasized an extension of the loan activities of the Farm Security Administration. This federal agency was set up in 1937 chiefly to extend loans and perform other services for needy farmers. Its low-interest, long-term loans enabled tenant farmers to acquire family-sized farms, converting some half-million defeated, hopeless families into financially independent farmers. It also helped itinerants by setting up a chain of sanitary migratory labor camps and by providing other services to the poor and dispossessed who tried to live off the land.[73]

The NCLC believed that the problem of eliminating child labor in agriculture—migrant and nonmigrant—could not be dissociated from the larger questions of living and working conditions for farm laborers as a whole. To restrict the employment of children of migratory workers or other farmers was futile unless measures were also taken to give their parents greater economic security. Thus from the start the NCLC was a strong supporter of the Farm Security Administration. Courtenay Dinwiddie, in fact, observed its operations during two summer field trips, finding complete evidence of its success.[74] The NCLC used his findings to increase public understanding and support of the FSA, which Southern landlords, large farm corporations, and their organizations were determined to kill so that their cheap farm labor, especially Negro tenants, would remain dependent.

Efforts to extend the Farm Security Administration's program, espe-

cially its loan activities, to another half-million families, as suggested
by the Tolan Committee, met with no success. The war provided its
critics, who were well represented in Congress, with the excuse to
label the program a "nonessential federal expenditure," and they
managed to get its modest appropriation so reduced as to limit its later
efforts.[75]

IX

World War II
and After

THE 1940 census figures showed a substantial decline in child labor since 1930. Only about 210,000 fourteen- and fifteen-year-old children worked in agriculture and industry, a drop of nearly 41 per cent. Some 660,000 sixteen- and seventeen-year-olds were employed, a drop of more than 30 per cent over the previous decade. In all, the number of employed children ages fourteen to seventeen reached an all-time low while the high schools enrolled their all-time high.[1]

The decline reflected a number of factors—some advances in state child labor laws and their enforcement, passage of the Fair Labor Standards Act, and the more limited job opportunities of the depression-ridden thirties. A slightly different definition of employment as used by census officials also tended to reduce the count, especially for seasonal workers.[2] But whatever the reason, there was cause for jubilation.

The early years of the 1940's presented a somewhat different picture. Under the stimulus of defense production the economy expanded enormously. By the time America entered the war in December 1941, employment certificate figures had risen rapidly, and violations of child labor statutes began to swell. For the first time in American history, public school enrollment and registration throughout the country declined.[3]

With the draft draining away men and the pace of war production accelerating, there were plenty of jobs for children of school age; in fact, in some areas there were acute labor shortages. It was easier and cheaper for employers to hire schoolchildren than to find adult workers. Schools that encouraged children to make a patriotic contribution through part-time work soon found that relatively high wages proved a greater attraction than the classroom. More and more children left school for the factory or worked too long after school. Some broke down physically under the combined strain of study and excessive work.

All the weak spots in existing state laws suddenly appeared: the many sixteen-year compulsory school attendance laws which contained exemptions for fourteen- and fifteen-year-olds if they were employed; the child labor laws which failed to include the innumerable nonmanufacturing businesses such as stores, offices, restaurants, laundries, bowling alleys, garages, and so forth; the dangerous occupations for which higher age limits were not set; poorly financed and inadequately staffed enforcing departments—all these and other shortcomings now took their toll.[4] Thus patriotism, high wages, high-pressure employment techniques, and faulty statutes combined to create a resurgence of child labor. Opponents of regulation began to think that the child labor laws might be abolished altogether, or at least modified.

Sensing an underground swell of opposition to regulation, the NCLC in January 1942 issued a policy statement. "The chief contribution a child can make to his country in the present crisis," the board pointed out, "is to remain in school and prepare himself for future work and for the future responsibilities of citizenship." The question was not whether American boys and girls could contribute to the winning of the war, but how best they could do so. The board went on to make clear its belief that the resources of the nation should be used to the utmost to preserve democratic freedom, and that protective standards achieved in peacetime might have to be modified from time to time in meeting emergency situations. Thus it recognized early in the war that rigid adherence to standards might not be possible or desirable in terms of actual war needs. It warned, however, that "any proposal which would lower existing standards relating to education and the employment of children should be examined with great care, both as to the reality and the urgency of the need for work by children and as to the degree of harm that might result to the children." [5]

Since the Committee could not prevent child labor during the war, it would do what it could to see that children took the right kinds of jobs with suitable protection. The real issue was not whether children should work, but under what conditions and for how long. The Children's Bureau, on its part, set up a Commission on Children in Wartime "to consider urgent steps for the protection and welfare of children in emergency situations resulting from the war." Comprising fifty-six members from agencies concerned with the welfare of children, the Commission, at its first meeting in March 1942, adopted a Children's Charter in Wartime. The paragraph on "School and Work" distinctly echoed the NCLC's recent policy statement.[6]

To be sure, the Children's Bureau was under constant pressure to modify its definitions and rulings under the Fair Labor Standards Act. But working closely with the War Manpower Commission and the federal procurement agencies, from which it received good co-operation, the Bureau maintained a realistic balance. It made concessions where the need was proved to be great, but none that exposed children to serious risk or undue strain. Thus, for example, some operations were exempted from the eighteen-year minimum age in occupations that previously had been defined as hazardous. Fourteen- and fifteen-year-old children were permitted to work until 10 P.M. (instead of 7 P.M.) in fruit and vegetable packing sheds, but only outside of school hours and for not more than forty hours a week or more than eight weeks a season. A similar modification was made in the shrimp canning industry, but with 8 P.M. the quitting time.[7] The Bureau's flexible policy resulted in surprisingly few attempts to weaken the provisions of the federal statute. The Fair Labor Standards Act proved to be far more important than anyone at the time of its enactment realized; it was the one bulwark that prevented a repetition of World War I conditions when thousands of young children flocked into munitions plants, canneries, mills, and other such places.

While the federal law and its vigorous enforcement by the Children's Bureau meant that young children were, for the most part, kept out of war and other interstate commerce industries, and those in them received good protection, this was not the case elsewhere. Each month, as manpower demands increased, it became clear that the child labor situation was getting completely out of hand in all but those industries covered by the federal law. The number of legally employed child workers, fourteen to seventeen years of age, reached three million by April 1944, more than three times the number employed in 1940. A million fewer students attended high school in 1944 than four years earlier.[8]

While state legislatures were flooded with bills to lower standards, the backward march in child labor and high school enrollment resulted not so much from a relaxation of legal regulations as from long-standing weaknesses in state laws (low standards and exemptions), the violation of those laws, and the inability of understaffed enforcement agencies to do much about it. During the depression, when children remained in school because there were no jobs for them, few states had strengthened their child labor laws or their administrative machinery against the day when employment would revive. Now, when working children numbered in the millions and three out of four were employed in unregulated local industries, in the service trades, and in agriculture, which offered little legal protection, those shortcomings were highlighted.[9]

The problem was best attacked at the local level, where measures could be taken to reduce school-leaving, establish more controls over part-time employment through the schools, and expose illegal employment. To help bring home the task of the community in checking the rush from school to jobs, the NCLC, in cooperation with twenty-seven other groups, prepared a Child Labor Manifesto. Published in January 1944, the booklet plainly stated that "demands for war production and essential civilian services can be met without exploiting children," and it urged all citizens to help keep children in school. It was clear, however, that policies alone could not stem the tide of child employment. The cooperating agencies therefore prepared suggestions for community action to help solve a problem which only local people could handle. The NCLC also cooperated locally in organizing Back-to-School and Stay-in-School campaigns which produced some favorable results.[10]

Once again, recalling World War I conditions, the second great war revealed unsuspected weaknesses in the nation's physical framework. The high percentage of draft rejections for illiteracy and physical and mental disability shocked a nation that took pride in its free educational system and its attention to public health.[11] It could not escape the fact that more and better education and health measures were basic needs and that, as the NCLC had been saying for a long time, problems involving the employment, education, and health of young people were inseparable.

The NCLC embarked upon a threefold program as the war came to an end. It would work for continued restrictive legislation to eliminate child labor and keep young people out of the labor market; it would help develop a constructive plan of educational reform so that children forced to remain in school longer as a result of higher labor standards would benefit from their further education, especially by way of being prepared for future employment; and it would support legislation providing economic security to all citizens so that it would be financially possible for their children to remain in school.[12] Specifically, the Committee would seek a sixteen-year minimum age for work in industry in all the states; it would have the schools develop educational programs related to the problems of youth employment; and it would strive to amend the Fair Labor Standards Act so as to broaden its coverage. To accomplish these goals the Committee would have to work closely with educational and welfare groups, something it could do quite well under its new general secretary, Gertrude Folks Zimand.

When Courtenay Dinwiddie died suddenly of a heart attack late in 1943, Mrs. Zimand, a Committee staff member since 1916, was made chief executive. Having served as a field worker, editor of the *American Child,* research director, and, since 1932, as associate general secretary, she was well prepared for her new position. But she brought more than experience to the job. She was identified in her work by a warm personal spirit coupled with a deep sense of responsibility for others. She had an eloquent voice and a powerful pen; through the spoken or written word she was able to lift the curtain of impersonal data and reveal social problems in human terms.

Moreover, as one who preferred action to talk, she had a special knack for implementing ideas. As an administrator, she inspired the confidence of board and staff alike, and thus was able to manage the Committee's affairs with considerable freedom. Most important, she had a lively and inquiring mind. While she always respected the past, she was never shackled to it. Ever imaginative and animated with the crusading spirit of her father, Homer Folks, and other pioneer social reformers, she constantly sought to reappraise existing policy with an eye to the future.[13]

As the evils of child labor in industry had lessened, Mrs. Zimand had become increasingly concerned with the financial, educational, and employment problems of youth, especially the transition from school to industrial life, and the need for a broad cooperative approach to these problems. It was her clear view at the war's end that "we can never fully eradicate child labor and give our young people what they need except through basic social and labor legislation that will give families economic security—and basic educational measures that will improve our schools and make it seem worthwhile to young people to remain in . . . [them]." [14] Mrs. Zimand was most concerned about the early school-leavers, as she called them; not only were they beginning to thicken the ranks of the unemployed as the war came to a close, but when they found work it was usually in dead-end routine jobs which only perpetuated the cycle of poverty and ignorance.

At Mrs. Zimand's suggestion, the NCLC, with the active support of educational and labor leaders, conducted two pioneer field studies.[15] The first, published in 1946, surveyed work-study (or school-work) programs developed during the war to meet manpower needs while keeping working children at their studies under well-planned school and work schedules. Such cities as Philadelphia, Tulsa, Los Angeles, Oakland, San Francisco, Detroit, and Minneapolis had set up these emergency programs. The Committee sought to determine their educational value and whether they were worthwhile as a regular part of the secondary-school curriculum.

The study revealed that the scheme had been extremely successful. In fact, the most constructive use of student manpower during the war was the paid employment of high school students under such programs organized and supervised by the schools. Where work-study programs had been in operation, school-leaving had been kept to a minimum and students received far better training and experience than they (or others not in the program) obtained in other after-school jobs. The NCLC recommended not only that they be continued, but that work-study programs be part of secondary-school curricula throughout the nation; they would provide worthwhile work experiences, add meaning and motivation for learning, and thus safeguard educational opportunities for many students who might otherwise leave school at an early age.[16]

The second study, published three years later, was designed to determine what caused students to drop out of high school, and what types of educational programs, if any, might encourage them to remain in class. Based on interviews and the school records of close to fourteen hundred drop-outs in five Ohio, Indiana, and Michigan communities, this survey indicated that while economic need and low intelligence were causes of school-leaving, other reasons were more important. Chief among them was lack of interest. Changes in the program and a "far more satisfactory school experience," it was concluded, "would appreciably reduce the number of [high school] students who leave school" for industry. The Committee suggested that the schools seek a better knowledge and understanding of each pupil; better testing, guidance, and counseling services to help students discover their aptitudes and interests; changes in the curriculum, including the adoption of work-study programs, to meet the needs and interests of all children; placement service for suitable employment after graduation; and educational work with both parents and students, as well as the use of public promotional devices, to emphasize the importance of completing at least high school.[17]

Both of these reports broke new ground and laid the pattern for subsequent studies of a problem that would consume more and more of the Committee's time and attention. Over the next few years Committee members participated in several conferences on child guidance, part-time school and work programs, and methods of increasing the holding power of the schools. The Committee published articles and distributed charts, color slides, and tape recordings that depicted the advantages of completing high school. It also produced radio broadcasts of youth panels on education and job plans, and recorded dramatic sketches on the drop-out problem which were distributed to high schools throughout the country. The Committee's position was that work was an important part of life; a person's attitude toward work and his satisfaction in it helped to determine his effectiveness as an individual and as a citizen; adequate schooling, supervised part-time employment, and proper placement services provided the best start toward job satisfaction.[18]

However important, secondary-school programs designed to increase student interest in completing high school were not enough. More and better legislation was also needed to achieve minimum standards for education and employment. Thus, in the field of education the Committee continued to work for compulsory education laws that prohibited full-time employment before the age of sixteen, for the extension of the school term to nine months in all areas of the country, and for improved enforcement machinery. Because laws designed to keep children in school necessitated more and better schools for them to attend, and because some states and localities lacked sufficient funds to support good schools, the Committee also continued its efforts for federal aid to education.[19]

In the field of labor legislation, the Committee never relaxed its efforts to improve state child labor laws. The legal standards of most states still lagged far behind the federal Wages and Hours Law;

thirty-three still permitted children to leave school for any employment at age fourteen, and two others for any employment except manufacturing. In 1927 the Committee had argued that "fourteen was too early"; surely that was even more so now. In 1945 the NCLC cooperated with state and local groups in a massive national campaign to raise the minimum age in state laws from fourteen to sixteen for all employment during school hours, and for factory employment at any time.[20] Within four years, six states—Illinois, Georgia, Virginia, Alabama, Kentucky, and Tennessee—were added to thirteen others that already had a sixteen-year minimum. By 1955 twenty-five states would reach that goal, a praiseworthy if not overly impressive advance.

Meanwhile, one of the most urgent needs in child labor legislation was improvement of the Fair Labor Standards Act. Its child labor provisions needed to be expanded and its loopholes plugged in order to give maximum protection to those children already covered by the statute. The thirty-day provision, which allowed evasion by employers whose business did not necessitate prompt shipment of goods, needed to be eliminated. Children working in all interstate industries, whether or not they actually produced or shipped goods, had to be brought within the law.

Above all, the provision that covered children working in agriculture only "while not legally required to attend school," had to be strengthened. Some 1,500,000 children under eighteen were employed in 1949 (well over half a million more than in 1940), about half of whom worked in the fields. Because of low compulsory school attendance standards and special exemptions for farm work in many states, and because in most cases migrants were not even subject to state laws, a large number of young farm laborers were in fact unprotected.[21]

Over the years the NCLC had drafted several amendments to the Wages and Hours Law aimed at repairing these shortcomings. It distributed leaflets explaining the proposed changes, and its members testified at public hearings. The Committee also used its legislative contact list of more than five hundred people and organizations throughout the country who were willing to work for progressive federal legislation, urging each to write to members of Congress in support of the proposals. At the same time it vigorously fought amendments that would have actually weakened the measure.[22]

In October 1949 the NCLC's activities started paying dividends; Congress began to strengthen the federal statute as advocated by the Committee. The measure was amended to apply to all nonagricultural establishments engaged in interstate commerce, regardless of whether or not goods were produced or shipped. This change brought under the law the communications (including Western Union), public utilities, transportation, and other child-employing industries previously exempt from its provisions. The act also was strengthened by an amendment that directly forbade the employment of oppressive child labor rather than merely prohibiting the shipment of goods on which children had worked. Finally, another amendment prohibited the employment of all children under sixteen years of age, including migrants, on commercial farms during school hours.[23]

Still, of course, there were loopholes (children could stay out of school to work on the family farm or could work unregulated outside of school hours) and areas in need of coverage (newsboys, for example),[24] but the amendments went a long way toward improving the law. Indeed, in 1952 Congress considered eight bills to break down the strengthened provisions for children in agriculture, and to make them inapplicable to migrants, but all were easily defeated. A last-minute attempt by one Southern Congressman to secure favorable action on one of the bills by offering it as an amendment to a defense bill received only ten supporting votes—encouraging evidence that the right of migrant children to attend school was at last recognized.[25]

This is not to say that they *did* attend school. Too often communities made little effort to bring the children into their classrooms or to enforce the law. Moreover, as the NCLC long realized, migratory child labor was not an isolated evil; it was part of a much larger problem, grievous in its dimensions. Transported under inhuman conditions, living in shelters that were incredibly congested and substandard, often with sanitary conditions that defied description, suffering a poor diet and little if any medical attention, these children,

America's most underprivileged citizens, had little incentive or stamina to attend school. Equally important, their parents were irregularly employed and excluded from virtually all social and labor legislation, including the minimum-wage provisions of the FLSA, the NLRA, the SSA, state workmen's compensation laws, and the like. The average annual income for migrant *families* in 1950 was somewhere between $500 and $1,000. Migrant children, then, were forced to work in violation of the law so that they and their families might have something to eat.

The NCLC worked with the Children's Bureau, the Public Health Service, the Office of Education, state and local governments, and many private agencies on numerous projects to promote the health, education, and welfare of boys and girls whose parents followed the crops. It also helped to organize, and then provided office space for, the National Citizens Council on Migrant Labor (later known as the National Citizens Council on Agricultural Life and Labor), which disseminated information and sponsored conferences on agricultural problems, consulted with experts, encouraged legislation, and in other ways acted as a clearing house for matters concerning the welfare of those who toiled in the fields.

With others, the NCLC urged Congress to regulate labor contractors, interstate transportation of migrant farm workers, and housing and health facilities in labor camps. The Committee asked the federal government to extend basic social and labor legislation to migrant farm workers, and to appropriate funds to the states for the establishment of day-care centers and public summer school and other educational programs for migrant children.[26]

As the NCLC approached its fiftieth anniversary it was clear that the organization was moving in a new direction. Certainly child labor still persisted, not only among migrants but also among thousands of others who worked too many hours after school, or late into the night on city streets, or illegally in industry. Yet the old abuses that had existed in the nation's mines, glass-making factories, cotton mills, and tenements had been wiped out, and the Committee's original goals of an elementary-school education for all and no full-time employment for those under fourteen had, with one notable exception, been achieved. Only among agricultural migrant workers did child labor in its traditional sense still exist to any considerable extent. This inexcusable blot on the American economy and the nation's conscience needed legislative attention, and the Committee vowed to do something about it.[27]

Yet each year the Committee's major concern was a problem still not yet generally recognized nor very sharply defined—that of youth employment, the preparation of boys and girls for their life's work. This became even more important during the early 1950's when sixteen- and seventeen-year-olds throughout the nation once again began dropping out of high school in large numbers. A precarious world situation, the Korean War, expectation of the draft, and uncertainty about the future contributed to the trend.[28] These young drop-outs, and even many of those who remained in class but whose formal education would terminate with high school, had little knowledge of the world of work. Many of them did not even know how to go about finding a job, nor did they know what kind of work they were interested in or fitted for. They had no idea of what was needed to make good on a job. They were, in short, unprepared for their future working life.

The NCLC turned to these children with constructive programs. The nation's youth had to be encouraged to remain in school longer, the secondary-school curriculum had to be adapted to their needs, adequate educational guidance and vocational counseling and placement services had to be set up, and job conditions and opportunities for training had to be regulated. These were matters of public welfare and concern that required the cooperation of public and private groups in the fields of welfare, labor, and education.[29]

Thus in 1954 the National Child Labor Committee was an historic and respected organization with an outdated name; its continued interest in child labor, chiefly agricultural, was now overshadowed by its broad interest in the problems of youth employment. Its fiftieth-anniversary observance offered the Committee an unusual opportunity to bring to public attention its past successes and the newer aspects of its work. In planning the big event it was agreed that the emphasis should be on the job that lay ahead.[30]

The celebration, held at New York's Hotel Commodore on April 21, 1954, was a memorable one. Editorials and news items in the press, a photographic feature in *Life* magazine, comments and articles in periodicals and professional journals, and the Committee's special anniversary publication, *The Changing Years, 1904–1954,* with its nostalgic Lewis Hine photographs of working children, created widespread interest. Letters of congratulation poured in. Eleanor Roosevelt, several Cabinet members, many United States Senators, labor and civic leaders, and even the President of the United States paid tribute to the organization. "In the fight to eliminate child labor and promote the welfare of the youth of this country," Dwight D. Eisenhower wrote to board chairman F. Ernest Johnson,

your committee has long been among the most energetic and dedicated participants. Many Americans today nearing their seventieth birthday can be grateful for the early efforts of your organization. I am sure that the benefits which your committee brought them in their youth are reflected today in their health, their welfare, and their effectiveness as active citizens of our nation.

As you start your second half-century of service to the nation's young people, you have my best wishes for continued effectiveness in your vital work.[31]

The Committee, which now had some fifteen thousand members, 194 of whom had been associated with it for more than forty-five years, could regard its past with pride. But like the President, it was determined to look ahead. As if to symbolize its commitment to the future and the newer phase of its work, it took the occasion to present to the Library of Congress all its records, reports, files, newspaper and magazine clippings, and other material of historical or research value; the venerable Owen Lovejoy, still spry and effective as a speaker, made the presentation.[32]

General Secretary Gertrude Folks Zimand captured the mood of the occasion when she reminded her audience:

No one who has been associated with the Committee for so long . . . or who has had occasion to delve into its earliest records, can be unaware of the extent to which its present is deeply rooted in the past. We, in the National Child Labor Committee of 1954, are grateful to the founders and staff of its early days for having launched the organization with vision, aware from the start that child labor was not an isolated evil but closely related to general social and economic health, and always insisting on a broad interpretation of the Committee's functions.

Today, as we enter our sixth decade, our broad objective is unaltered —to secure for all children the kind of life America wants its growing citizens to enjoy. But while our objective has remained steadfast, our program has changed as old evils have gone, as new ones have emerged, and especially as new knowledge has come to light about children, their needs, and the nature of the growing-up process.[33]

So, while the Committee viewed with satisfaction the many reforms it had helped to achieve—reforms which brought a greater measure of dignity to the lives of a vast number of American children—it did not intend to stand on past performances. Many children were still being physically and mentally impaired as a result of restrictive policies.[34]

Even more than in the past, the organization needed a new name. In November 1955 the board named a committee to review the issue and such other questions as future financial policy, programs, and possible internal changes.[35] Several years of self-evaluation and often heated debate followed. While the corporate name was retained, in effect two separate committees, one on the employment of youth and another on the education of migrant children, were informally paired under the NCLC banner. As time passed, the Committee found itself stressing even more the problems of youth in a rapidly changing world. As a result, late in 1957 the board decided to give up the old name and call the organization the National Committee on Employment of Youth. It subsequently discovered, however, that such a change was unwise from a legal standpoint, inasmuch as the National Child Labor Committee's congressional charter had many advantages (including tax-exempt status) which might not necessarily be transferred to the National Committee on Employment of Youth. The organization also received bequests in the name of the National Child Labor Committee, and the receipt of such gifts would be complicated by a change in name. Therefore, on December 11, 1958, the board decided to retain the National Child Labor Committee as the corporate and legal entity, but for program purposes to use the name National Committee on Employment of Youth, effective January 1, 1959.[36] As some 26,000,000 young people came of working age in the 1960's, over seven million of whom entered the labor market without finishing high school, the National Committee on Employment of Youth of the NCLC led the nation in setting up programs to help many of them select, receive, and hold suitable and satisfying jobs.

Meanwhile, the Committee continued to protect children from harmful employment by acting as a watchdog to prevent the breakdown of child labor laws. It also continued to help the nation's itinerant children in their struggle against exploitation and deprivation. In fact, when it became clear that not enough was being done to assist these sorely neglected youngsters, the Committee decided to give added impetus to this phase of its work by establishing the National Committee on the Education of Migrant Children. Founded in 1963 on the principle that the children of migrant farm workers must be educated in order to break the cycle of poverty in which they have lived for generations, the NCLC's National Committee on the Education of Migrant Children was (and still is) the only private national organization in America devoted solely to improving the education of these children, some 300,000 in number. In this and in still other ways the National Child Labor Committee continues to render important aid to America's youth in building a future for itself through receiving a meaningful education and developing worthwhile job skills.[37]

When the fifty-year-old National Child Labor Committee began changing its focus, its original objectives had been nearly achieved. Problems certainly remained, but child labor had been dramatically reduced and, in fact, if defined by 1904 standards, largely eliminated.

Where injustice did remain, as in the fields, all signs indicated that it was rapidly decreasing. Throughout the 1950's statistics showed a continuing decline in the number of agricultural child laborers. Much of the reduction was due to the invention and application of machines —tomato and cucumber pickers, cherry shakers, bean and berry harvesters, and the like. Just as the drive toward industrial efficiency in factories helped lead to increased worker output and the replacement of many young hands by machines, so the problem in commercial agriculture was being solved by technology.

Thus, while it would be satisfying to give the NCLC and its allies full credit for the decline of child labor, it would be quite erroneous to do so. Other, perhaps more powerful, forces were at work. Aside from technology, structural changes in the economy demanded more skilled and semi-skilled workers and thus reduced job opportunities for children. An increase in the number of working women, the growing strength of organized labor, the passage of minimum-wage legislation, the rising real income of the wage-earning class, a reluctance on the part of employers to hire young men eligible for draft—these and other factors were all responsible for curtailing the injustice.

Yet one should not belittle the NCLC's efforts or accomplishments. Certainly, to the extent that legislation helped to reduce child labor— and it did—the Committee was primarily responsible. It aroused public opinion, drafted legislation, lobbied and propagandized at the state and federal levels, and recruited aid from other groups that helped mightily in the passage of numerous child labor and compulsory school attendance laws and in their enforcement. While the impulse which led to the formation of the Committee sprang from a demand for constructive change, the NCLC in turn created and sustained a great deal of new public interest in the child labor issue and captured the necessary support for needed legislation.

Fundamental to its work were a profound regard for the worth and dignity of every child and a conviction that American democracy could and indeed must meet the needs of all its children. The safety of the future rested on some sort of progressive movement based upon the principle of equal opportunity and the provision of adequate food, shelter, health, and education for all American children so that they could develop their inner capacities and grow into productive, creative citizens. Carried to its fullest implications, this was a radical idea, yet the Committee's philosophy and program were moderate. At the outset its leaders had faith in a slow process of education and the accumulation of state child labor legislation. To most, the steps toward the goal were as important as the goal itself. Willing to accomplish their ends slowly, Committee members attacked child labor on a patient trial-and-error basis.

To its credit, however, the Committee never relied solely on persuasion or the molding of a national "social conscience" as its instrument of reform. Members realized from the start that laws were necessary to regulate the economy in the public interest, and they easily shifted from state to federal legislation. By advocating the extension of state and federal power so as to protect society from industrial evils, and by stressing the social duty of the individual, the NCLC contributed to the decline of laissez faire.

To the NCLC, which published some four hundred reports based on original research, knowledge was essential. Protective and prohibitive legislation was always based on the results of investigation. Yet the Committee also used the techniques of modern organization and propaganda. Reform had to be full time, well organized, and proficient; the efficient organization of human affairs in a complex industrial society required the same degree of planning and coordination that prevailed, for example, in the business world.

In a sense, progressive reformers who sought an efficient use of the nation's human resources were, in Roy Lubove's words, "humanitarian efficiency experts." Anxious to organize the economic and social environment so that every individual could attain his maximum physical, mental, and cultural development, they exemplified the ideals of social engineering that emerged in the early twentieth century and became increasingly evident over the next two decades, especially during the New Deal.

As a reform group, the NCLC demonstrated an amazing capacity for adaptation and change. Always expanding, it never stood still and attempted to consolidate its gains. Its original interest in mines, factories, and mills came to include canneries, the street trades, industrial homework, commercial agriculture, stores, the service trades, and many other areas not covered by this account, such as bowling alleys, the theater, and even baby-sitting. Its remarkable flexibility, growth, and foresight were never more clearly evident than in the course it plotted after the reduction in child labor. The new emphasis on youth employment reflected a depth of vision and an understanding of changing times and circumstances (as well as a reminder of the progress that had been made) not often found in private agencies.

Another of the NCLC's unusual qualities was its appreciation of the importance of cooperation between voluntary and governmental agencies, both to encourage the formation of public opinion as a foundation for sound policy, and to aid in the formulation and implementation of that policy. Thus the Committee held joint staff meetings with the Children's Bureau and other federal and state agencies to get more efficient use of limited staffs, to prevent duplication of effort, and to share learning experiences.

Finally, while the vast majority of Committee members were not prepared to reconstruct society in order to abolish child labor, most had a pretty broad vision. One should not underestimate the difficulties they faced. Given the strength of the opposition and other problems, including popular myth and prejudice and an indifferent if not hostile Supreme Court, they had to move forward step by step.

From the beginning the Committee took a broad approach to the problem: child labor was only one thread in the wider fabric of child and family welfare. Thus the Committee was never solely concerned with the regulation and prohibition of child labor. It always worked for various constructive measures in the fields of health, education, recreation, and welfare to provide badly needed individual and social services and resources to all. Too, it did not underestimate the economic necessity that drove some children to work; long before the War on Poverty it saw the connection between want and other social problems, pointing out, however, that child labor was as much a cause as an effect of poverty.

The National Child Labor Committee, then, never ignored the

whole individual or the total environment of the working child, nor did it advocate piecemeal solutions for interrelated problems in the ecology of want. On the contrary, it recognized the need to get at the entire "culture of poverty."

The crusade against child labor in the first half of the twentieth century illustrated the gropings of American democracy; peaceful reform was possible, but slow. Hopefully, constructive change will come more rapidly during the second half of the century, including the alleviation of poverty and elimination of the remnants of child labor. Until then, however, it is comforting to recall that reformers usually do not have to repeat themselves. The history of child labor legislation does not record very many backward steps; most bills, once passed, remained on the books. Thus it is not only, say, 150,000 children helped in one year by the passage of this or that statute who are to be considered, but the children of all the future years who are also helped by its enactment—some 1,500,000 over the following decade, 4,500,000 over the next generation, and so on.[38] The history of the National Child Labor Committee lives on in those unnumbered citizens.

Notes

Preface

1. Felix Adler, "Child Labor: A Menace to Civilization," *Proceedings of the Seventh Annual Conference on Child Labor* (New York, 1911), p. 2 (hereafter cited as *Proc. ACCL*). Also see Alexander J. McKelway, "Child Labor and Democracy," *Child Labor Bulletin*, I (June 1912), 127; Felix Adler, "The Attitude of Society Toward the Child as an Index of Civilization," *Proc. Third ACCL* (New York, 1907), pp. 135–41.

I
The Problem Emerges

1. Vincent A. McQuade, *The American Catholic Attitude on Child Labor Since 1891* (Washington, D.C., 1938), p. 1 ff.; O. J. Dunlop, *English Apprenticeship and Child Labor* (London, 1912), *passim*; John Spargo, *The Bitter Cry of the Children* (New York, 1906), p. 127 ff.

2. Quoted in McQuade, *American Catholic Attitude*, p. 2.

3. Ibid., p. 4; Grace Abbott, ed., *The Child and the State*, 2 vols. (Chicago, 1947), I, 91–101; Edith Abbott, "A Study of the Early History of Child Labor in America," *American Journal of Sociology*, IV (July 1908), 17.

4. Machines ranked higher than children on the balance sheet; they cost money and therefore were to be handled with care. Children, however, did not represent dollars but rather only a few cents, perhaps the small margin necessary to outstrip a competitor. Since children were plentiful they could, without expense, easily be replaced. Only when the state required employers to

observe child labor laws, and fined them heavily for breaking those laws, was a standard of value placed on children. See Abbott, *The Child and the State,* I, 106–9.

5. Quoted in John L. and Barbara B. Hammond, *The Town Laborer* (New York, 1917), p. 174. Also see Thomas S. Adams and Helen L. Sumner, *Labor Problems* (New York, 1905), p. 21 ff.; Stuart A. Queen, *Social Work in the Light of History* (Philadelphia, 1922), pp. 158–59; McQuade, *American Catholic Attitude,* p. 4; Abbott, *The Child and the State,* I, 79–185.

6. Quoted in Abbott, "Early History of Child Labor," p. 19; Ralph and Muriel Pumphrey, *The Heritage of American Social Work* (New York, 1964), pp. 19–26; Abbott, *The Child and the State,* I, 199–204.

7. Abbott, "Early History of Child Labor," pp. 15–16; Edmund S. Morgan, *The Puritan Family* (New York, 1966), pp. 65–66.

8. Abbott, "Early History of Child Labor," pp. 17–18; Alexander J. Mc-Kelway, "The Herod Among Industries," manuscript dated March 9, 1911, in Alexander J. McKelway Papers, Manuscript Division, Library of Congress, Washington, D.C. (hereafter cited as McKelway Papers); Abbott, *The Child and the State,* I, 199–200.

9. Abbott, "Early History of Child Labor," pp. 19–20.

10. Ibid., pp. 20–21; Abbott, *The Child and the State,* I, 195–98, 200–1; Alexander J. McKelway, "Southern Aspects of the Child Labor Problem," manuscript dated April 11, 1910, McKelway Papers.

11. Abbott, "Early History of Child Labor," pp. 21–23.

12 Ibid., p. 24; NCLC, *Handbook on the Federal Child Labor Amendment* (New York, 1937), p. 7; Caroline F. Ware, *The Early New England Cotton Manufacturer* (Boston, 1931), p. 23; William R. Bagnall, *Samuel Slater and the Early Development of Cotton Manufacture in the United States* (Middletown, Conn., 1890), *passim.* The most authoritative account of child labor conditions in America during the nineteenth century is Elizabeth L. Otey, "The Beginnings of Child Labor Legislation in Certain States," in U.S. Senate Document No. 645, *Report on the Condition of Women and Child Wage-Earners in the United States,* 19 vols. (Washington, D.C., 1910–13), IV.

13. U.S. Department of Labor, *Growth of Labor Law in the United States* (Washington, D.C., 1962), p. 10.

14. Abbott, "Early History of Child Labor," pp. 27–28; Alexander J. Mc-Kelway, "The Long Curse of Child Labor," undated manuscript in McKelway Papers; McQuade, *American Catholic Attitude,* p. 9. The same economic factors which encouraged the use of children in the mills acted to put women there as well. See Arthur M. Schlesinger, *A Political and Social History of the United States, 1829–1925* (New York, 1928), p. 6.

15. Quoted in Abbott, "Early History of Child Labor," p. 26.

16. Quoted in Alexander J. McKelway, "The Child Labor Problem—A Study in Degeneracy," *Annals of the American Academy of Political and Social Science,* XXVII (March 1906), 323 (hereafter cited as *Annals*); Abbott, *The Child and the State,* I, 107; Hammond and Hammond, *The Town Laborer,*

149–50. Fifty years later, when England fought a handful of South African farmers in the Boer War and discovered that its physical vigor was sapped, Macaulay's prophecy appeared to have come true.

17. See Thomas Burke, "Child Labor in England," *Charities,* IX (August 9, 1902), 141–43; "Child Slavery: Democracy's Present Battle with the Moloch of Greed," *Arena,* XXXVII (February 1907), 176; Abbott, *The Child and the State,* I, 84–90, 177–83; Adams and Sumner, *Labor Problems,* p. 21 ff.; Queen, *Social Work in the Light of History,* pp. 158–59; McKelway, "Child Labor Problem—Degeneracy"; Alexander J. McKelway, untitled manuscript dated May 24, 1905, and "The Economic Fallacy of Child Labor," manuscript dated March 1, 1911, in McKelway Papers.

18. Quoted in Abbott, *The Child and the State,* I, 278; Rush Welter, *Popular Education and Democratic Thought in America* (New York, 1962), pp. 103–5; Elizabeth Sands Johnson, "Child Labor Legislation," in John R. Commons, et al., *History of Labor in the United States,* 4 vols. (New York, 1918–35), III, 423–24; Ware, *The Early New England Cotton Manufacturer,* p. 282; W. L. Chenery, *Industry and Human Welfare* (New York, 1922), p. 49.

19. Otey, "The Beginnings of Child Labor Legislation," p. 36.

20. Ibid., p. 38.

21. Miriam E. Loughran, *The Historical Development of Child Labor Legislation in the United States* (Washington, D.C., 1921), *passim;* Owen R. Lovejoy, "Child Labor in the United States," manuscript dated June 23, 1923, National Child Labor Committee Papers, Manuscript Division, Library of Congress, Washington, D.C. (hereafter cited as NCLC Papers).

22. Noticeably lacking, however, were night work provisions, workmen's compensation, laws requiring the fencing of machinery, and special provisions for dangerous or hazardous occupations.

23. Herbert J. Lahne, *The Cotton Mill Worker* (New York, 1944), pp. 107–8; Abbott, "Early History of Child Labor," p. 33.

24. *New York Times,* October 6, 1869.

25. See Thomas C. Cochran and William Miller, *The Age of Enterprise* (New York, 1961), pp. 129–227.

26. Ibid., pp. 119–28; Ralph H. Gabriel, *The Course of American Democratic Thought* (New York, 1940), pp. 216–33.

27. Adams and Sumner, *Labor Problems,* p. 57; Eva McDonald Valesh, "Child Labor," *American Federationist,* XIV (March 1907), 158; Graham Taylor, "A Human View of Child Labor," *Charities,* XV (January 6, 1906), 434–35.

28. Kirk H. Porter and Donald B. Johnson, eds., *National Party Platforms, 1840–1960* (Urbana, Ill., 1961), p. 58; Otey, "The Beginnings of Child Labor Legislation," p. 41; Norman J. Ware, *The Labor Movement in the United States, 1860–1895* (New York, 1929), p. 379 ff.; Donald D. Lescohier and Elizabeth Brandeis, *History of Labor in the United States, 1896–1932* (New York, 1935), p. 404 ff.; Ben E. Salinsky, "A History of Federal Child Labor Legislation" (master's essay, University of Wisconsin, 1931), p. 326.

29. McQuade, *American Catholic Attitude,* p. 21. For whatever reason, whether self-interest or humanitarianism, from the beginning the movement to abolish child labor from industry received the constant support of trade unionism. This was especially true of the AFL, founded by Samuel Gompers, a cigar-maker, at a time when about half the cigars produced in New York City were made in homes and tenements by about ten thousand nonunion workers, including several thousand youngsters. See Jeremy P. Felt, *Hostages of Fortune* (New York, 1965), p. 10; Frederick L. Hoffman, "The Social and Medical Aspects of Child Labor," *Proceedings of the National Conference of Charities and Correction* (Atlanta, 1903), p. 144 (hereafter cited as *Proc. of NCCC*).

30. Porter and Johnson, *National Party Platforms,* p. 89.

31. Ibid., p. 142.

32. Mrs. Arthur O. Granger, "The Work of the General Federation of Women's Clubs Against Child Labor," *Annals,* XXV (May 1905), 516–21. Also see Eleanor Flexner, *Century of Struggle: The Woman's Rights Movement in the United States* (Cambridge, Mass., 1959), pp. 179–80; Mary I. Wood, *The History of the General Federation of Women's Clubs* (New York, 1912), pp. 22–118.

33. The best study of the National Consumers' League is Louis L. Athey, "The Consumers' Leagues and Social Reform, 1890–1923" (doctoral dissertation, University of Delaware, 1965). Also see Maud Nathan, *The Story of an Epoch-making Movement* (New York, 1926).

34. Josephine Goldmark, *Impatient Crusader: Florence Kelley's Life Story* (Urbana, Ill., 1953); Felt, *Hostages of Fortune,* pp. 32, 43; Robert Bremner, *From the Depths: The Discovery of Poverty in the United States* (New York, 1956), p. 79; Frances Perkins, "My Recollections of Florence Kelley," *Social Service Review,* XXVIII (March 1954), 12–19; Donald Fleming, "Social Darwinism," in A. M. Schlesinger, Jr., and Morton White, eds., *Paths of American Thought* (Boston, 1963), pp. 143–44.

35. Florence Kelley, "Child Labor Legislation," *Annals,* XX (July 1902), 155; Florence Kelley Wischneivetsky, "White Child Slavery," *Arena,* I (April 1890), 595. Also see Romona T. Mattson, "A Critical Evaluation of Florence Kelley's Speaking on the Child Labor Issue" (doctoral dissertation, State University of Iowa, 1956).

36. Johnson, "Child Labor Legislation," p. 431. Also see William F. Ogburn, *Progress and Uniformity in Child Labor Legislation* (New York, 1912).

37. Department of Interior, Census Office, *Report on Population of the United States at the Eleventh Census: 1890* (Washington, D.C., 1897), part II, pp. 66, 138 (hereafter cited as *Census*).

38. John G. Van Osdell, Jr., "Cotton Mills, Labor, and the Southern Mind, 1880–1930" (doctoral dissertation, Tulane University, 1966), p. 4.

39. Ibid., p. 8. Also see Herbert J. Doherty, Jr., "Voices of Protest from the New South, 1875–1910," *Mississippi Valley Historical Review,* XLII (June 1955), 45–66; C. Vann Woodward, *Origins of the New South, 1877–1913* (Baton Rouge, La., 1951), pp. 112–41. Mill owner D. A. Tompkins, one of

the most practical and effective of the preachers of the gospel of Southern industrialization, always insisted that he was leading not an industrial revolution but a revival. There was some truth to this appealing idea of an industrial renaissance, which went back not only to the antebellum period but to the region's earliest settlers. The original Scotch-Irish settlers of the Piedmont section of Virginia, the Carolinas, and the upper part of Georgia and Alabama had been a manufacturing people in Ireland. They had left that country largely because of oppressive restrictions passed by Parliament for the protection of English industries against competition. The climate and soil of the South, the growth of slavery, and the demand for raw cotton had turned them primarily toward agriculture. After the war, however—with the abolition of slavery, the depletion of the South's resources, and the demand for manufactured goods—it was hardly surprising that the descendants of these settlers should set up manufacturing establishments in the region.

40. Van Osdell, "Cotton Mills, Labor, and the Southern Mind," pp. 8, 36; Woodward, *Origins of the New South*, pp. 131–33, 306–8. In 1870 the South consumed 8.6 per cent of the nation's cotton used in manufacturing; New England, 69.2 per cent. In 1910 the figures were 47 per cent for the South and only 46 per cent for New England. The Cotton Exposition at Atlanta in 1881 gave a tremendous impetus to cotton manufacturing (as well as to the diversification of southern industries). The climax of enthusiasm at that exposition was reached when the governor of Georgia appeared one evening wearing a suit completely manufactured that same day. Spectators had followed the entire process, from the picking of the cotton in the morning to the tailoring and finishing. See Elizabeth H. Davidson, *Child Labor Legislation in the Southern Textile States* (Chapel Hill, 1939), pp. 6–7; Alexander J. McKelway, "Child Labor in the Cotton Mill Industry of the Southern States," undated manuscript in the McKelway Papers.

41. Woodward, *Origins of the New South*, p. 222. It is interesting that Southern propagandists, seeking to entice Northern capital to the Southern mills, painted a picture of the Southern mill hand very similar to that of the Negro slave painted during the antebellum period (and equally incorrect): a simple, untutored creature possessing the old-fashioned virtues of impassioned piety, oxlike docility, and unquestioning loyalty to his betters who philanthropically provided him with work.

42. Woodward, *Origins of the New South*, pp. 222–24, 418; Leonora Beck Ellis, "A Study of Southern Cotton Mill Communities," *American Journal of Sociology*, VIII (March 1903), 623–30. Eighty-seven per cent of the cotton textile workers in the South were living in company-owned houses in 1908. The mills owned and controlled not only the houses in the village but everything else as well. It was quite possible for a mill hand to be born in a mill-owned hospital (after his mother had attended a prenatal clinic established by the mill owner), having been delivered by a mill-paid doctor; to receive what little education he had in a mill-supported school; to be married in a mill-subsidized church to a girl he had met in the mill; to live all his life

in housing belonging to the mill; and, when he died, to be buried in a mill-owned cemetery in a coffin supplied by the mill. See Lahne, *The Cotton Mill Worker*, p. 124.

43. Davidson, *Child Labor Legislation in the Southern Textile States*, p. 16.

44. Some states felt that nothing would bring in capital more quickly than a large supply of child labor. In fact, they advertised that children within their borders were helpless and could be used, without restriction, by private industry for individual profit. In 1898, for example, one Southern state sent out a circular which read in part: "No strikes, no laws regulating the hours of employment and the age of employees, cheap labor and the home of the cotton plant." Quoted in John P. Frey, "Social Costs of Child Labor," *Child Labor Bulletin*, I (June 1912), 118.

45. Quoted in Woodward, *Origins of the New South*, p. 134; Davidson, *Child Labor Legislation in the Southern Textile States*, pp. 52–68; August Kohn, "Child Labor in the South," in Samuel C. Mitchell, ed., *History of the Social Life of the South*, 13 vols. (Richmond, Va., 1909), X, 590.

46. See Hayes Robbins, "The Necessity for Factory Legislation in the South," *Annals*, XX (July 1902), 181–88; Mary A. Bacon, "Child Labor in the Cotton Mills of Georgia," *Charities*, XI (July 18, 1903), 60–61.

47. Most of the early publicity on the child labor question in the South appeared either in periodicals published in the North or in union journals, such as the AFL's *American Federationist*. See Davidson, *Child Labor Legislation in the Southern Textile States*, pp. 21–36; Neal L. Anderson, "Child Labor Legislation in the South," *Annals*, XXV (May 1905), 500, and "Legislation and Methods in the Southern States," *Charities*, XIII (March 4, 1905), 538–39; Alton DuMar Jones, "The Child Labor Reform Movement in Georgia," *Georgia Historical Society Quarterly*, XLIX (December, 1965), 397.

48. Anderson, "Child Labor Legislation in the South," p. 504; Lahne, *The Cotton Mill Worker*, p. 108; Bremner, *From the Depths*, p. 216; W. H. Hand, "Need of Compulsory Education in the South," *Child Labor Bulletin*, I (June 1912), 73–84; Woodward, *Origins of the New South*, p. 416; Alexander J. McKelway, "The Illiteracy in the Mill Districts," undated manuscript in the McKelway Papers.

49. In states outside the South, for example, 15.6 per cent of the cotton mill industry operatives in 1880 were under fifteen years of age. In 1900 the percentage was down to 7.7, and most of these young workers were between fourteen and fifteen years old. In the South, about 25 per cent of the cotton mill operatives in 1880 were under the age of fifteen. In 1900 the percentage was still 25, and the number of these workers had increased from 9,000 to 25,000. Almost half of them were under twelve, many as young as six and seven.

50. Johnson, "Child Labor Legislation," pp. 404–5; Bremner, *From the Depths*, pp. 212–17. Only fifteen states set a fourteen-year age limit, and only one state had an eight-hour day for children under sixteen. Seventeen states

had no school attendance laws at all, and twenty-seven had no educational requirements for child laborers.

51. Felix Adler, "Child Labor in the United States and Its Great Attendant Evils," *Annals*, XXV (May 1905), 422; "Child Labor in New Jersey," *Charities*, XII (January 9, 1904), 60–62; Pauline Goldmark, "Children Who Work at Night," *Charities*, X (June 6, 1903), 573; Florence Kelley, "Use and Abuse of Factory Inspection," *Proc. of NCCC* (Atlanta, 1903), pp. 135–38; Edgar T. Davies, "The Difficulties of a Factory Inspector," *Annals*, XXIX (January 1907), 125–31.

52. *Twelfth Census: 1900*, "Occupations," p. 142. The 1,750,178 working children between the ages of ten and fifteen comprised 18.2 per cent of the total child population between those ages. Both the total number and the percentage of working children between the ages of ten and fifteen had increased since 1880—the former from 1,118,356 and the latter from 16.8 per cent. In 1890, however, the total number of working children aged ten to fifteen was 1,503,771, or 18.1 per cent of all the children in that age group. So although the number of child laborers continued to mount, the rate of increase for the nation declined between 1890 and 1900.

Census figures gave an incomplete count of child workers. They included only children ten years of age or over, although there were many child laborers under that age. Even for the age group covered (ten to fifteen years), youngsters "attending school" were not listed as working, yet they might labor seven or eight hours a day before or after school. Thus most street traders and tenement home workers were not counted. Then too, because the census was taken in April, when farming was not in full swing in most states—especially the hand processes for which children were primarily used—the number of child laborers in agriculture was grossly understated. Again, since most states had no compulsory birth registration, children's ages had to be guessed at. The fact that most states requiring work permits for children under fourteen did not ask adequate proof of age no doubt resulted in the employment of many underaged children. Taking these and other shortcomings into account, one appears justified in increasing the reported figure by about 25 per cent.

II
The National Child Labor Committee

1. The literature on the so-called progressive movement is voluminous, but for a good brief account see Arthur S. Link and William B. Catton, *American Epoch: A History of the United States Since the 1890's* (New York, 1963), pp. 17–45, 68–91.

2. Robert Bremner, *From the Depths: The Discovery of Poverty in the United States* (New York, 1956), p. 123–63. Also see Eric Goldman, *Rendezvous*

with Destiny (New York, 1958), pp. 73–124. The accumulation and mastery of data was one of the most fundamental principles of successful reform. Because of public apathy, those who had opposed change had been able to assert that a proposed reform was unnecessary. After the reformers began marshaling overwhelming evidence to the contrary, they were unable to do so.

3. Robert Hunter, *Poverty* (New York, 1904), p. 98. Also see pp. 1–65, 223–55. Hunter, and others, argued that child labor, which lowered the wage scale and produced much physical harm, was both a cause and an effect of poverty.

4. Theodore Roosevelt, "The Conservation of Childhood," *Proceedings of the Seventh Annual Conference on Child Labor* (New York, 1911), p. 16 (hereafter cited as *Proc. ACCL*). Child labor reformers deliberately took advantage of the growing enthusiasm for the conservation of natural resources, pointing out that child labor reform and conservation of human resources were related to the larger movement to conserve the nation's water, timber, and mineral resources. The careless, unregulated exploitation of children, they argued, robbed the community of its most important asset—the manpower necessary to keep industry operating in the future. In the words of Felix Adler, the child labor reform movement "has for its object to conserve the human resources, the best human assets of the nation—the health, the intelligence, and the character of the children." So if for no other reason than national self-interest, the nation's children had to be protected. See Felix Adler, "Annual Address of the Chairman of the National Child Labor Committee," *Proc. Sixth ACCL* (New York, 1910), p. 1. Also see Stephen S. Wise, "Justice to the Child," ibid., p. 39; NCLC, *Why Conserve Our Natural Resources and Not the Generations That Are to Use Them?* (New York, 1910).

5. There is no adequate general study of child welfare which treats all these developments. For a brief discussion of many of them, however, see Walter I. Trattner, *Homer Folks: Pioneer in Social Welfare* (New York, 1968), pp. 17–119. See also Homer Folks, *The Care of Destitute, Neglected, and Dependent Children* (New York, 1902); Emma O. Lundburg, *Unto the Least of These: Social Services for Children* (New York, 1947); Grace Abbott, ed., *The Child and the State,* 2 vols. (Chicago, 1938); Children's Aid Society, *The Crusade for Children* (New York, 1928); Philip Van Ingen, "The History of Child Welfare," in Mazyck P. Ravenel, ed., *A Half Century of Public Health* (New York, 1921), pp. 290–322; Helen I. Clarke, ed., *Social Legislation: American Laws Dealing with the Family, Child, and Dependent* (New York, 1940); C. C. Carstens, "Public Pensions to Widows with Children," *Survey,* XXIX (January 4, 1913), 459–66; Ada J. Davis, "Evolution of the Institution of Mothers' Pensions in the United States," *American Journal of Sociology,* XXXV (January 1930), 573–87; Elizabeth Sands Johnson, "Child Labor Legislation," in John R. Commons, et al., *History of Labor in the United States,* 4 vols. (New York, 1918–35), III, 403–56; and Homer Folks, *Changes and Trends in Child Labor and Its Control* (New York, 1938).

6. Florence Kelley, "What Should We Sacrifice to Uniformity?," *Proc.*

Seventh ACCL (New York, 1911), pp. 24–30; Louis Athey, "The National Consumers' Leagues and Social Reform, 1890–1923" (doctoral dissertation, University of Delaware, 1965), p. 115; Madeleine W. Sikes, *Child Labor Legislation* (New York, 1902). The model law was revised in succeeding years to include the best provisions of new state laws as they were enacted. It was replaced in 1909 by a uniform child labor law, worked out by the Conference of Commissioners on Uniform State Laws in cooperation with the National Child Labor Committee. Thereafter, the NCLC, rather than the National Consumers' League, assumed responsibility for revising and publicizing the model measure.

7. *Annals of the American Academy of Political and Social Science,* XX (July 1902), part IV, 155–220 (hereafter cited as *Annals*).

8. John A. Ryan, "What Wage Is a Living Wage?," *Catholic World,* LXXV (April 1902), 8. For the Pope's view of child labor see *Encyclical Letter of Pope Leo XIII on the Condition of Labor* [*Rerum Novarum,* 1891] (New York, n.d.). Father Ryan's book, *A Living Wage,* published in 1906, was the first to explore scientifically the bearing of the encyclical on industrial reform in the United States.

9. The miners, in fact, pointed to the prevalence of child labor in the industry as one justification for their demands, and also said that the low wages they received made child labor a necessity for their families. For a brief account of the coal strike, see George E. Mowry, *The Era of Theodore Roosevelt* (New York, 1962), pp. 134–40.

10. Capitalizing upon the excitement this aroused, the *Cosmopolitan* launched a Child Labor Federation with Gustavus Myers as its secretary and the slogan "Child Labor Must Go." The *Woman's Home Companion* also sponsored a reform organization, the Anti-Child Slavery League, which in October 1906 was absorbed by the National Child Labor Committee.

11. Ernest Poole, *The Street: Its Child Workers* (New York, 1903); Robert Hunter, *Poverty* (New York, 1904); John Spargo, *The Bitter Cry of the Children* (New York, 1906). All three presented facts and figures to disprove the cherished notion that child laborers learned the lessons of industry and enterprise and thus began to ascend the ladder of success at an early age. Their research indicated that child labor not only usually failed to provide useful training for a later trade or business, but also that it bred bad habits and physical conditions that were positive handicaps to steady employment in manhood. They found that far more child laborers became unskilled, low-paid adult laborers or vagabonds, criminals, prostitutes, public dependents, and the like, than became successful, self-supporting citizens. See, too, Robert Hunter, "The Children Who Toil," *World's Work,* XI (December 1905), 6991–95.

12. See, for example, Felix Adler, *The Attitude of Society Toward the Child as an Index of Civilization* (New York, 1907), or Homer Folks, "The Charity Side of the Child Labor Problem," *Charities,* XII (March 19, 1904), 293–94.

13. James A. Britton, "Child Labor and the Juvenile Court," *Proc. Fifth ACCL* (New York, 1909), pp. 111–15; Owen Lovejoy, *Child Labor and*

Philanthropy (New York, 1907); George M. Kober, "The Physical and Physiological Effects of Child Labor," *Proc. Second ACCL* (New York, 1906), pp. 27–34; Albert H. Freiberg, "Some of the Ultimate Physical Effects of Premature Toil," *Proc. Third ACCL* (New York, 1907), pp. 19–25; Ben B. Lindsey, "Juvenile Delinquency and Employment," *Survey,* XXVII (November 4, 1911), 1097–1100; NCLC, *The Cost of Child Labor* (New York, 1905); Emil G. Hirsch, "Child Labor from the Employer's Point of View," *Annals,* XXV (May 1905), 554; Felix Adler, "Child Labor in the United States and Its Great Attendant Evils," ibid., XXV (May 1905), 424; William E. Harmon, *Handicaps in Later Years from Child Labor* (New York, 1909).

14. Folks, "The Charity Side of the Child Labor Problem," pp. 293–94; Homer Folks, "Poverty and Parental Dependence as an Obstacle to Child Labor Reform," *Annals,* XXIX (January 1907), 1–8, and "Effective and Adequate Child Care Work," in Homer Folks, *Public Health and Welfare: The Citizens' Responsibility* (New York, 1958), p. 52; Elizabeth Gilman, "School Scholarships—A Branch of Child Labor Work," *Charities,* XVII (March 2, 1907), 971–73; NCLC, *Dependent Parents* (New York, 1905); NCLC, *Both Sides of the Poverty Question in Child Labor Cases* (New York, 1910); George Hall, *Poverty and Child Labor* (New York, 1907), and "Meeting the Poverty Excuse," *Charities,* XV (January 20, 1906), 527; Florence Kelley, "The Child Breadwinner and the Dependent Parent," *Child Labor Bulletin,* II (May 1913), 1–6. The reformers also pointed out, and statistically demonstrated, that the longer children remained in school, the greater would be their eventual earnings.

15. Lovejoy, *Child Labor and Philanthropy,* p. 204; Thomas S. Adams and Helen L. Sumner, *Labor Problems* (New York, 1905), pp. 65–66; John Kingsbury, "Child Labor and Poverty: Both Cause and Effect," *Child Labor Bulletin,* II (May 1913), 27–34; Alexander J. McKelway, *Child Wages in the Cotton Mills: Our Modern Feudalism* (New York, 1913).

16. Kingsbury, "Child Labor and Poverty," p. 34.

17. Murphy received a master's degree from Yale University in 1904 and an honorary doctor of civil law degree from the University of the South in 1912. He withdrew from the ministry in 1903 in order to pursue further his interests in education, labor legislation, and race relations, serving as executive secretary of the Southern Education Board from 1903 to 1908. He also was the first executive of the Rosenwald Fund, devoted to improving Negro education, vice-president of the Conference for Education in the South, and an organizer of the Southern Society for Consideration of Race Problems and Conditions of the South. He resigned from active work in 1908 because of ill-health, and died on June 23, 1913. See Maud King Murphy, *Edgar Gardner Murphy: From Records and Memories* (New York, 1943); Hugh C. Bailey, *Edgar Gardner Murphy: Gentle Progressive* (Miami, Florida, 1968); *New York Evening Post,* July 2, 1913; *Outlook,* CIV (July 5, 1913), 496–97; Elizabeth H. Davidson, *Child Labor Legislation in the Southern Textile States* (Chapel Hill, 1939), p. 26; Herbert H. Doherty, "Voices of Protest from

the New South, 1875–1910," *Mississippi Valley Historical Review*, XLII (June 1955), 58–59.

18. Davidson, *Child Labor Legislation*, pp. 19–25; Alexander J. McKelway, "Child Labor in Southern Industry," *Annals*, XXV (May 1905), 434.

19. Davidson, *Child Labor Legislation*, pp. 26–28; Doherty, "Voices of Protest," pp. 58–59; Hugh C. Bailey, "Edgar Gardner Murphy and the Child Labor Movement," *Alabama Review*, XVIII (January 1965), 47–51.

20. Davidson, *Child Labor Legislation*, pp. 42–46, 125; Edgar Gardner Murphy, "Child Labor in the United States," manuscript dated March 20, 1904, Edgar Gardner Murphy Papers, Southern Historical Collection, University of North Carolina Library, Chapel Hill, N. C. (hereafter cited as Murphy Papers).

21. Quoted in Bremner, *From the Depths*, p. 217. To the argument that Southern families were better off in the mill villages than on their former mountain farms, Murphy answered, "Let us not be guilty of mental confusion. Let us not credit the good fortune of the family to the misfortune of the child." Edgar Gardner Murphy, "Child Labor as a National Problem," *Proceedings of the National Conference of Charities and Correction* (Atlanta, 1903), p. 128 (hereafter cited as *Proc. NCCC*). Also see Alexander J. McKelway, "Edgar Gardner Murphy," manuscript dated December 7, 1913, Murphy Papers.

22. Quoted in Davidson, *Child Labor Legislation*, p. 36.

23. "Of all the sections of the World," wrote Murphy, "the South—the land of chivalry, of tenderness, of home, the land where, if we have learned anything, we have learned to suffer for our ideals—the South is the very last place in which to laugh at sentiment, least of all at the sentiment which touches the promise and freedom of our children." Quoted in Bailey, "Edgar Gardner Murphy," p. 53; Murphy, "Child Labor in the United States."

24. Davidson, *Child Labor Legislation*, pp. 32–33; Doherty, "Voices of Protest," pp. 58–59; Bailey, "Edgar Gardner Murphy," p. 54; Edgar Gardner Murphy, "The National Child Labor Committee," *Charities*, XII (June 4, 1904), 574–75.

25. Davidson, *Child Labor Legislation*, p. 33.

26. Ibid., pp. 49–51; Maud King Murphy, *Edgar Gardner Murphy*, pp. 47–50; Doherty, "Voices of Protest," pp. 58–60; *Outlook*, LXX (February 14, 1903), 373–74.

27. Sands, "Child Labor Legislation," p. 409; Edgar Gardner Murphy, "Southern Prosperity Not Shackled to Child Labor," *Charities*, X (May 2, 1903), 453–56.

28. McKelway, "Edgar Gardner Murphy."

29. Murphy, "Child Labor as a National Problem," pp. 121–34. Murphy did not deny the culpability of the South in permitting large numbers of young children to work long hours, but he again asserted that Northern capitalists who had established mills in the South were as responsible as Southerners for imposing the practice on the region. He also pointed out that if the proportion

of child to adult laborers was larger in the South than elsewhere, the actual number of working children was greater in the state of Pennsylvania than in all the Southern states combined.

30. Ibid., p. 121. Also see Edgar Gardner Murphy, *Problems of the Present South* (New York, 1904), p. 129.

31. Jeremy P. Felt, *Hostages of Fortune* (New York, 1965), pp. 42–45; Josephine Goldmark, *Impatient Crusader: Florence Kelley's Life Story* (Urbana, Ill., 1953), p. 81.

32. Felt, *Hostages of Fortune*, pp. 45–46; "Child Labor Reform in New York," *Charities*, X (January 10, 1903), 52–56.

33. Felt, *Hostages of Fortune*, p. 46.

34. Jeremy P. Felt, "The Regulation of Child Labor in New York State, 1886–1942, with Emphasis upon the New York Child Labor Committee" (doctoral dissertation, Syracuse University, 1956), p. 1.

35. Ibid., pp. 115 ff.; Felt, *Hostages of Fortune*, pp. 48 ff.; "Child Labor Then and Now," *Independent*, LX (March 29, 1906), 746–47.

36. Felix Adler, Jane Addams, Stanley McCormick, John W. Wood, William Baldwin, V. Everit Macy, Lillian Wald, Florence Kelley, and Edgar Gardner Murphy, "The National Child Labor Committee: A Suggested Organization," National Child Labor Committee Papers, Manuscript Division, Library of Congress, Washington, D.C. (hereafter cited as NCLC Papers). Also see Goldmark, *Impatient Crusader*, p. 79; Felt, *Hostages of Fortune*, pp. 74–75.

37. Adler, et al., "A Suggested Organization"; *New York Times*, April 23, 1904.

38. *Minutes* of the first general meeting of the National Child Labor Committee, April 15, 1904, NCLC Papers (hereafter cited as NCLC *Minutes*).

39. Ibid.; Edgar Gardner Murphy, "The National Child Labor Committee," *Charities*, XII (June 4, 1904), 574–76; "A National Child Labor Committee," ibid., XII (April 23, 1904), 409–11; Homer Folks, "Child Labor and the Law," ibid., XIII (October 1, 1904), 21. When the Committee was incorporated by an act of Congress on Feb. 21, 1907, its objects, as stated in its charter, were:

To promote the welfare of society with respect to the employment of children in gainful occupations; to investigate and report the facts concerning labor; to raise the standard of parental responsibility with respect to the employment of children; to assist in protecting children, by suitable legislation, against premature or otherwise injurious employment, and thus to aid in securing for them an opportunity for elementary educational and physical development sufficient for the demands of citizenship and the requirements of industrial efficiency; to aid in promoting the enforcement of laws relating to child labor; to coordinate, unify and supplement the work of State or local child labor committees, and encourage the formation of such committees where they do not exist.

40. Adler, et al., "A Suggested Organization"; NCLC *Minutes,* April 15, 1904.

41. NCLC *Minutes,* April 15, 1904; *New York Times,* April 23, 1904.

42. NCLC *Minutes,* May 4 and July 19, 1904; *New York Times,* June 4, 1904.

43. Among the earliest subscribers, each of whom contributed at least $500, were John D. Rockefeller, A. T. Cassatt, William E. Harmon, Henry Phipps, Adolph Lewisohn, E. H. Harriman, Isaac N. Seligman, Annie B. Jennings, John Huyler, R. Fulton Cutting, S. W. Bowne, V. Everit Macy, Paul Warburg, Jacob H. Schiff, James Stillman, J. P. Morgan, Henry C. Frick, and Andrew Carnegie. Samuel McCune Lindsay to members of the Finance Committee, November 25, 1904, and NCLC Finance Committee to Jefferson Coolidge, Feb. 17, 1905, NCLC Papers; NCLC, *Extracts from the First Annual Report of the Secretary* (New York, 1905).

44. *Who's Who in America, 1903–1905* (Chicago, 1906), p. 903; Obituary, *New York Times,* November 13, 1959.

45. Lindsay resigned as secretary in the fall of 1907. Thereafter he served on the board until 1935, from 1923 to 1935 as its chairman.

46. NCLC *Minutes* October 3, 1904.

47. Ibid.; *Charities,* XIII (October 8, 1904), 47.

48. Homer Folks to Edgar Gardner Murphy, September 2, 1904, Murphy Papers; Owen R. Lovejoy, "Dr. Alexander Jeffrey McKelway, 1866–1918," *Child Labor Bulletin,* VII (May 1918), 21–27; NCLC press release, December 8, 1913, NCLC Papers; Robert J. Doherty, "Alexander J. McKelway: Preacher to Progressive," *Journal of Southern History,* XXIV (May 1958), 177–90; Alexander J. McKelway, untitled manuscript dated April 28, 1916, NCLC Papers. Before joining the NCLC, McKelway had fought in the Carolinas for temperance and anti-gambling as well as child labor laws. In later years he espoused almost every reform associated with the Progressive movement: employers' liability and workmen's compensation laws; abolition of the convict-lease system; juvenile offender laws; extended public education; state aid for needy families; reformatories for criminals; women's suffrage; prohibition; the initiative, referendum, and recall, etc.

49. "The New Child Labor Secretary," *Charities and The Commons,* XIX (November 2, 1907), 951–52; NCLC press release, October 18, 1915, NCLC Papers; Owen R. Lovejoy, untitled manuscript dated May 11, 1915, NCLC Papers; Clarke A. Chambers, *Seedtime of Reform* (Minneapolis, 1964), p. 48. Lovejoy had a deep religious conviction of the divine purposefulness of life lived in conformity with God's will. His presidential address before the National Conference of Social Work in 1920 bore witness to this faith. Regardless of one's formal religious commitment, he said, the social worker and social reformer were in the line of the devoted—the communion of those who did good works. Concern for the youth of the nation, he declared, had to take precedence over all else, for it was through an uplifted and liberated youth that the kingdom of God on earth would be achieved.

50. NCLC press release, October 18, 1915, NCLC Papers; NCLC *Minutes*, July 19, 1904.

51. NCLC *Minutes*, November 10 and 28, 1904.

52. "Felix Adler," in *Dictionary of American Biography*, 22 vols. (New York, 1944), XXI, 13–14; *New York Times*, April 26, 1933. Adler, born in Alzey, Germany, in 1851, came to America at the age of six, when his father, a rabbi, was called to Temple Emanuel in New York City. As he later recalled, his interest in the child labor problem began in 1872. Then, for the first time, he read "with a beating heart and with horror" the chapter in Karl Marx's *Das Kapital* in which Marx culled from English bluebooks facts about the maltreatment of little children in early nineteenth-century England, especially the emptying of orphanages in order to provide child laborers for machines in the mills. See *Child Labor Bulletin*, IV (August 1915), 92.

53. Walter I. Trattner, *Homer Folks: Pioneer in Social Welfare* (New York, 1968), especially pp. 96–103.

54. *Who's Who in America, 1906–1907* (Chicago, 1908), p. 1167.

55. The Committee's initial members are listed in its first publication. *Leaflet* [No. 1] (New York, 1904). Also see *Charities*, XIII (October 8, 1904), 47–48.

56. Ibid.

57. For the variations in thought and action among progressives, see Link and Catton, *American Epoch*, pp. 68–91; Irwin Yellowitz, *Labor and the Progressive Movement in New York State, 1897–1916* (New York, 1965), pp. 1–17; Daniel Levine, *Varieties of Reform Thought* (Madison, 1963).

58. Felix Adler, "Annual Address of the Chairman," *Child Labor Bulletin*, IV (August 1915), 95; "A Word from Dr. Adler," *American Child*, XII (January 1930), 5; Roy Lubove, *The Progressives and the Slums* (Pittsburgh, 1962), p. 214.

59. Samuel McCune Lindsay, "The Work, Policy, and Plans of the National Child Labor Committee," manuscript dated 1907, NCLC Papers; *Child Labor Bulletin*, II (November 1913), 5.

III

A Slow Start

1. From the outset the Committee assumed that to accomplish its goal it had to work for both child labor and compulsory school attendance laws. It also assumed that if laws were to be passed, and adequately enforced, the public must be educated. See Introduction to the *Minutes* of the first meeting of the National Child Labor Committee, April 15, 1904, Manuscript Division, Library of Congress, Washington, D.C. (hereafter cited as NCLC *Minutes* and NCLC Papers). Also see Arthur T. Vance, "The Value of Publicity in Reform," *Annals of the American Academy of Political and Social Science*, XXIX (January 1907), 87–92 (hereafter cited as *Annals*).

2. NCLC *Minutes,* December 14, 1904; Elizabeth Sands Johnson, "Child Labor Legislation," in John R. Commons, et al., *History of Labor in the United States,* 4 vols. (New York, 1918–35), III, 409.

3. Their general survey showed that the facts were as bad as they had anticipated. Not only were working conditions terrible but, as suspected, the number of working children was far greater than the figure reported in the 1900 census. Samuel McCune Lindsay to the Executive Committee, November 10, 1904, NCLC Papers; NCLC *Minutes,* February 15 and April 27, 1905, October 27, 1909. Also see NCLC, *Unprotected Children: In Occupations Not Usually Covered by Child Labor Legislation* (New York, 1905) and *Sixth Annual Report* (New York, 1910), *passim.*

4. The relationship between the NCLC and the state and local committees was never very clearly defined. For the most part, the NCLC merely provided leadership, materials, and information to those bodies, never dictating policy to them. See the memorandum from Owen Lovejoy to the Board of Trustees, December 31, 1908, NCLC Papers; Owen Lovejoy, "The National Child Labor Movement," *Proceedings of the National Conference of Charities and Correction* (St. Louis, 1910), pp. 232–35 (hereafter cited as *Proc. NCCC*); Edward W. Frost, "Relation of the National Child Labor Committee to State and Local Committees," *Proceedings of the Sixth Annual Conference on Child Labor* (New York, 1910), pp. 155–59 (hereafter cited as *Proc. ACCL*); NCLC, *Extracts from First Annual Report* (New York, 1905).

5. Samuel McCune Lindsay to the Board of Trustees, October 12, 1905, NCLC Papers; A. J. McKelway, "Child Labor and Social Progress," *Charities and The Commons,* XX (April 18, 1908), 104–7.

6. Francis H. Nichols, "Children of the Coal Mines," *Review of Reviews,* XXVII (February 1903), 214–15; Owen Lovejoy, "Child Labor in the Soft Coal Mines," *Annals,* XXIX (January 1907), 26–34, and "The Extent of Child Labor in the Anthracite Coal Industry," *Proc. Third ACCL* (New York, 1907), pp. 35–49; Fred S. Hall, "Pennsylvania's Child Labor Laws," *Survey,* XXII (May 29, 1909), 321.

7. The majority of children employed in the anthracite mines were used in the breakers separating slate from the coal. Since there was no slate picking in the bituminous mines, those employed in that industry worked inside the mines. See Owen Lovejoy, "Child Labor in the Coal Mines," *Proc. Second ACCL* (New York, 1906), pp. 35–41, and "Child Labor in the Soft Coal Mines," pp. 26–34.

8. Owen Lovejoy, *Child Labor in the Coal Mines* (New York, 1906), p. 5.

9. Lovejoy, "Child Labor in the Soft Coal Mines," p. 41, or "Child Labor in the Coal Mines," *Annals,* XXVII (March 1906), 293–99.

10. Nichols, "Children of the Coal Mines," pp. 214–15; Owen Lovejoy, *In the Shadow of the Coal Breakers* (New York, 1907).

11. Lovejoy, *Child Labor in the Coal Mines,* p. 5. Gob is mining waste, in this case piles of the discarded slack and slate.

12. Lovejoy, *In the Shadow of the Coal Breakers*, p. 10. Also see Owen Lovejoy, "School-House or Coal-Breaker," *Outlook*, LXXX (August 26, 1905), 1011–19.

13. Lovejoy, *In the Shadow of the Coal Breakers*, p. 10.

14. Lovejoy, "Child Labor in the Coal Mines," p. 294, or "Child Labor in the Soft Coal Mines," p. 26. Adequate provision for documentary proof of age began in 1903 when New York required as evidence of age a birth certificate, passport, baptismal certificate, or other religious record; a parent's affidavit was no longer sufficient. See Johnson, "Child Labor Legislation," pp. 428–30.

15. Pennsylvania Department of Mines, *Report* (Harrisburg, 1907), part I, p. 17.

16. Lovejoy, "Child Labor in the Coal Mines," p. 295; Helen Marot, "Progress in Pennsylvania," *Charities*, XIV (June 10, 1905), 834–36; Florence Kelley, "Judge-Made Ignorance in Pennsylvania," *Charities*, XVI (May 5, 1906), 189–90; Frank Watson, "The Child Labor Situation in Pennsylvania," *Charities and The Commons*, XVII (March 30, 1907), 1110–12; *Proc. Second ACCL*, in *Annals*, XXVII (March 1906), p. 385.

17. "New Pennsylvania Laws for Women and Children," *Survey*, XXII (May 15, 1909), 243–44; Hall, "Pennsylvania's Child Labor Laws," pp. 321–24; "Child Labor Revolution Under Pennsylvania Law," *Survey*, XXII (February 26, 1910), 791–92.

18. NCLC *Minutes*, January 25 and October 24, 1906. For the Committee's early financial records and statements, see Box 5, NCLC Papers; NCLC, *Fifth Annual Report* (New York, 1909), *passim.*

19. NCLC *Minutes*, September 31 and October 4, 1906; NCLC, *Second Annual Report* (New York, 1906); Elizabeth H. Davidson, *Child Labor Legislation in the Southern Textile States* (Chapel Hill, 1939), p. 129.

20. Those named in the act of incorporation were Felix Adler, Francis G. Caffey (lawyer and later federal judge), Robert W. de Forest, Edward T. Devine, Homer Folks, William E. Harmon (real estate broker and developer), John S. Huyler, Florence Kelley, James H. Kirkland, V. Everit Macy, Isaac N. Seligman, Lillian D. Wald, Paul M. Warburg, John W. Wood.

21 NCLC, *Extracts from the First Annual Report of the Secretary* (New York, 1905), *passim.*

22. See Box 14 and the Child Labor Day scrapbook, Box 34, NCLC *Papers*. Also see NCLC, *Selections for Child Labor Day* (New York, 1908); John Haynes Holmes, "Indifference of the Church to Child Labor Reform," *Annals*, XXXV (March 1910), 23–32.

23. Owen Lovejoy, "Child Labor in the Glass Industry," *Annals*, XXVII (March 1906), 301; John William Larner, Jr., "The Glass House Boys: Child Labor Conditions in Pittsburgh's Glass Factories, 1890–1917," *Western Pennsylvania Historical Magazine*, XLVIII (October 1965), 362–63.

24. Florence Kelley, "A Boy-Destroying Industry," *Review of Reviews*, XXVIII (August 1903), 221–22, and "A Boy-Destroying Trade," *Charities*, XI (July 4, 1903), 19; Larner, "Glass House Boys," p. 357; Johnson, "Child

Labor Legislation," pp. 421–23. The remainder of the leading glass-producing states—Ohio, Illinois, and New York—maintained a fairly decent standard, a fourteen-year minimum age for factory work during the day and a sixteen-year minimum for night work.

25. Quoted in Lovejoy, "Child Labor in the Glass Industry," p. 302. Generally each glassblower needed two or three helpers; sometimes he was required to furnish them. Because glassblowers would not use their own children, they frequently took youngsters from orphan asylums or child-placing societies. See Kelley, "A Boy-Destroying Industry," pp. 221–22, and Thomas S. Adams and Helen L. Sumner, *Labor Problems* (New York, 1905), p. 45. Also see Larner, "Glass House Boys," pp. 358–62; Harriet Vander Vaart, "Children in the Glass Works of Illinois," *Annals,* XXIX (January 1907), 77–83; NCLC, *What the Government Says About Child Labor in Glass Factories* (New York, 1911) and *Night-Work and Day-Sleep* (New York, 1911).

26. Lovejoy, "Child Labor in the Glass Industry," pp. 300–11; Johnson, "Child Labor Legislation," p. 422.

27. Owen Lovejoy, *Child Labor in the Glass Industry* (New York, 1906), *passim.* Also see Lovejoy, "Child Labor in the Glass Industry," p. 304. Box 3, NCLC *Papers,* contains reports of many glass factory investigations carried out by the Committee's agents.

28. Quoted in Lovejoy, "Child Labor in the Glass Industry," p. 309. Also see Owen Lovejoy, *Children in the Glass Industry in Pennsylvania* (New York, 1907).

29. Owen Lovejoy, "The Year in Child Labor Reform," *Survey,* XXII (May 29, 1909), 324–26; "New Jersey Prohibits Night Work by Children," *Survey,* XXIV (April 16, 1910), 98–99; Larner, "Glass House Boys," pp. 355–56; Charles L. Chute, "Women and Children in the Glass Industry," *Survey,* XXVI (June 17, 1911), 437–38, and *The Glass Industry and Child Labor Legislation* (New York, 1911).

30. Johnson, "Child Labor Legislation," p. 423.

31. While conditions in New England were far from ideal, they had improved considerably and were far better than those in the South. The two leading Northern cotton textile-producing states—Massachusetts and Rhode Island—had fourteen- and thirteen-year minimum ages and certain educational requirements for factory work. Moreover, the laws were enforced. For that reason, the Committee concentrated on the Southern mill states, especially North and South Carolina, Georgia, and Alabama.

32. Almost two-thirds of the nation's cotton mill operatives from ten to fifteen years of age were in the South. This was due not so much to the concentration of industry in that section as to the greater tendency in the South to employ children. It was, however, extremely difficult to ascertain the exact number of children in the mills, for parents were allowed to take their youngsters to work with them as "assistants" and thus were able to tend a larger number of looms. Of course, the children's names did not appear on the company's books; the parents merely received increased earnings. See Eva

McDonald Valesh, "Child Labor," *American Federationist*, XIV (March 1907), 164–65; Alexander J. McKelway, "Child Labor in the Southern Cotton Mills," *Annals*, XXVII (March 1906), 266, and "Child Labor in Southern Industry," ibid., XXV (May 1905), 433.

33. Wiley H. Swift, "Why It Is Hard to Get Good Child Labor Laws in the South," *Child Labor Bulletin*, III (May 1914), 72–78. Southern textile manufacturers also carried a great deal of weight in Washington where for a long time they blocked federal child labor legislation.

34. Johnson, "Child Labor Legislation," pp. 412–15; George F. Milton, "Compulsory Education in the South," *Annals*, XXXII (July 1908), Supplement, 57–66; McKelway, "Child Labor in Southern Industry," pp. 430–36; Neal Anderson, *Child Labor Legislation in the South* (New York, 1906).

35. See, for example, E. E. Pratt, "Child Labor: A Rational Statement," *Arena*, XXXVII (June 1907), 613–19. Also see August Kohn, "Child Labor in the South," in Samuel C. Mitchell, ed., *History of the Social Life of the South*, 13 vols. (Richmond, 1909), X, 582–97, and Davidson, *Child Labor Legislation in the Southern Textile States*, p. 92.

36. These figures were derived from the federal *Report on Women and Child Wage-Earners in the United States*, XIV (Washington, D.C., 1910). See Florence Taylor, "Mortality Among Cotton Operatives," *Child Labor Bulletin*, III (November 1914), 62–65. Mill fever (or byssinosis, sometimes referred to as "brown lung"), caused by the inhalation of cotton dust over a long period of time and characterized by chronic bronchitis sometimes complicated by emphysema or asthma, is still a chronic industrial disease among textile workers today.

37. The relationship between child labor and illiteracy was quite clear. Seven Southern states contained over 50 per cent of the native-born white illiterates in the entire country, and those states with the highest percentage of child labor had the highest illiteracy rates. Approximaely 52 per cent of the mill children under fourteen years of age were unable to read or write. See Alfred E. Seddon, "The Education of Mill Children in the South," *Annals*, XXXII (July 1908), Supplement, 72–79; "In the South: Child Labor and Compulsory Education," *Outlook*, LXXXV (April 20, 1907), 870–71; NCLC, *The Child in the Cotton Mill* (New York, 1916), p. 9.

38. NCLC *Minutes*, February 15, 1905.

39. Samuel McCune Lindsay to Board of Trustees, March 23, 1905, NCLC Papers; Davidson, *Child Labor Legislation in the Southern Textile States*, p. 128.

40. Alexander J. McKelway, "History of Child Labor Legislation in the South," undated manuscript in the Alexander J. McKelway Papers, Manuscript Division, Library of Congress, Washington, D.C. (hereafter cited as McKelway Papers). Also see Davidson, *Child Labor Legislation in the Southern Textile States*, pp. 152–54.

41. One Southerner defending the employment of children said that in a

certain mill seventy-one children were employed, and "every one [of them] was working to support a widowed mother." The federal *Report on Women and Child Wage-Earners in the United States* stated that less than one-fourth of the children under fourteen years of age working in mills could be considered children of widowed mothers. See NCLC, *The Child in the Cotton Mill*, p. 9.

The fact that many of the reformers were women, who generally were felt to be sentimentalists lacking business sense, or labor union advocates, who were regarded with distrust, made it easier for mill owners to convince Southern legislators that they were the natural protectors of their workers' interests.

42. Davidson, *Child Labor Legislation in the Southern Textile States*, p. 178; J. F. Hanson, "Child Labor from the Employer's Point of View," *Charities*, X (May 16, 1903), 494–95.

43. Quoted in Davidson, *Child Labor in the Southern Textile States*, p. 106.

44. Ibid., pp. 106, 117. Manufacturers (not only in the South), never raised objections to state interference when it benefited them, as in the case of tariffs.

45. *South Carolina News and Courier*, January 7, 1901. For a mill operator's classic defense of child labor in the South, see Lewis W. Parker, "Compulsory Education: The Solution of the Child Labor Problem," *Proc. Fourth ACCL* (New York, 1908), pp. 40–56 [reprinted in *Annals*, XXXII (July 1908), Supplement, 40–56]. Also see Hanson, "The Employer's Point of View," pp. 494–95.

46. Milton, "Compulsory Education in the South," pp. 57–66.

47. Alexander J. McKelway, "Compulsory Education and Child Labor," undated manuscript (approximately 1905) in McKelway Papers.

48. Alexander J. McKelway, "Southern Aspect of the Child Labor Problem," undated manuscript (approximately 1910) in McKelway Papers. McKelway did not, however, argue that blacks and whites should receive the same education, nor did he say what "the proper education of the Negro should be, [or] how it should be adapted to his peculiar needs and capacities."

49. Alexander J. McKelway, "Child Labor in Its Relation to Education," undated manuscript in McKelway Papers. Also see Seddon, "The Education of Mill Children in the South," p. 74.

50. McKelway was a racist in that he explained differences between groups, i.e., blacks and whites, in terms of durable hereditary characteristics. He hailed the disfranchisement of the Negro as a measure for the preservation of civilization. Even the illiterate white, he thought, was a more intelligent voter than the Negro. Others were saying the same things about Orientals, Filipinos, southeastern European immigrants, etc. See Herbert J. Doherty, Jr., "Alexander J. McKelway: Preacher to Progressive," *Journal of Southern History*, XXIV (May 1958), 188–89; Dewey W. Grantham, Jr., "The Progressive Movement and the Negro," *South Atlantic Quarterly*, LIV (October 1955), 461–77; Charles Crowe, "Racial Violence and Social Reform—Origins of the Atlanta

Riot of 1906," *Journal of Negro History,* LIII (July 1968), 234–56; John B. Wiseman, "Racism in Democratic Politics, 1904–1912," *Mid-America,* LI (January 1969), 38–58.

51. Alexander J. McKelway to Commissioner of Labor Charles P. Neill, November 8, 1906, McKelway Papers; Alexander J. McKelway, "Child Labor in the South," *Proc. NCCC* (Buffalo, 1909), pp. 38–39; Alexander J. McKelway, *Child Labor and Its Consequences* (New York, 1908); Alexander J. McKelway, "Conditions of Factory Labor in the South and the Child Labor Question," manuscript dated July 5, 1909, McKelway Papers; Alexander J. McKelway, "In Behalf of Children," manuscript dated December 30, 1905, NCLC Papers; Doherty, "McKelway, Preacher-Progressive," p. 188. In the South, 98 per cent of the cotton mill operatives between the ages of ten and fifteen were native whites, while in the Northern states only about 12 per cent were in that category. See Herbert J. Lahne, *The Cotton Mill Worker* (New York, 1944), pp. 71–36.

52. Alexander J. McKelway, "The Child Labor Problem—A Study in Degeneracy," *Annals,* XXVII (March 1906), 312–26. Also see Davidson, *Child Labor Legislation in the Southern Textile States,* p. 62.

53. NCLC *Minutes,* November 16, 1905; Samuel McCune Lindsay, "The New Child Labor Law in Georgia," *Charities,* XVI (September 1906), 337–38.

54. Quoted in Davidson, *Child Labor Legislation in the Southern Textile States,* p. 197. Also see pp. 194–202.

55. Ibid., p. 202; "A Child Labor Law in Georgia," *Outlook,* LXXXIII (August 18, 1906), 872–73; Doherty, "McKelway, Preacher-Progressive," p. 180; Alexander J. McKelway, "The Awakening of the South Against Child Labor," *Proc. Third ACCL* (New York, 1907), pp. 9–18; Dewey Grantham, Jr., *Hoke Smith and the Politics of the New South* (Baton Rouge, 1967), pp. 131–55; NCLC *Minutes,* August 3, 1907; Alton DuMar Jones, "The Child Labor Reform Movement in Georgia," *Georgia Historical Society Quarterly,* XLIX (December 1965), 404–5.

56. John Braeman, "Albert J. Beveridge and the First National Child Labor Bill," *Indiana Magazine of History,* LX (March 1964), 17. For a discussion of Beveridge's motives, which were a combination of outrage over the inhumanity of the evil, fear of racial degeneracy, and political ambition, see Braeman, p. 17 ff. Also see Albert J. Beveridge to Albert Shaw, October 16 and November 22, 1906, and Albert Beveridge to William H. Loeb, November 12, 1906, Albert J. Beveridge Papers, Manuscript Division, Library of Congress, Washington, D.C. (hereafter cited as Beveridge Papers).

57. NCLC *Minutes,* November 23, 1906; Samuel McCune Lindsay to Edgar Gardner Murphy, November 24, 1906, Edgar Gardner Murphy Papers, Southern Historical Collection, University of North Carolina, Chapel Hill, N.C. (hereafter cited as Murphy Papers); "A Bill to Prevent the Employment of Children in Factories and Mines," S.6562 and H.R.21404 (1906), reprinted in *Annals,* XXIX (July 1907), Supplement, 56; U.S. *Congressional Record,* 59th

Congress, 2nd Session (1906), pp. 50, 159. The bill was based on federal authority under the interstate commerce clause of the U.S. Constitution. Beveridge felt that since the U.S. Supreme Court had upheld several federal laws prohibiting the transfer across state boundaries of goods deemed in some way injurious to the nation's welfare (including lottery tickets), Congress had the power to pass a child labor law. See Albert J. Beveridge, "Child Labor and the Constitution," *Proc. NCCC* (Minneapolis, 1907), pp. 188–96.

58. Francis G. Caffey to Edgar Gardner Murphy, November 30, 1906, Murphy Papers; Robert W. de Forest to Paul M. Warburg, December 6, 1906, NCLC *Minutes*, December 6, 1906.

59. Samuel McCune Lindsay to George F. Peabody, January 25, 1907, Murphy Papers; Samuel McCune Lindsay to members of the National Child Labor Committee, January 17, 1907, NCLC Papers; *New York Evening Post*, January 24, 1907. The chief proponents of federal child labor legislation on the board were Lindsay, Addams, Folks, Kelley, and Wald.

60. Alexander J. McKelway, "Legislative Hints for Social Reformers," undated manuscript in the McKelway Papers; *Proc. Third ACCL*, pp. 29–45; Samuel McCune Lindsay, "Child Labor and the Republic," *Charities*, XVII (January 5, 1907), 639–49.

61. Braeman, "Albert J. Beveridge," pp. 22–23; Valesh, "Child Labor," pp. 166–73. Also see Samuel Gompers, "Organized Labor's Attitude Toward Child Labor," *Proc. Second ACCL* (New York, 1906), pp. 79–83.

62. Braeman, "Albert J. Beveridge," p. 23; Allen F. Davis, *Spearheads for Reform: The Social Settlements and the Progressive Movement, 1890–1914* (New York, 1967), pp. 133–35; "National Child Labor Standards," *Child Labor Bulletin*, III (July 1914), 25–33.

63. At first the investigation was planned on the basis of a $150,000 appropriation. While they would not have been so exhaustive, the investigation and report would have been finished and made public before the 1908 election. Apparently, to postpone publication of the results before the 1909 congressional session, at which the tariff was to be considered, another $150,000 was appropriated, the investigation enlarged, and the report delayed.

64. Braeman, "Albert J. Beveridge," p. 23; "Child Labor in the District of Columbia," *Charities*, XV (December 2, 1905), 270–71; Charles P. Neill, "Child Labor at the National Capital," *Annals*, XXVII (March 1906), 270–80; "Child Slavery," *Arena*, XXXVII (February 1907), 178; "Child Labor in the District of Columbia," *Survey*, XXII (August 7, 1909), 612.

65. U.S. *Congressional Record*, 59th Congress, 2nd Session (1907), pp. 1552–57, 1792–1826, 1867–83; Albert J. Beveridge, "Child Labor and the Nation," *Annals*, XXIX (January 1907), 119–24; McKelway, "Legislative Hints for Social Reformers." The NCLC decided to reprint Beveridge's speech and distribute it throughout the country. NCLC *Minutes*, March 26, 1907.

66. Edgar Gardner Murphy to Felix Adler, May 27, 1907, Murphy Papers, and Murphy to Adler, December 18, 1906, NCLC Papers; NCLC *Minutes*, January

29, 1907; "Against Federal Child Labor Legislation," *Outlook*, LXXXV (March 16, 1907), 583; Hugh C. Bailey, "Edgar Gardner Murphy and the Child Labor Movement," *Alabama Review*, XVIII (January 1965), 56–57.

67. Edgar Gardner Murphy, *The Federal Regulation of Child Labor: A Criticism of the Policy Represented in the Beveridge-Parsons Bill* (New York, 1907); Davidson, *Child Labor Legislation in the Southern Textile States*, p. 133; Edgar Gardner Murphy to President Theodore Roosevelt, February 4, 1907, Murphy Papers; Robert W. de Forest to Edgar Gardner Murphy, May 28, 1907, Murphy Papers.

68. Florence Kelley to Albert Beveridge, August 5, 1907, Beveridge Papers.

69. Samuel McCune Lindsay to Albert Beveridge, November 8, 1907, Beveridge Papers; NCLC *Minutes*, October 25, 1907.

70. Alexander J. McKelway, "The National Child Labor Bill," undated manuscript in the NCLC Papers in the basement of the Columbia University School of Social Work, New York City. Also see Alexander J. McKelway, "The Awakening of the South Against Child Labor," *Annals*, XXIX (January 1907), 9–18. Here (p. 16), he wrote: "Shall we, for the sake of one application of one constitutional theory, fail to ask the aid of our national government in securing an effective law and condemn a generation of our precious children that might be saved?"

71. Albert Beveridge to Isaac N. Seligman, November 13, 1907, and Albert Beveridge to Samuel McCune Lindsay, November 5, 1907, Beveridge Papers.

72. NCLC *Minutes*, November 26, 1907.

73. Samuel McCune Lindsay to Albert Beveridge, November 27, 1907, Beveridge Papers; Robert W. de Forest to Edgar Gardner Murphy, January 8, 1908, and Owen Lovejoy to Edgar Gardner Murphy, January 6, 1908, Murphy Papers.

74. Undaunted, Beveridge continued to introduce his bill; he intended to force the Senate to go on record by offering it as an amendment to the District of Columbia child labor bill each time that measure came up for consideration. Finally, however, at the urging of NCLC members and President Roosevelt, all of whom wanted the D.C. bill passed, Beveridge withdrew his measure and it died—for the time being. The D.C. bill, which the NCLC drafted, became law on May 28, 1908. See Braeman, "Albert J. Beveridge," pp. 31–33; Theodore Roosevelt to Albert Beveridge, March 30, 1908, and Owen Lovejoy to Albert Beveridge, March 13, 1908, Beveridge Papers; NCLC, *Appeal for Immediate Action* (New York, 1908).

IV
Broadening the Field

1. Robert L. Duffus, *Lillian Wald: Neighbor and Crusader* (New York, 1938), p. 42; Alice E. Padgett, "The History of the Establishment of the United States Children's Bureau" (master's essay, University of Chicago, 1936),

pp. 2–3; Julia Lathrop, "The Children's Bureau," in *Proceedings of the National Conference of Charities and Correction* (Cleveland, 1912), p. 30 (hereafter cited as *Proc. NCCC*). Florence Kelley made the suggestion in the summer of 1900 in a series of lectures on child labor that were repeated at various colleges and universities and later incorporated in *Some Ethical Gains Through Legislation* (New York, 1905). She proposed what she called a National Commission for Children, which should do for all phases of child life what the U.S. Department of Agriculture did for life on the farm—that is, "to make available and interpret the facts concerning the physical, mental, and moral conditions and prospects of the children of the United States." See Josephine Goldmark, *Impatient Crusader: Florence Kelley's Life Story* (Urbana, Ill., 1953), pp. 94–95, 97–99.

2. Dorothy E. Bradbury, *Five Decades of Action for Children: A History of the Children's Bureau* (Washington, D.C., 1962), pp. 1–2; Padgett, "Establishment of the U.S. Children's Bureau," pp. 5–6. As Lillian Wald later recalled, the morning she arrived at the White House to talk to President Roosevelt about her idea, the Secretary of Agriculture was departing for the South to consider that serious threat to the Southern cotton crop—the boll weevil. The realization that no threat to the nation's children could have evoked similar official action convinced her even more strongly of the need for a federal children's bureau.

3. *Minutes* of the meetings of the Board of Trustees of the National Child Labor Committee, April 27, 1905, National Child Labor Committee Papers, Manuscript Division, Library of Congress, Washington, D.C. (hereafter cited as NCLC *Minutes* and NCLC Papers).

4. NCLC *Minutes*, October 12, 1905; Samuel McCune Lindsay, testimony before the House Committee on Expenditures (Interior Department), "Establishment of Children's Bureau in the Interior Department," January 27, 1909, pp. 18–19, typescript in the National Child Labor Committee Papers at the Columbia University School of Social Work, New York (hereafter cited as Committee Hearings, "Establishment of Children's Bureau").

5. Samuel McCune Lindsay to the Board of Trustees, October 12, 1905, NCLC Papers; Padgett, "Establishment of the U.S. Children's Bureau," p. 32; Bradbury, *Five Decades of Action*, p. 2; Samuel McCune Lindsay, *The Federal Children's Bureau* (New York, 1909); "Child Labor a National Disgrace," *Annals of the American Academy of Political and Social Science*, XXVIII (September 1906), 302 (hereafter cited as *Annals*).

6. Homer Folks, "The National Children's Bureau," *Proc. NCCC* (St. Louis, 1910), pp. 90–96; Frank J. Bruno, *Trends in Social Work, 1874–1956* (New York, 1957), p. 153; Goldmark, *Impatient Crusader*, pp. 99–100.

7. Padgett, "Establishment of the U.S. Children's Bureau," pp. 6–8, 11–12, 15–20, 33–34. Interestingly, Senator Albert Beveridge did not support the bill because he "feared that this project might be used as a means of delaying real legislation for the ending of child labor in this republic." See Albert Beveridge to Jane Addams, November 27, 1909, Albert J. Beveridge Papers, Manuscript

Division, Library of Congress, Washington, D.C. (hereafter cited as Beveridge Papers).

8. For the NCLC's organized letter-writing campaign and other activities in behalf of the Children's Bureau bill, see Box 14, NCLC Papers. Also see NCLC, *Fourth Annual Report* (New York, 1908), *passim.;* NCLC, *What Congress Can Do to Protect the Rights of Childhood* (New York, 1906) and *A National Children's Bureau: What Is Proposed* (New York, 1908); Florence Kelley, "The Federal Government and the Working Child," *Annals,* XXVII (March 1906), 289–92.

9. Lillian Wald, Jane Addams, et al., *The Federal Children's Bureau: A Symposium* (New York, 1909); Owen Lovejoy, "Some Unsettled Questions About Child Labor," *Charities and The Commons,* XXI (January 16, 1909), 673–75; Padgett, "Establishment of the U.S. Children's Bureau," pp. 11–12.

10. Bradbury, *Five Decades of Action,* p. 3; Walter I. Trattner, *Homer Folks: Pioneer in Social Welfare* (New York, 1968), pp. 107–8; Owen R. Lovejoy to all participants in the 1909 White House Conference, January 15, 1909, NCLC Papers; Conference on the Care of Dependent Children, Washington, D.C., *Proceedings* (Washington, D.C., 1909), p. 6.

11. Alexander J. McKelway, "Suggested Draft of a Special Message to Congress," undated manuscript in the Alexander J. McKelway Papers, Manuscript Division, Library of Congress, Washington, D.C. (hereafter cited as McKelway Papers); Bradbury, *Five Decades of Action,* p. 1; *New York Tribune,* February 16, 1909; *New York Times,* February 16, 1909.

12. Committee Hearings, "Establishment of Children's Bureau"; "Report of the General Secretary to the Board of Trustees," March 4 and May 12, 1909, and "Report of the General Secretary to the Twenty-fifth Meeting of the Board of Trustees," October 20, 1909, NCLC Papers; Samuel McCune Lindsay to Charles D. Norton, November 7, 1910, NCLC Papers. Also see Isaac N. Seligman to President William H. Taft, November 16, 1911, Florence Kelley to Taft, November 17, 1911, Jane Addams to Taft, November 20, 1911, Lillian Wald to Taft, November 23, 1911, President William H. Taft Papers, Manuscript Division, Library of Congress, Washington, D.C.; U.S. *Congressional Record,* 62nd Congress, 2nd Session (1912), part II, pp. 702–5, 1255, 1571–82, 4226–27. Also see "The Children's Bureau Bill," *Survey,* XXVIII (April 13, 1912), 83–84, and "The Trend of Things," ibid., XXVIII (September 28, 1912), 793.

13. Alexander J. McKelway, "Child Labor in the Carolinas," *Charities and The Commons,* XXI (January 30, 1909), 743–57; "A Year's Progress in Child Labor," ibid., XXI (November 7, 1908), 175–77; Josephine Goldmark, "Summary Changes in Child Labor Law," ibid., XIX (October 5, 1907), 770–72.

14. Alexander J. McKelway, "The Fight for Child Labor Reform in the Carolinas," *Charities and The Commons,* XXI (March 20, 1909), 1224–26; "Factory Inspectors for South Carolina," *Survey,* XXII (May 15, 1909), 248; Alexander J. McKelway, "Child Labor in the South," *Proc. NCCC* (Buffalo,

1909), pp. 38–42, and "Child Labor Campaign in the South," *Survey,* XXVII (October 21, 1911), 1023–26; Owen R. Lovejoy, "Better Child Labor Laws," ibid., XXVI (September 2, 1911), 773–78.

15. *American Federation,* XII (April 1905), 205–9; *Saturday Evening Post* (January 16, February 23, and July 20, 1905, June 21, 1906); *Cosmopolitan* (September 1906); Elizabeth H. Davidson, *Child Labor Legislation in the Southern Textile States* (Chapel Hill, 1939), pp. 128, 138; E. E. Pratt, "Child Labor: A Rational Statement," *Arena,* XXXVII (June 1907), 613–19.

16. Davidson, *Child Labor Legislation in the Southern Textile States,* p. 141. Later David Clark, editor of the *Southern Textile Bulletin,* made the editorial columns of that journal a leading medium for attacks on the Committee in general and on McKelway in particular.

17. Alexander J. McKelway, "Memorandum as to Cooperation with the Cotton Manufacturers in the South" (1909), NCLC Papers; Alexander J. McKelway, "Child Labor in Southern Industry," *Annals,* XXV (May 1905), 432, and "The Awakening of the South Against Child Labor," ibid., XXIX (January 1907), 9–18; McKelway, "Fight for Reform in the Carolinas," pp. 1224–26.

18. NCLC *Minutes,* March 8, 1909.

19. Owen R. Lovejoy, "Memorandum: Work of the National Child Labor Committee, Especially in North and South Carolina, March 25 to April 15," NCLC Papers; NCLC *Minutes,* May 12, 1909; Davidson, *Child Labor Legislation in the Southern Textile States,* pp. 141–43.

20. NCLC *Minutes,* May 12 and October 27, 1909.

21. In reading the history of child labor in England, New England, and the South, one is immediately struck by the similarity of the arguments used against restriction in all three places. See NCLC, *Sixth Annual Report* (New York, 1910), *passim.;* Homer Folks, "Poverty and Parental Dependence as an Obstacle to Child Labor Reform," *Annals,* XXIX (January 1907), 1–2.

22. Thomas F. Parker, "The South Carolina Cotton Mill—A Manufacturer's View," *South Atlantic Quarterly,* VIII (October 1909), 328–37. Also see August Kohn, "Child Labor in the South," in Samuel C. Mitchell, ed., *History of the Social Life of the South,* 13 vols. (Richmond, 1909), X, 582–97.

23. "The Constructive Philanthropy of a Southern Cotton Mill," *South Atlantic Quarterly,* VIII (January 1909), 82–90; "The Child-Labor Problem: Fact Versus Sentimentality," *North American Review,* CLXXXVI (October 1907), 245–56; Thomas R. Dawley, Jr., *The Child That Toileth Not: The Story of a Government Investigation Hitherto Suppressed* (New York, 1912); Davidson, *Child Labor in the Southern Textile States,* pp. 140, 147. Also see W. L. Stoddard, "The Child That Toileth Not," *Survey,* XXIX (February 15, 1913), 705–8.

24. Gertrude Beeks, "Welfare Work and Child Labor in the Southern Cotton Mills," *Charities and The Commons,* XVII (November 10, 1906), 271; Mrs. J. Borden Harriman, "The Cotton Mill: A Factor in the Development of the South," *Proceedings of the Sixth Annual Conference on Child Labor* (New

York, 1910), pp. 47–51 (hereafter cited as *Proc. ACCL*); "Child Slavery,"
Arena, XXXVII (February 1907), 179–80; Jeremy P. Felt, *Hostages of Fortune*
(New York, 1965), pp. 78–79; *New York World*, April 21, 1907. Also see
Box 136, National Civic Federation Papers, New York Public Library, New
York, especially Ralph Easley to D. A. Tompkins, February 13, 1907, and
Ralph Easley to A. T. Ankeny, September 16, 1907. Morris Hillquit, the famed
Socialist, said of the National Civic Federation: "To the organized labor
movement, the policy of the Civic Federation is the most subtle and insidious
poison." Quoted in Norman Hapgood, *Professional Patriots* (New York, 1927),
p. 140.

25. Quoted in "The Argument for Child Labor," *Literary Digest*, XLIV
(March 23, 1912), 594–95. Also see Davidson, *Child Labor Legislation in the
Southern Textile States*, p. 146; "Child Labor Conference Disagrees with Dr.
Stiles," *Survey*, XXIV (April 23, 1910), 131–32.

26. NCLC, *Sixth Annual Report* (New York, 1910). A still more intimate
connection with mountain whites was made in 1913 when the Committee took
on its staff a native mountaineer, Wiley H. Swift. Because of Lovejoy's and
McKelway's trip, McKelway's residence in the section, and Swift's background,
the Committee could speak with authority.

27. Alexander J. McKelway, "The Mill or the Farm?," *Annals*, XXXV
(March 1910), 52–57. Also see Alexander J. McKelway, "Welfare Work and
Child Labor in Southern Cotton Mills," *Charities and The Commons*, XVII
(November 10, 1906), 371–73; John C. Campbell, *From Mountain Cabin to
Cotton Mill* (New York, 1913).

28. McKelway, "The Mill or the Farm?," p. 25. Also see McKelway, "Child
Labor in the Carolinas," pp. 743–57, and *Child Labor in the Carolinas* (New
York, 1908).

29. Not only were Hine's photographs made into slides, which were used
to illustrate lectures, but the pictures were developed into striking exhibits,
which became an important phase of the Committee's work. Later these were
exhibited at the Museum of Modern Art in New York City and reproduced
in numerous books and periodicals throughout America, including *Life Magazine*. See NCLC *Minutes*, October 27, 1909; NCLC, *Fifth Annual Report* (New
York, 1909), p. 7; "They Led Child Labor Crusade," *Milwaukee Journal*,
September 21, 1966.

30. According to the study, 52 per cent of the mill children under fourteen
were unable to read or write, and less than one-fourth of them were children
of widowed mothers. The author also discussed the difficulties involved in
eliminating the problem and, through a comparative analysis of the South and
New England, provided sufficient evidence to demonstrate that child labor in
the textile industry was unnecessary and that an eight-hour day was feasible.
U.S. Congress, Senate Document 645, *Report on the Condition of Women and
Child Wage-Earners in the United States*, 19 vols. (Washington, D.C., 1910–
13), I, *The Cotton Textile Industry, passim*. Also see Edward N. Clopper,
The Education of Factory Children in the South (New York, 1911), p. 3;

Samuel McCune Lindsay, "National Child Labor Standards," *Child Labor Bulletin*, III (May 1914), 25–33; Richard K. Conant, "The Textile Industry and Child Labor," ibid., II (May 1913), 91–95.

31. For a good breakdown of the 1910 census figures on child labor, see Edward N. Clopper, "The Extent of Child Labor Officially Measured," *Child Labor Bulletin*, III (November 1914), 30–36. Also see Homer Folks, *Changes and Trends in Child Labor and Its Control* (New York, 1938), p. 7. North Carolina had over four thousand children aged ten to thirteen working in its mills, more than one-third of the mill children under fourteen reported for the entire country. It had not only a larger number of them than all other states but the highest proportion of cotton mill workers below that age.

32. Pauline Goldmark, "Child Labor in the Canneries," *Annals*, XXXV (March 1910), 152–54; Lewis W. Hine, "The Child's Burden in the Oyster and Shrimp Canneries," *Child Labor Bulletin*, II (May 1913), 105–11; Rheta Claude Door, "When Is a Factory Not a Factory?," *Hampton Magazine*, XXVIII (February 1912), 34–39; René Bach, "Shrimps and Babies," *Technical World*, XVI (January 1912), 499. Box 2, NCLC Papers, contains the reports of many Committee investigations of various kinds of canneries throughout the country.

33. Edward F. Brown, "The Neglected Human Resources of the Gulf Coast States," *Child Labor Bulletin*, II (May 1914), 112–16; Hine, "The Child's Burden," pp. 105–11, and "Child Labor Conditions in the Oyster Industry" (1911), NCLC Papers. When President Wilson visited an oyster cannery at Pass Christian, Mississippi, he did not go inside the shed because the odor was too unpleasant. When an NCLC agent entered it, he found six-, seven- and eight-year-old children working there. NCLC press release, March 13, 1914, NCLC Papers.

34. Bach, "Shrimps and Babies," p. 497; Door, "When Is a Factory Not a Factory?," pp. 34–39; Lewis W. Hine, "Baltimore to Biloxi and Back: The Child's Burden in the Oyster and Shrimp Canneries," *Survey*, XXX (May 3, 1913), 167–72.

35. Quoted in Felt, *Hostages of Fortune*, p. 170.

36. Ibid., pp. 170–76; Door, "When Is a Factory Not a Factory?," p. 36; Ernest S. Whitin, "Children in the Canning Industry," *Outlook*, LXXIX (January 21, 1905), 177–79.

37. "When a Shed Is Not a Shed," *Survey*, XXII (April 10, 1909), 85; Goldmark, "Child Labor in the Canneries," p. 152; Felt, *Hostages of Fortune*, pp. 175–76; Door, "When Is a Factory Not a Factory?," p. 35.

38. Reformers hoped to use workmen's compensation laws to bring about more effective control of hazardous child labor, especially through statutes providing for double or triple compensation for minors injured while illegally employed. The employer was personally responsible for this "added" or increased compensation; he could not relieve himself from the liability by taking out insurance. See Elizabeth S. Johnson, "Child Labor Legislation," in John R. Commons, et al., *History of Labor in the United States*, 4 vols. (New York, 1918–35), III, 455.

39. The best comprehensive account of street trading and all its ramifications is Edward N. Clopper, *Child Labor in City Streets* (New York, 1912). Also see Edward N. Clopper, *Child Labor in Street Trades* (New York, 1910). In some places, newspaper "carriers" (delivery boys in residential areas) were eventually covered by child labor laws; "sellers," on the other hand, were not. Thus those in a less dangerous occupation, carriers, were prevented from working until age fourteen, while those in a more dangerous one, sellers, could work at any age.

40. Quoted in Felt, *Hostages of Fortune,* p. 41. Also see Clopper, *Child Labor in City Streets,* pp. 128–29.

41. Johnson, "Child Labor Legislation," pp. 434–35; Felt, *Hostages of Fortune,* p. 61; "Child Laborers of the Street—The New York Bill," *Charities,* X (March 7, 1903), 205–6; Myron E. Adams, "Municipal Regulation of Street Trades," *Proc. NCCC* (Portland, Me., 1904), pp. 294–300; George Hall, "The Newsboy," *Proc. Seventh ACCL* (New York, 1911), pp. 100–102.

42. Study after study based on the records of juvenile courts, reformatories, and prisons conclusively demonstrated a direct relationship between child labor, especially in the streets, and crime. Usually anywhere from 50 to 75 per cent of the inmates of correctional institutions had been newsboys at a young age. While other factors no doubt contributed to their antisocial behavior, street work certainly was in large measure responsible for it. See Josephine Goldmark, "Street Labor and Juvenile Delinquency," *Political Science Quarterly,* XIX (September 1904), 417–38; NCLC, *Newsboy Life: What Superintendents of Reformatories and Others Think About Its Effects* (New York, 1910); "Street Trades and Delinquency," *Survey,* XXVI (May 20, 1911), 285; Edward N. Clopper, *Street Work and Juvenile Delinquency* (New York, 1914), and "Child Labor in Street Trades," *Annals,* XXXV (March 1910), 139; Fred S. Hall, "Child Labor and Delinquency," *Child Labor Bulletin,* III (November 1914), 37–51; Ben B. Lindsey, "Juvenile Delinquency and Employment," *Survey,* XXVII (November 4, 1911), 1097–1100; Felt, *Hostages of Fortune,* p. 160.

43. There was an interesting inconsistency here. Newspaper publishers washed their hands of the newsboys and any pecuniary obligations which might occur by virtue of their being employees, claiming that the boys were "little merchants" on their own. On the other hand, each time someone tried to pass protective legislation for newsboys, the publishers jumped to their rescue, stating that they themselves looked after and took such good care of the boys that no legislation was necessary. Johnson, "Child Labor Legislation," p. 435. Also see Felt, *Hostages of Fortune,* pp. 57–58; Edward N. Clopper, "Street Trades Regulation," *Child Labor Bulletin,* V (August 1916), 99–100.

44. Johnson, "Child Labor Legislation," pp. 436–37; "Milwaukee Regulates Its Street Traders," *Survey,* XXII (July 31, 1909); Edward N. Clopper, *Children on the Streets of Cincinnati* (New York, 1908), p. 589; "A Legislative Victory for Working Children," *Charities and The Commons,* XX (June 20, 1908), 392–93; Lettie Johnston, "Street Trades and Their Regulation," *Proc. NCCC* (Baltimore, 1915), pp. 518–26.

45. The NCLC did not attack the day messenger service. Its investigators found that in the early morning and during business hours messenger boys catered to the needs of stores, factories, hotels, and private homes. For the most part, their contacts with business and professional people tended to develop enterprise, efficiency, and honor. Frequently, promising boys were advanced to higher and better positions, either by the messenger company itself or by local business or professional people whom they had come in contact with in the course of their duties. The night messenger service, however, was another matter.

46. Owen R. Lovejoy, *Child Labor and the Night Messenger Service* (New York, 1910), and "Child Labor and the Night Messenger Service," *Survey,* XXIV (May 21, 1910), 311–16; Felt, *Hostages of Fortune,* pp. 156–57. Also see Box 59, NCLC Papers, which contains a scrapbook full of clippings on the Committee's various investigations of the night messenger service, 1909–1910.

47. Quoted in Felt, *Hostages of Fortune,* pp. 156–57.

48. NCLC press release, November 16, 1910, NCLC Papers.

49. *New York Tribune,* May 22, 1910; *New York Times,* May 25, 1910; Lovejoy, "Child Labor and the Night Messenger Service," pp. 311–16; Felt, *Hostages of Fortune,* pp. 157–58. The New York State statute, however, applied only to first- and second-class cities; not until 1934 did the Committee succeed in extending the law to all cities in the state.

50. Johnson, "Child Labor Legislation," p. 423.

51. *Child Labor Bulletin,* II (November 1913), 45, and III (November 1914), 9; NCLC press release, October 26, 1914, NCLC Papers.

52. In an investigation of child labor, the Department of Labor found that an American flag was hoisted atop a Southern cotton mill to warn people that government inspectors were in town and children should be kept away from the mill. When the inspectors left, the flag was taken down to show that the children could return to work. *New York Post,* July 29, 1916.

53. NCLC, *Sixth Annual Report* (New York, 1910), p. 14, and *Seventh Annual Report* (New York, 1911), *passim;* Owen R. Lovejoy, *Seven Years of Child Labor Reform* (New York, 1911), and *Uniform Child Labor Laws* (New York, 1911); "A Model Uniform Child Labor Law," *Outlook,* XLIX (October 21, 1911), 401–2; Alexander J. McKelway, "Standards of Legislation for Women and Children in the Southern States," *Proc. NCCC* (Boston, 1911), pp. 186–90, and "Ten Years of Child Labor Reform," ibid. (Memphis, 1914), pp. 138–46. The chief differences between the 1910 uniform child labor law and the 1904 model law were the following: The latter statute provided (1) that messengers under twenty-one years of age should not be employed in cities between the hours of ten P.M. and five A.M.; (2) that the street trades should be regulated and that boys under twelve and girls under sixteen should be forbidden from such employment; and (3) that the canning industry should be brought under the provisions of child labor legislation.

54. According to an NCLC estimate, the states appropriated thirty-three cents a year for factory inspection for each working man, woman, and child. See

NCLC press release, March 9, 1914, NCLC Papers. Also see Florence Kelley, "Factory Inspection in Pittsburgh," *Charities and The Commons,* XXI (March 6, 1909), 1105–16, and *Obstacles to the Enforcement of Child Labor Legislation* (New York, 1907); Charles L. Chute, "The Enforcement of Child Labor Laws," *Child Labor Bulletin,* I (August 1912), 108–13; Homer Folks, "Enforcement of Child Labor Laws," *Annals,* XXXV (March 1910), 91–95, and "Child Labor and the Law," *Charities,* XIII (October 1, 1904), 23; Herschel A. Jones, "European and American Methods of Training Factory Inspectors," *Child Labor Bulletin,* III (May 1914), 122–29; Owen R. Lovejoy to Friends of the Working People, November 2, 1911, NCLC Papers, and "The Year in Child Labor Reform," *Survey,* XXII (May 29, 1909), 325. Enforcement of child labor laws was, of course, one of the Committee's chief objectives at the time it was created, as stated in its charter: "to aid in promoting the enforcement of laws relating to child labor." The Committee called for large appropriations to establish effective, adequately manned departments to carry on systematic inspection of all child-employing industries. To do this, and successfully resist corruption and the introduction of spoils politics, it urged staffing such departments with well-paid, full-time public officials selected for the work from a civil service list. As late as 1914 only nine states had a merit system for choosing factory inspectors. See John H. Morgan, *Essentials in Factory Inspection* (New York, 1908).

55. Running through the NCLC Minutes for these years was a persistent refrain that went something like this: "The campaign was a failure, but Mr. ———— reports that progress is being made and that things have now been brought to the point where in another year, with proper effort on our part, the public can be roused and the states will pass decent legislation in the interests of the children."

V
Federal Child Labor Legislation

1. "The Children's Bureau Bill," *Survey,* XXVIII (April 13, 1912), 83–84; Julia Lathrop, "The Federal Children's Bureau," *Child Labor Bulletin,* II (May 1913), 56–62; Owen Lovejoy, "Creation of the Children's Bureau," *American Child,* XXIX (February 1947), 3; J. J. Eschenbrenner to Alexander J. McKelway, April 12, 1912, National Child Labor Committee Papers, Manuscript Division, Library of Congress, Washington, D.C. (hereafter cited as NCLC Papers); Owen Lovejoy to the Board of Trustees, May 1, 1912, NCLC Papers. The establishment of the Children's Bureau was a historic event, marking a departure in government policy. For the first time the government recognized the importance of children and the advisability of creating special machinery to study and protect them.

2. *Minutes* of the meetings of the Board of Trustees of the National Child Labor Committee, April 3, 1912, May 1, 1912, NCLC Papers (hereafter cited as

NCLC *Minutes*); Owen Lovejoy to the Board of Trustees, May 1, 1912, NCLC Papers; Alice E. Padgett, "The History of the Establishment of the United States Children's Bureau" (master's essay, University of Chicago, 1936), pp. 77–80; Owen Lovejoy, "Child Labor in 1912," *Child Labor Bulletin*, I (May 1912), 10; Jane Addams and Julius Rosenwald to Julian W. Mack, April 12, 1913, William H. Taft to Jane Addams, April 15, 1912, Charles Nagel to Taft, April 17, 1912, George Wickersham to Taft, April 15, 1912, William H. Taft Papers, Manuscript Division, Library of Congress, Washington, D.C.

3. Quoted in Allen F. Davis, *Spearheads for Reform* (New York, 1967), pp. 132–33. Also see Lillian Wald, "The Right Woman in the Right Place," *American City*, VI (June 1912), 847; Padgett, "Establishment of the U.S. Children's Bureau," p. 80; James Weber Linn, *Jane Addams: A Biography* (New York, 1935), p. 138.

4. "Act Establishing the Children's Bureau (42 U.S.C. Ch. 6) Approved April 9, 1912," in Dorothy E. Bradbury, *Five Decades of Action for Children* (Washington, 1962), p. 132; "Immediate Work of the Children's Bureau," *Survey*, XXIX (November 16, 1912), 189–90.

5. Paul U. Kellogg, "The Industrial Platform of the New Party," *Survey*, XXVIII (August 24, 1912), 668–70; *New York Times*, August 14, 1912; George E. Mowry, *Theodore Roosevelt and the Progressive Movement* (New York, 1960), pp. 266, 273; William Allen White, *The Autobiography of William Allen White* (New York, 1946), pp. 487–88.

6. Davis, *Spearheads for Reform*, pp. 195–96; Owen Lovejoy, "Report of the Committee on Standards of Living and Labor," *Proceedings of the National Conference of Charities and Correction* (Cleveland, 1912), pp. 376–95 (hereafter cited as *Proc. NCCC*); NCLC press release, June 4, 1912, NCLC Papers.

7. Davis, *Spearheads for Reform*, pp. 196–97; Walter I. Trattner, *Homer Folks: Pioneer in Social Welfare* (New York, 1968), pp. 101–3.

8. "Governor Wilson and the Social Worker," *Survey*, XXIX (February 8, 1913), 639–40; *New York Post*, January 29, 1913; Trattner, *Homer Folks*, p. 102.

9. Woodrow Wilson, *Constitutional Government in the United States* (New York, 1908), p. 179.

10. "Governor Wilson and the Social Worker," p. 640.

11. "Federal Control over Anti-Social Labor," *Survey*, XXX (August 16, 1913), 615; Stephen B. Wood, *Constitutional Politics in the Progressive Era* (Chicago, 1968), p. 28.

12. The problem of enforcement was particularly vexing to reformers. Most states simply did not provide enough funds to hire the number of inspectors needed for effective administration of their child labor laws. Equally troublesome, however, was the fact that, when inspectors did uncover illegal practices, frequently nothing happened. In many communities, especially semirural ones or those with seasonal industries or one dominant industry, prosecutors often were reluctant to institute proceedings, juries to convict, and judges to impose

penalties. It was felt, however, that federal courts (unlike local ones) would convict violators and thus at the same time act as a deterrent to potential law-breakers. See NCLC press release, November 13, 1913, NCLC Papers.

13. Alexander J. McKelway, "Child Labor and Poverty," *Survey,* XXX (April 12, 1913), 60–62, and "Ten Years of Child Labor Reform in the South," *Child Labor Bulletin,* I (February 1913), 35; Felix Adler, "The Abolition of Child Labor: A National Duty," ibid., III (May 1914), 20-24; NCLC *Minutes,* May 12, 1913.

14. NCLC *Minutes,* April 7, May 12, and December 8, 1913, January 22, 1914; Owen Lovejoy, "The Federal Government and Child Labor," *Child Labor Bulletin,* II (February 1914), 19–25; NCLC press release, January 26, 1914, NCLC Papers. For an excellent account of the legal principles involved in the proposed federal statute see Wood, *Constitutional Politics,* pp. 28–37. Also see Thomas I. Parkinson, "Precedents for Federal Child Labor Legislation," *Child Labor Bulletin,* IV (May 1915), 2. For a discussion of the chief differences between the NCLC's bill and the other federal child labor bills, see Owen Lovejoy's "Memo to the Board of Trustees," Jan. 22, 1914, NCLC *Minutes.* The two Cabinet members, both of whom strongly favored the bill, were Secretary of the Interior Franklin K. Lane and Secretary of Labor William B. Williams.

15. NCLC *Minutes,* January 22 and September 24, 1914; NCLC, *Federal Child Labor Bill Endorsed by the National Child Labor Committee* (New York, 1914).

16. "Report of the General Secretary to the Board of Trustees," NCLC *Minutes,* April 20, 1914; *Child Labor Bulletin,* III (May 1914), 3. Also see Arthur S. Link, *Wilson: The New Freedom* (Princeton, N.J., 1956), pp. 256–57.

17. NCLC press release, February 21 and February 23, 1914, NCLC Papers; "Report of the General Secretary to the Board of Trustees," NCLC *Minutes,* April 20, 1914; NCLC *Minutes,* January 26, 1915; Wood, *Constitutional Politics,* pp. 31 ff.; Robert Bremner, *From the Depths: The Discovery of Poverty in the United States* (New York, 1956), p. 225. For some idea of the Committee's promotional activities in behalf of the bill, see Box 15, NCLC Papers.

18. Grace Abbott, ed., *The Child and the State,* 2 vols. (Chicago, 1938), I, 476–80; Wood, *Constitutional Politics,* pp. 32–42; *New York Times,* January 7, 1915.

19. Elizabeth H. Davidson, *Child Labor Legislation in the Southern Textile States* (Chapel Hill, 1939), pp. 255–56; Wood, *Constitutional Politics,* pp. 42–46; David Clark, "A Demand for a Square Deal," *Child Labor Bulletin,* IV (May 1915), 37–44; *Southern Textile Bulletin,* May 18, 1922.

20. Quoted in Wood, *Constitutional Politics,* p. 41. Also see U.S. *Congressional Record,* 63rd Congress, 3rd Session (1915), pp. 3834–36; "Federal Child Labor Bill Passes the House," *Survey,* XXXIII (February 27, 1915), 569.

21. NCLC *Minutes,* March 15, 1915; NCLC press release, March 16, 1915, NCLC Papers; Wood, *Constitutional Politics,* pp. 41–42; Davidson, *Child Labor*

Legislation in the Southern Textile States, p. 257; *New York Times,* March 16, 1915.

22. NCLC, *Supporters of the Keating-Owen Bill* (New York, 1916).

23. Abbott, *The Child and the State,* I, 480–81; "Special Memorandum on Keating-Owen Bill for *Collier's Weekly,*" January 22, 1916, NCLC Papers. The bill was introduced in Congress on the opening day of the session. It was not immediately sent to committee, however, because the interests opposed to it were trying to have the bill referred to the House Committee on Interstate Commerce, known to oppose the measure. The NCLC fought to have it referred to the House Committee on Labor, which had handled the Palmer-Owen bill favorably the previous year. See Davidson, *Child Labor Legislation in the Southern Textile States,* pp. 439–40.

24. Abbott, *The Child and the State,* I, 480–81; *Outlook,* CXII (January 26, 1916), 169; *New Republic,* VI (February 15, 1916), 9; Arthur S. Link, *Wilson: Campaigns for Progressivism and Peace, 1916–1917* (Princeton, 1965), p. 57. Some last-minute opposition came from a Mrs. A. A. Birney and Mary S. Garrett who, claiming to represent the 100,000 members of the National Congress of Mothers, objected to the provision for a fourteen-year minimum working age.

25. U.S. *Congressional Record,* 64th Congress, 1st Session (1916), pp. 2007–35.

26. Davidson, *Child Labor Legislation in the Southern Textile States,* p. 257; Wood, *Constitutional Politics,* pp. 56–57. The Keating-Owen bill affected children working in Maine canneries, New York City manufacturing establishments, West Virginia glass factories, Indiana mines, Vermont quarries, etc., as much as Southern cotton mills. Yet, with very few exceptions, only Southern cotton manufacturers (who labeled the measure a deliberate attack on the South) opposed it. Nine states already had all the standards embodied in the bill. Of the thirty-nine other states that would therefore be affected by the measure, only four, all Southern cotton mill states which employed about one-sixth of the children covered by its provisions, voted against it. See Helen C. Dwight, "On the Inside of a Cotton Mill," undated manuscript, NCLC Papers.

27. "Working Children and the Senate," *Survey,* XXXVI (April 15, 1916), 69.

28. Ibid.; Wood, *Constitutional Politics,* p. 65.

29. Link, *Wilson: Campaigns,* p. 39.

30. Ibid., p. 40. The Republican party platform went further, stating, "We favor . . . the enactment and rigid enforcement of a Federal child labor law." See Kirk H. Porter and Donald B. Johnson, eds., *National Party Platforms, 1860–1964* (Urbana, Ill., 1966), pp. 207, 199.

31. Alexander J. McKelway to Woodrow Wilson, July 17, 1916, Alexander J. McKelway Papers, Manuscript Division, Library of Congress, Washington, D.C. (hereafter cited as McKelway Papers). Also see Link, *Wilson: Campaigns,* p. 58, and *Woodrow Wilson and the Progressive Era* (New York, 1954), p. 227; NCLC press release, July 18, 1916, NCLC Papers; Wood, *Constitutional*

Politics, p. 65; Robert J. Doherty, "Alexander J. McKelway: Preacher to Progressive," *Journal of Southern History,* XXIV (May 1958), 184–86. Actually, as early as 1910, McKelway had urged Wilson to express himself clearly on child labor reform for the sake of his own and his party's future. See Alexander McKelway to Woodrow Wilson, December 16, 1910, McKelway Papers.

32. Woodrow Wilson to Alexander McKelway, July 19, 1917, McKelway Papers; Link, *Wilson: Campaigns,* pp. 58–59, and *Woodrow Wilson and the Progressive Era,* p. 277; *Survey,* XXXVI (July 22, 1916), 424; Alexander J. McKelway, "Passing the Federal Child Labor Law," *Child Labor Bulletin,* V (August 1916), 91–93; "President Urges Child Labor Bill," *Independent,* LXXXVII (July 31, 1916), 150; "The President and the Mill-Child," *Literary Digest,* LIII (August 5, 1916), 290; Wood, *Constitutional Politics,* p. 68; NCLC press release, July 18, 1916, NCLC Papers.

33. U.S. *Congressional Record,* 64th Congress, 1st Session (1916), pp. 12034, 12062 ff., esp. 12289–94. Also see Wood, *Constitutional Politics,* pp. 69–77; "The Democrat's Child-Labor Law," *Literary Digest,* LII (September 2, 1916), 547.

34. U.S. *Congressional Record,* 64th Congress, 1st Session (1916), pp. 12055, 12281, 12284. In both these instances the U.S. Supreme Court recognized the enlarging sphere of federal police power under congressional power to regulate interstate commerce. Specifically, in *Champion v. Ames* [188 U.S. 321 (1903)] the Supreme Court, by a 5–4 vote, upheld a federal law forbidding the shipment of lottery tickets in interstate commerce. In so doing, the Court dwelt at length upon the supreme and plenary powers of Congress in the field of interstate commerce. Such powers, the Court stated, were absolute and could rightfully touch upon any problem that could be correctly construed as interstate commerce. In *Hoke v. United States* [227 U.S. 308 (1913)] the Court upheld the constitutionality of the (Mann) White Slave Traffic Act of 1910 which, by making it a felony to transport a woman from one state to another for immoral purposes, was another instance of the congressional use of police power to regulate interstate commerce.

35. The full text of the measure ("An Act to Prevent Interstate Commerce in the Products of Child Labor and for Other Purposes") appears in Abbott, *The Child and the State,* I, 483–86. Also see Wood, *Constitutional Politics,* p. 77.

36. *New York Times,* September 2, 1916; Wood, *Constitutional Politics,* p. 78.

37. Albert J. Beveridge to Albert Shaw, August 16, 1916, and Moses E. Clapp to Albert Beveridge, August 9, 1916, Albert J. Beveridge Papers, Manuscript Division, Library of Congress, Washington, D.C.; *Child Labor Bulletin,* V (November 1916), 141; Alexander J. McKelway, "Another Emancipation Proclamation, the National Child Labor Law," *American Review of Reviews,* LIV (October 1916), 424. Regarding President Wilson's role in enacting the law, Senator Thomas W. Hardwick (Democrat, Georgia), a staunch opponent of the measure, stated, "I am not sure that the President has changed his mind

on the question, even if he has changed his position." See U.S. *Congressional Record,* 64th Congress, 1st Session (1916), p. 12070.

38. Quoted in Link, *Wilson: Campaigns,* p. 60, and "The Democrat's Child-Labor Law," *Literary Digest,* LIII (September 2, 1916), 547. Also see "A Victory for the Children," *Outlook,* CXIII (August 16, 1916), 882.

39. *New York Post,* October 14, 1916; Jane Addams, *Second Twenty Years at Hull-House* (New York, 1930), p. 46; E. David Cronon, *The Political Thought of Woodrow Wilson* (Indianapolis, 1965), Introduction, p. iv; Allen F. Davis, "The Social Workers and the Progressive Party, 1912–1916," *American Historical Review,* LXIX (April 1964), 688.

40. NCLC *Minutes,* September 30, and October 3, 1916; NCLC press releases, September 23 and November 23, 1916, NCLC Papers; Helen Dwight, "The New Child Labor Law," manuscript dated September 19, 1916, NCLC Papers; Owen Lovejoy, "The Rest of the Working Children," *Child Labor Bulletin,* V (November 1916), 141–42, and "The Federal Child Labor Law," manuscript dated May 25, 1917, NCLC Papers; Helen Dwight, "Beyond the Reach of the Law," *Survey,* XXXVII (January 6, 1917), 397. According to Arthur Link, the Keating-Owen Act encompassed the "first systematic use of Federal police power to accomplish rearrangement of economic relationships" and thus "represented a significant shift in the balance between the public and private spheres." It was the "first step toward a potentially comprehensive national social and economic regulation" that came to fruition during the New Deal. See Arthur Link, *American Epoch* (New York, 1961), p. 69, and *Wilson: The New Freedom,* p. 256.

41. State regulation of child labor in local industry was nowhere as thorough as the federal regulation of industries engaged in interstate commerce. In November 1916, twenty-eight states allowed children to work more than eight hours a day in stores and other local establishments; nineteen states allowed children to work at night in such establishments; twenty-eight states had no regulation of street work by children, and in many states the regulation was poor; twenty-three states needed night messenger laws; twelve states had no educational requirements for work permits. See NCLC press releases, October 21, November 9, and November 27, 1916, NCLC Papers; NCLC *Minutes,* November 9, 1916; Florence Taylor, *Child Labor in Your State—A Study Outline* (New York, 1916).

42. Edith Abbott, "Grace Abbott—A Sister's Memories," *Social Service Review,* XIII (September 1939), 351–407, especially 380 ff.; Florence Kelley, "The Federal Child Labor Law," *Survey,* XXXVIII (September 1, 1917), 484–86.

43. Julia C. Lathrop, "Administration of the Federal Child Labor Law," *Child Labor Bulletin,* VI (May 1917), 23–26; "Enforcement of the Child Labor Law," *Survey,* XXXVIII (July 21, 1917), 357–58; NCLC, *Thirteenth Annual Report* (New York, 1917), *passim;* NCLC *Minutes,* March 30, June 15, and October 3, 1917; Elizabeth Sands Johnson, "Child Labor Legislation," in John R. Commons, et al., *History of Labor in the United States,* 4 vols. (New

York, 1918–35), III, 442; Alexander McKelway to William B. Williams, August 7, 1917, McKelway Papers. For the work of the Advisory Board see Box 34 in the Abbott Papers, University of Chicago Library, Chicago, Illinois (hereafter cited as Abbott Papers). Also see the correspondence between McKelway and Grace Abbott, June–August, 1917, Abbott Papers. The policy adopted for administering the law was to cooperate with state officials and to refrain from stepping in above them or duplicating their work, except in states where administration practices were too poor to be tolerated under the federal statute. In most states, state inspectors were given federal authority; the work of federal inspectors would be confined to states with standards below those of the federal act and states where opposition to the state law prevented its enforcement.

44. NCLC press release, March 26, 1917, NCLC Papers; *New York Post,* April 11, 1917; NCLC, *What Shall We Do for the Children in Time of War?* (New York, 1917); Anna Rochester, "Child Labor in the Warring Countries," *Child Labor Bulletin,* VI (February 1918), 230–40.

45. Wood, *Constitutional Politics,* pp. 81–93; *Child Labor Bulletin,* VI (November 1917), 144–46. Clark's action was against the wishes of a large majority of Southern mill owners who, despite their dislike of the law, felt that the suit was ill advised and fruitless. In the *Southern Textile Bulletin* (October 16, 1924), p. 54, Clark described the steps leading to the test case. "It can be stated," he wrote, "that Dagenhart never had an idea of making a test case until approached by David Clark and was only a figurehead."

46. See Box 1, McKelway Papers, especially Alexander McKelway to Felix Adler, August 29, 1917, and Alexander McKelway to Owen Lovejoy, September 1, 1917; Florence Kelley to Julia Lathrop, August 28, 1917, Florence Kelley to Felix Adler, August 28, 1917, and Julia Lathrop to Felix Adler, August 29 and September 6, 1917, Abbott Papers; Wood, *Constitutional Politics,* pp. 100–101. For an extremely lucid and detailed account of the court proceedings, see Alexander McKelway to Attorney General Thomas Gregory, September 3, 1917, McKelway Papers.

47. Quoted in Wood, *Constitutional Politics,* pp. 105, 110; also see pp. 106–7.

48. NCLC *Minutes,* October 31, 1917; "On the Way to the U.S. Supreme Court," *Survey,* XXXVIII (September 8, 1917), 507. For an excellent account of the Supreme Court, its personnel, and the legal questions involved in the case, see Wood, *Constitutional Politics,* pp. 119–54.

49. *Hammer v. Dagenhart* [247 V.S. 251 (1918)]; Alpheus T. Mason and William M. Beaney, *American Constitutional Law* (Englewood Cliffs, N.J., 1958), pp. 277–81; "States' Rights vs. the Nation," *New Republic,* XV (June 15, 1918), 194–95; Wood, *Constitutional Politics,* pp. 154–59. With reference to the earlier rulings in the Lottery and White Slave cases, the Court drew a distinction between prohibiting the shipment of injurious articles and prohibiting the shipment of articles harmless in themselves as a means of regulating the conditions under which they were produced. In his dissenting opinion Justice

Holmes held that "If an act is within the powers specifically conferred upon the Congress [and the statute in question was], . . . it is not made any less constitutional because of the indirect effects that it may have," and "we are not at liberty upon such grounds to hold it void." The Court, by the way, did not condemn the law as a deprivation of substantive rights without due process, as Boyd had done. Six years later a reporter asked Reuben Dagenhart, "What benefit did you get out of the suit which you won in the U.S. Supreme Court?" "You mean the suit the Fidelity Manufacturing Company won?" he replied.

> I don't see that I got any benefit. I guess I'd been a lot better off if they hadn't won it. Look at me! A hundred and five pounds, a grown man and no education. I may be mistaken, but I think the years I've put in the cotton mills stunted my growth. They kept me from getting any schooling. I had to stop school after the third grade and now I need the education I didn't get. . . . But I know one thing, I ain't going to let them put my kid sister in the mill.

Quoted in Abbott, *The Child and the State,* I, 515–17.

50. Owen Lovejoy, "Federal Child Labor Legislation," manuscript dated December 13, 1918, NCLC Papers; Wood, *Constitutional Politics,* pp. 169–76; "The Child-Labor Defeat," *Literary Digest,* LVII (June 15, 1918), 16.

51. Quoted in Owen Lovejoy, "The New Child Labor Program," manuscript dated June 18, 1918, NCLC Papers. Also see Wood, *Constitutional Politics,* pp. 169–71; *Southern Textile Bulletin* (June 6, 1918), p. 5.

52. Davidson, *Child Labor Legislation in the Southern Textile States,* pp. 170–71, 192, 263.

53. NCLC press releases, June 7 and August 29, 1918, NCLC Papers; U.S. Children's Bureau, *Seventh Annual Report* (Washington, 1919), *passim;* Owen Lovejoy, "Federal Child Labor Legislation"; Edith Abbott, "A Sister's Memories," pp. 381–82; Grace Abbott, *Administration of the First Federal Child Labor Law* (Washington, 1921), and "The Enforcement of the Federal Child Labor Law," *Child Labor Bulletin,* VII (February 1919), 256–57; Wood, *Constitutional Politics,* pp. 171–73.

54. NCLC press releases, June 4 and June 5, 1918, NCLC Papers; Wood, *Constitutional Politics,* pp. 178–79. As Julia Lathrop put it (p. 179): "The Court's ruling might seem, at first, conclusive, but analysis of the opinions justifies the conviction that federal regulation to protect children has received not a defeat but only a stimulating setback. . . . It remains only to find a method of national limitation not repugnant to the Constitution."

55. NCLC *Minutes,* June 7, 1918; NCLC press release, June 8, 1918, NCLC Papers.

56. NCLC press release, July 16, 1918, NCLC Papers; *Child Labor Bulletin,* VII (August 1918), 80; Wood, *Constitutional Politics,* pp. 199–200; "A Reprieve for the Children," *New Republic,* XVI (August 3, 1918), 7–8. The American Cotton Manufacturers' Association protested the edict and urged its

state affiliates not to accept government contracts under the provisions stated in the clause. Enforcement of the clause was entrusted to Grace Abbott and the Child Labor Division of the Children's Bureau. See E. Abbott, "A Sister's Memories," p. 383.

57. See Box 24 and NCLC press releases, August 16 and October 29, 1918, NCLC Papers; *New York Tribune,* September 22, 1918; Thomas I. Parkinson, "The Federal Child Labor Law Decision," *Child Labor Bulletin,* V (August 1916), 89–97; Wood, *Constitutional Politics,* pp. 201–2; Raymond G. Fuller, "Uncle Sam's Child-Labor Policy," manuscript dated October 22, 1918, NCLC Papers; "War Power to Restrict Child Labor," *Survey,* XLI (October 26, 1918), 103–4.

58. There were objections to using the taxing power of Congress to restrict child labor on these grounds: that it would appear to be a recognition by the federal government of employers' rights to hire young children provided they paid the tax, and, furthermore, that by means of such exploitation the federal government would make money. On the other hand, it was felt that the situation was critical and that amending the U.S. Constitution would take too long. See Wood, *Constitutional Politics,* pp. 195 ff.; "Tax Child Labor Out of Existence," unsigned manuscript dated October 14, 1918, NCLC Papers.

59. The main difference between the Pomerene amendment and the NCLC's measure was that the latter vested administrative responsibility in the Child Labor Division of the Children's Bureau and the former in the Treasury Department. For the implications of this difference, see Wood, *Constitutional Politics,* pp. 203–4. Also see Johnson, "Child Labor Legislation," p. 443; NCLC *Minutes,* November 6, 1918; "Taxes to Drive Out Child Labor," *Survey,* XLI (November 23, 1918), 221. The full text of the bill appears in *Child Labor Bulletin,* VII (February 1919), 4.

60. NCLC *Minutes,* December 17, 1918; NCLC, *Tax on Employment of Child Labor* (New York, 1918); Wood, *Constitutional Politics,* p. 204.

61. *Child Labor Bulletin,* VII (February 1919), 229–34; Irvine L. Lenroot, "Taxing Child Labor Out of Industry," ibid., pp. 254–56; Thomas Reed Powell, "Child Labor and the Constitution," ibid., p. 258; NCLC press release, November 13, 1919, NCLC Papers; Wood, *Constitutional Politics,* pp. 205–6, 214–16. The only Northern Senator to vote against the Pomerene Amendment was Charles S. Thomas of Colorado, a state where sugar beet growers had an enormous economic stake in child labor.

62. *American Child,* I (May 1919), 77; NCLC, *Fifteenth Annual Report* (New York, 1919); "North Carolina Goes It Alone," *Survey,* XLII (May 24, 1919), 312; *Southern Textile Bulletin* (May 18, 1922), p. 18; Wood, *Constitutional Politics,* pp. 221–29. This time, however, Boyd did not contend that the measure violated the due-process clause of the Fifth Amendment.

63. Quoted in NCLC press release, May 8, 1919, NCLC Papers. For press comment on Boyd's ruling, see Box 28, NCLC Papers. Also see Raymond G. Fuller, "Child Labor and the Constitution," *Weekly Review,* III (September

29, 1920), 266; David Brady, "A Forecast of the Supreme Court on the Child Labor Tax Law," *American Child,* I (August 1919), 115–17.

64. NCLC press releases, November 26, 1919, May 16, 1922, NCLC Papers; Abbott, *The Child and the State,* I, 528–31; Owen Lovejoy, "The Salvage of Childhood in the South," *Survey,* XLIV (April 10, 1920), 72.

65. *Bailey* v. *Drexel Furniture Co.* [259 U.S. 42 (1922)]; Mason and Beaney, *American Constitutional Law,* pp. 327–29; Wood, *Constitutional Politics,* pp. 277–81; "Invalid," *Survey,* XLVIII (May 20, 1922), 266–67. The new Chief Justice was William H. Taft, who, since the Beveridge bill had been proposed, had consistently expressed the belief that control over child labor was vested exclusively in the states and that their power was protected from federal interference by the Tenth Amendment. See ibid., p. 285.

VI
Tenements, Farms, and Schools

1. The decision raised important questions regarding the ability of the American people to express their will through legislation. For editorial comment on the decision, see *American Child,* IV (August 1922), 91–96. In a long letter to a lawyer friend shortly after the court decision, Florence Kelley voiced the frustration, and determination, many reformers felt. After forty years of effort, she said,

> We have all failed . . . [for] the state laws are a crazy quilt. No two of them are uniform. The children and the employers alike have a grievance because of the lack of uniformity. States' rights have meant, and do mean, the right to hand over the children as low-paid wage-earners to the exploiters. State child-labor laws will not do except as supplements to a federal law. Congress has now been told twice in four years by the Supreme Court that under the present Constitution it cannot act. Unless we are a nation of morons we must recognize from forty years of failure in the states and these two decisions of the Court that the Constitution must be changed.

Quoted in Louis L. Athey, "The Consumers' Leagues and Social Reform, 1890–1923" (doctoral dissertation, University of Delaware, 1965), p. 133.

2. Raymond G. Fuller, "Child Labor and the Constitution," *Weekly Review,* III (September 29, 1920), 266, and *Child Labor and the Constitution* (New York, 1923), p. 244; Owen Lovejoy to the Board of Trustees, *Minutes* of the meetings of the Board of Trustees of the National Child Labor Committee, September 30, 1922, National Child Labor Committee Papers, Manuscript Division, Library of Congress, Washington, D.C. (hereafter cited as NCLC *Minutes* and NCLC Papers); Stephen B. Wood, *Constitutional Politics in the Progressive Era* (Chicago, 1968), p. 291.

3. NCLC press release, May 16, 1922, NCLC Papers. Also see Owen Lovejoy, "Child Protection Up to the States," manuscript dated May 19, 1922, NCLC Papers, and "Child Labor in the United States," *Current History,* XVI (July 1922), 619–20; "Working Children," *Survey,* XLVIII (June 15, 1922), 381.

4. Jeremy P. Felt, *Hostages of Fortune* (New York, 1965), pp. 7, 146; NCLC, *What the United States Government Says About Child Labor in Tenements* (New York, 1911), *passim.;* Elizabeth Watson, "Homework in Tenements," *Survey,* XXV (February 4, 1911), 772–81.

5. While manufacturers contended that homework was a godsend to the poor widow who had to support her children, the poor widow with young children was seldom found among homeworkers. Even if she had been a factor, her children would have starved, since the pay for this kind of labor was so low. As late as 1924–25, the wages of homeworkers in the men's clothing industry, for example, averaged only one-third of the wages of regular factory workers. See NCLC press release, January 9, 1913, NCLC Papers; Felt, *Hostages of Fortune,* p. 141. Also see Elizabeth Shepley Sergeant, "Toilers of the Tenements: Where the Beautiful Things of the Great Shops Are Made," *McClure's Magazine,* XXXV (July 1910), 231–48; Mary Van Kleeck, "Child Labor in New York City Tenements," *Charities and The Commons,* XIX (January 1908), 1405–20; Rheta Childe Door, "The Child Who Toils at Home," *Hampton Magazine,* XXVIII (April 1912), 183–88.

6. Quoted in Louis L. Athey, "The Consumers' Leagues and Social Reform, 1890–1923," p. 141. Also see Felt, *Hostages of Fortune,* pp. 143–45; Henry White, "Perils of the Home Factory," *Harper's Weekly,* LV (February 11, 1911), 10; Mary Van Kleeck, "Child Labor in Home Industries," *Annals of the American Academy of Political and Social Science,* XXXV (March 1910), 145–49 (hereafter cited as *Annals*); Door, "The Child Who Toils at Home," p. 187; Sergeant, "Toilers of the Tenements," p. 231. Homeworkers couldn't understand why a disease in the household should prevent them from continuing their work. Illness meant that money was urgently needed, so they frequently concealed the sick person and pleaded with the doctor not to "tell on them." Often the doctor, out of sympathy, refrained from reporting the case.

7. Felt, *Hostages of Fortune,* pp. 144–45. Maud Miner, secretary of the NYC Probation Association, told the NYS Factory Investigating Commission (p. 143) how the fatigue of overwork at home drove young girls into prostitution.

8. See Box 4, NCLC Papers; NCLC press release, December 12, 1912, NCLC Papers; Van Kleeck, "Child Labor in N.Y.C. Tenements," pp. 1410–20. The purpose of licensing was to induce better standards of sanitation; it was useless, however, without an adequate force of inspectors. In most areas, because of small staffs, even licensed tenements were not inspected more than once or twice a year. Also see *American Child,* I (May 1919), 19; Mary G. Schonberg, "Tenement Homework in New York City," ibid., II (November 1920), 257–61; Raymond G. Fuller, "Child Labor and Tenement Homework," manuscript dated December 8, 1920, NCLC Papers.

9. Bureau of Census, Department of Commerce and Labor, *Child Labor in the United States* (Washington, D.C., 1907), Bulletin 69, pp. 7–8. Also see John M. Gillette, "Rural Child Labor," *Child Labor Bulletin,* I (June 1912), 154–60.

10. Quoted in Grace Abbott, ed., *The Child and the State,* 2 vols. (Chicago, 1947), I, 474.

11. Quoted in Gertrude F. Zimand, "Brief Historical Sketch on the National Child Labor Committee," 3, manuscript dated May 6, 1965, in the author's possession.

12. Beatrice McConnell, "Child Labor in Agriculture," *Annals,* CCXXXVI (November 1944), 92–100; Homer Folks, *Changes and Trends in Child Labor and Its Control* (New York, 1938), p. 9; Paul S. Taylor, "Hand Laborers in the Western Sugar Beet Industry," *Agricultural History,* XLI (January 1967), 19–26.

13. See Box 2, NCLC Papers; Felt, *Hostages of Fortune,* p. 182; Abbott, *The Child and the State,* I, 572–75. Actually farm producers preferred hiring workers with many children because family labor was cheap.

14. NCLC *Minutes,* April 27, 1905.

15. See, for example, Owen Lovejoy, "Some Unsettled Questions About Child Labor," *Proceedings of the Fifth Annual Conference on Child Labor* (New York, 1909), p. 59 (hereafter cited as *Proc. ACCL*); Woods Hutchinson, "Overworked Children on the Farm and in School," ibid., pp. 116–21; NCLC, *Seventh Annual Report* (New York, 1911), p. 7; Edward F. Brown, "Child Laborers in the Cranberry Bogs of New Jersey" (1910), or Charles L. Chute, "The Cranberry Pickers of New Jersey" (1911), NCLC Papers; Edward N. Clopper and Lewis W. Hine, "Child Labor in the Sugar-Beet Fields of Colorado," *Child Labor Bulletin,* IV (February 1916), 176–206; Edward N. Clopper, "Farmwork and Schools in Kentucky," ibid., V (February 1917), 178–205; Harry M. Bremer, "Agricultural Work and School Attendance," ibid., III (November 1914), 153–58; NCLC press releases, February 3, February 7, and October 16, 1916, NCLC Papers; Florence I. Taylor, "Child Labor on the Farm," manuscript dated December 8, 1916, NCLC Papers; Ruth McIntre, "Effects of Agricultural Employment upon School Attendance," *Elementary School Journal,* XVIII (March 1918), 533–42; Edward N. Clopper, "November in the Beet Fields," *Survey,* XXXVII (November 25, 1916); Gertrude Folks, "Child Labor in Agriculture," *American Child,* III (November 1921), 267–73. As one would expect, the states with the highest percentage of children in agriculture were those with the highest percentage of illiteracy. At the top of the list in both categories were Alabama, Arkansas, Florida, Georgia, and Kentucky. See *Child Labor Bulletin,* V (November 1916), 156.

16. *Child Labor Bulletin,* VI (August 1917), 86; Ruth McIntre, "American Children and the War," ibid., VII (November 1918), 178–84; NCLC press releases, April 21 and May 7, 1917, NCLC Papers; Florence I. Taylor, "Child Protection in Time of War," manuscript dated June 28, 1917, NCLC Papers; NCLC, *Children in Food Production* (New York, 1917); NCLC, *What the*

United States Government Says About Taking Care of Our Children in War Time (New York, 1918); "A Plan to Safeguard Children in Farm Work," *Survey,* XXXVIII (April 28, 1917), 86; "Emptying the School to Work on the Farm," ibid., (September 29, 1917), 576.

17. NCLC press release, January 10, 1919, NCLC Papers; "Rural Child Labor and Farm Truancy," manuscript dated January 14, 1921, NCLC Papers; "Children and War Industry," *Survey,* XLI (October 12, 1918), 49–50.

18. NCLC *Minutes,* May 18, June 29, and December 15, 1921; NCLC press release, August 9, 1921, NCLC Papers; "Rural Child Labor: A Symposium," *American Child,* III (May 1921), 33–45; ibid. (August 1921), 100–103; Felix Adler, "The Next Step to Be Taken by the National Child Labor Committee," *Proceedings of the National Conference of Social Work* (New Orleans, 1920), pp. 62–64. Before serving as Secretary of Agriculture (1913–1920) and Secretary of the Treasury (1920–1921), Houston had been active in educational affairs as a teacher, school superintendent, college professor of political and social science, president of Texas A. and M. College, dean and later president of the University of Texas, and chancellor of Washington University. For the Committee's back-to-school drive, see Box 25, NCLC Papers.

19. Edward N. Clopper, "What Is Child Labor?," *American Child,* II (February 1921), 325–29; "Notes on Compilation of Child Labor and Compulsory Attendance Laws as They Affect the Employment of Children in Agriculture," ibid., pp. 310–19; Charles E. Gibbons, "What Is Rural Child Labor?," ibid., III (August 1921), 171–76, and *Child Labor and Rural Tenancy* (New York, 1921); Owen Lovejoy, "Helping the Farmer Through His Children," manuscript dated September 15, 1921, NCLC Papers; NCLC *Minutes,* October 13, 1921; George B. Mangold and Lillian B. Hill, *Migratory Child Workers* (New York, 1929).

20. "Shall Charitable Societies Relieve Family Distress by Finding Work for Children?," *Child Labor Bulletin,* II (May 1913), 35–41; ibid., VII (February 1919), 236; Owen Lovejoy, *Child Labor and Health* (New York, 1913); Samuel McCune Lindsay, *How to Make Child Labor Legislation More Effective* (New York, 1913); NCLC press release, January 16, 1915, NCLC Papers; Raymond G. Fuller, *Economics and Needs of Child Welfare* (New York, 1922).

21. Edward N. Clopper, "The Draft as a Test of the Nation's Physical Stamina," *Child Labor Bulletin,* VI (February 1918), 216–18; NCLC press release, September 1921, NCLC Papers.

22. Quoted in Clarke A. Chambers, *Seedtime of Reform: American Social Service and Social Action, 1918–1933* (Minneapolis, 1963), p. 30. Also see Box 25, NCLC Papers; Mabel Brown Ellis, "Rural Child Welfare and the Red Cross," *Child Labor Bulletin,* VII (August 1918), 126–36; ibid., VII (February 1919), 237; NCLC, *Fourteenth Annual Report* (New York, 1918), *passim.*

23. NCLC press releases, March 7 and May 19, 1919, NCLC Papers; *American Child,* I (May 1919), 1; National Child Labor Committee to librarians, form letter dated May 31, 1919, NCLC Papers.

24. NCLC, *Fifteenth Annual Report* (New York, 1919), pp. 170 ff., and

Sixteenth Annual Report (New York, 1920), *passim*. Also see, for example, Edward N. Clopper, *Child Welfare in Oklahoma* (New York, 1917), and *Child Welfare in Alabama* (New York, 1918); Wiley H. Swift, *Child Welfare in North Carolina* (New York, 1918); Edward N. Clopper, *Child Welfare in Kentucky* (New York, 1919) and *Child Welfare in Tennessee* (Nashville, 1920).

25. *Child Labor Bulletin*, VII (November 1918), 163–64; NCLC *Minutes*, March 20, 1918; NCLC, *Sixteenth Annual Report* (New York, 1920), pp. 6–7. Lovejoy served as secretary and V. Everit Macy as treasurer of the NCHO. The NCLC also played a part in organizing the Council for Co-ordinating Child Health, a body designed to coordinate the child health work of its six member organizations with that of public departments and private organizations engaged in similar activities. See NCLC, *Sixteenth Annual Report* (New York, 1920), p. 7.

26. James H. Kirkland, "The School as a Force Arrayed Against Child Labor," *Annals*, XXV (May 1905), 558–59; Samuel McCune Lindsay, "Child Labor and the Public Schools," ibid., XXIX (January 1907), 104–9; Felix Adler, "Child Labor in the United States and Its Great Attendant Evils," ibid., XXV (May 1905), 428; William Noyes, "Overwork, Idleness, or Industrial Education," ibid., XXVII (March 1906), 342–53; NCLC *Minutes*, January 29, 1907. Compulsory education laws were far more enforceable than child labor statutes. It was easier for a truant officer than for a labor inspector to find a working boy. When a labor inspector found a boy at work, the child might have been working a year or more—since establishments were not ordinarily inspected oftener than once a year. A boy's absence from school, however, could be detected within a day or two, and a call at his home would immediately reveal the violation. See Elizabeth Sands Johnson, "Child Labor Legislation," in John R. Commons, et al., *History of Labor in the United States*, 4 vols. (New York, 1918–35), III, 411 ff.

27. See, for example, Charles W. Dabney, "Child Labor and the Public Schools," *Annals*, XXIX (January 1907), 110–14; Jean M. Gordon, "Why the Children Are in the Factory," ibid., XXXII (July 1908), 67–71; Jane Addams, "Child Labor and Education," *Proc. NCCC* (Richmond, 1908), pp. 364–69; Owen Lovejoy, "The Function of Education in Abolishing Child Labor," *Proc. Fourth ACCL* (New York, 1908), pp. 80–91; Graham Taylor, "National Front Against Child Labor," *Charities and The Commons*, XXI (January 30, 1909), 741–42; "Child Workers and the Nation," ibid., pp. 760–61; Owen Lovejoy, "Will Trade Training Solve the Child Labor Problem?," *North American Review*, CXCI (June 1909), 773–84, and *Vocational Guidance and Child Labor* (New York, 1914); Theresa Wolfson, "Why, When, and How Children Leave School," *American Child*, I (May 1919), 59–64; Helen C. Dwight, "The Future of Child Labor in the United States," manuscript dated October 20, 1916, NCLC Papers. Also see Sol Cohen, "The Industrial Education Movement, 1906–1917," *American Quarterly*, XX (Spring 1968), 95–110; Timothy Smith, "Progressivism in American Education, 1880–1900," *Harvard*

Educational Review, XXXI (Spring 1961), 168–93; Lawrence A. Cremin, *The Transformation of the School: Progressivism in American Education, 1876–1957* (New York, 1961); William I. Issel, "Teachers and Educational Reform During the Progressive Era," *History of Education Quarterly,* VII (Summer 1967), 220–33. The NCLC did not assume that vocational education was necessarily "progressive" or democratic; in fact, the Committee realized that in practice it could mean class education. If working-class children received a vocational education and middle-class children made up a majority of those who took academic and college preparatory courses, it could serve to widen the gap in social classes. Yet vocational education was necessary in an industrial society. One way to get around the problem, as the NCLC suggested, was to have all schoolchildren take some vocational courses.

28. NCLC *Minutes,* February 21 and April 29, 1908.

29. NCLC *Minutes,* November 2 and December 6, 1910, February 8, 1911, November 17, 1912, November 9, 1916, October 31 and December 26, 1917; Felix Adler, "National Aid to Education," *Child Labor Bulletin,* I (June 1912), 1–5; NCLC press release, March 17, 1917, NCLC Papers; John Dewey and P. P. Claxton, *Federal Aid to Elementary Education* (New York, 1917); John Dewey, "Federal Aid to Elementary Education," *Child Labor Bulletin,* VI (May 1917), 61–66; Cremin, *Transformation,* pp. 50–57; Johnson, "Child Labor Legislation," pp. 452–53; Lloyd E. Blauch, *Federal Cooperation in Agricultural Extension Work, Vocational Education, and Vocational Rehabilitation* (Washington, 1935), pp. 52–71.

30. Alexander McKelway, *The Next Federal Campaign* (New York, 1918); A. C. Monahan, "The Rural Child Labor Problem," *Child Labor Bulletin,* VI (May 1917), 50–55; Edward N. Clopper, "Federal Aid to Education," ibid., VII (May 1918), 57–74; ibid., VII (November 1918), 155, 161; NCLC *Minutes,* May 14, 1918; Owen Lovejoy, "Federal Aid to Education," manuscript dated May, 1918, NCLC Papers; NCLC press releases, June 12 and December 7, 1918, NCLC Papers; Gertrude Folks, *Farm Labor and School Attendance* (New York, 1920). The NCLC also advocated changes in rural educational organization and administration. It especially favored the adoption of the county unit of school organization, more school consolidation, stricter administration of attendance laws through state supervision, the distribution of state funds in part on the basis of attendance, and the adaptation of the school curriculum to rural life.

31. NCLC *Minutes,* March 20, 1918. Actually this matter had come up before. In 1911 and again in 1913, the board considered both a name change and a merger with other child welfare agencies. On both occasions, however, the ideas were rejected. See NCLC *Minutes,* October 26, 1911, December 8, 1913.

32. NCLC *Minutes,* May 14, 1918, November 18, 1919.

33. NCLC *Minutes,* March 5, November 18, and December 8, 1919; Owen Lovejoy to Samuel McCune Lindsay. December 4, 1919, NCLC Papers.

34. NCLC *Minutes,* June 9, 1920, February 2, February 7, April 11, and December 15, 1921, January 24 and March 17, 1922; David Houston,

"Purpose and Scope of the National Child Labor Committee," NCLC *Minutes*, March 17, 1922; Edward N. Clopper to Owen Lovejoy, December 20, 1920, Lovejoy to Clopper, January 3, 1921, Clopper to Lovejoy, February 3, 1921, NCLC Papers; *American Child*, IV (May 1922); Owen Lovejoy to Mrs. Alexander J. McKelway, September 30, 1932, and Edward N. Clopper to Mrs. Alexander J. McKelway, May 11, 1932, McKelway Papers.

35. "Census Figures and Child Labor," *American Child*, IV (November 1922), 1; Ellen N. Matthews, "Child Labor and the Fourteenth Census," *Survey*, XLVIII (September 15, 1922), 727–29.

36. Florence I. Taylor, "The Passing of the Breaker Boy," *Child Labor Bulletin*, V (August 1916), 101–2; Wood, *Constitutional Politics*, pp. 172, 251–52; Herbert J. Lahne, *The Cotton Mill Worker* (New York, 1944), p. 124; Walter Armentrout, "Trade Union Activity for Child Protection," *American Child*, III (February 1922), 332–42; ibid., I (November 1919), 156–57; Broadus Mitchell, "The End of Child Labor," *Survey*, XLII (August 23, 1919), 747–50. In the South two other factors were important in reducing child labor: (1) the declining growth rate of cotton textile mills, which put less pressure on employers for additional workers; and (2) increasing travel and mobility, which meant that the mill village no longer had to be the sole source of labor for the plant.

37. Census returns were based upon parents' replies, which frequently were unreliable. For a breakdown of the figures in terms of area, see Abbott, *The Child and the State*, I, 526. The census also revealed, by the way, that nearly five million Americans over ten years of age (three million of whom were native born), about 6 per cent of the total population, were illiterate.

VII
The Proposed Federal Child Labor Amendment

1. *New York Times*, May 18 and May 20, 1922. Also see Grace Abbott, "Neglected Fundamentals in Children's Work," *Proceedings of the National Conference of Social Work* (Providence, 1922), pp. 21–24 (hereafter cited as *Proc. NCSW*).

2. Some of the other organizations represented at the meeting were the U.S. Children's Bureau, the National Council of Jewish Women, the National Education Association, the National Congress of Mothers and Parent-Teacher Associations, the National Federation of Teachers, the General Federation of Women's Clubs, the National League of Women Voters, the YWCA, the American Association of University Women, and the National Women's Christian Temperance Union.

3. Gompers was chosen chairman, Florence Kelley vice-chairman, and Matilda Lindsay secretary of the Permanent Conference. See *New York Times*, June 2, 1922, November 21, 1923; NCLC, *Handbook on the Federal Child Labor Amendment* (New York, 1937), pp. 12–13; Richard B. Sherman, "The Re-

jection of the Child Labor Amendment," *Mid-America,* XLV (January 1963),
4; NCLC press release, December 11, 1922, National Child Labor Committee
Papers, Manuscript Division, Library of Congress, Washington, D.C. (hereafter
cited as NCLC Papers).

4. *Minutes* of the meetings of the Board of Trustees of the National Child
Labor Committee, November 3, 1920, May 16, May 31, June 9, and June 19,
1922, NCLC Papers (hereafter cited as NCLC *Minutes*). Also see NCLC press
releases, September 7, September 27, and October 9, 1921, June 27, 1922,
NCLC Papers; *American Child,* IV (August 1922), 68–70; Elizabeth H. Davidson, *Child Labor Legislation in the Southern Textile States* (Chapel Hill,
1939), p. 268. There was some opposition to an amendment among NCLC board
members. A few felt that the Committee should turn away from national
legislation and return to state action. Some other friends of child labor legislation felt the same way. See, for example, Felix Frankfurter, "Child Labor and
the Court," *New Republic,* XXXI (July 26, 1922), 250.

5. NCLC press release, September 1, 1922, NCLC Papers; Grace Abbott,
"Federal Regulation of Child Labor, 1906–38," *Social Service Review,* XIII
(September 1939), 419.

6. See Box 15, NCLC Papers; NCLC press release, December 11, 1922, NCLC
Papers; NCLC *Minutes,* November 18, 1922, January 11, 1923; *New York Times,*
June 28, October 11, and December 9, 1922. The Hoover quote is in Sherman,
"Rejection of the Amendment," p. 5. Also see Herbert Hoover, "The Future
of a Community in an Industrial Civilization," *Proc. NCSW* (Providence,
1922), pp. 64–67; *American Child,* II (November 1920), 203–4, and IV
(December 1922), 1.

7. Elizabeth Sands Johnson, "Child Labor Legislation," in John R. Commons et al., *History of Labor in the United States,* 4 vols, (New York, 1918–
35), III, 443–44; NCLC press releases, February 3 and February 13, 1923,
NCLC Papers; *American Child,* V (February 1923), 1, and V (September
1923), 1; *New York Times,* March 11, August 2, and September 2, 1923;
Raymond G. Fuller, *Child Labor and the Constitution* (New York, 1923), p. 4.

8. *New York Times,* February 20, 1923; NCLC *Minutes,* January 11 and
March 8, 1923; *American Child,* V (February 1923), 1. The original Mc-
Cormick amendment read:

> The Congress shall have the power to limit or prohibit the labor of persons
> under 18 years of age, and power is also reserved to the several states to
> limit or prohibit such labor in any way which does not lessen any limitation
> of such labor or the extent of any prohibition thereof by Congress. The
> power vested in the Congress by this article shall be additional to and not
> a limitation on the powers elsewhere vested in the Congress by the Constitu-
> tion with respect to such labor.

9. NCLC *Minutes,* February 23, March 8, April 27, May 24, and October 25,
1923, February 6, 1924; Grace Abbott to Florence Kelley, December 5, 1923,

and Florence Kelley to G. W. B. Cushing, December 5, 1923, National Consumers' League Papers, Manuscript Division, Library of Congress, Washington, D.C. (hereafter cited as NCL Papers); Owen Lovejoy to the Board of Trustees, December 21, 1923, NCLC Papers; Grace Abbott to Samuel Gompers, August 21, 1923, Samuel McCune Lindsay to Samuel Gompers, November 26, 1923, Owen Lovejoy to Elizabeth Tilton, December 18, 1923, Owen Lovejoy to Lillian Wald, December 20, 1923, Julia Lathrop to Owen Lovejoy, January 3, 1924, and Florence Kelley to Grace Abbott, December 26, 1923, Abbott Papers, University of Chicago Library, University of Chicago, Chicago, Illinois (hereafter cited as Abbott Papers); Grace Abbott, ed., *The Child and the State,* 2 vols. (Chicago, 1943), I, 536. The agreed-upon amendment read:

Section 1. The Congress shall have power to prohibit the labor of persons under the age of eighteen years and to prescribe the conditions of such labor.

Section 2. The reserved power of the several states to legislate with reference to the labor of persons under eighteen years of age shall not be impaired or diminished except to the extent necessary to give effect to legislation enacted by Congress.

10. Chief financial supporters of the Sentinels, which later became the American Liberty League and opposed Franklin Roosevelt and the New Deal, especially Social Security, were Raymond Pitcairn of the Pittsburgh Plate Glass Co., E. T. Stotesbury of J. P. Morgan and Co., and Alfred P. Sloan of General Motors. See Norman Hapgood, *Professional Patriots* (New York, 1927), pp. 170 ff.; George Soule, "Liberty in Politics," *New Republic,* LXXXVIII (September 2, 1936), 97 ff. Also see James A. Emery, *An Examination of the Proposed Twentieth Amendment to the Constitution of the United States* (New York, 1924).

11. "Foes of the Amendment," *American Child,* VI (March 1924), 1; Hapgood, *Professional Patriots,* p. 175. Also opposing the proposed amendment were Henry W. Moore of the Pennsylvania Manufacturers' Association and Simon Miller, a Pennsylvania textile and garment manufacturer.

12. U.S. *Congressional Record,* 68th Congress, 1st Session (1924), part 7, p. 7295; Davidson, *Child Labor Legislation in the Southern Textile States,* p. 270; Geddes Smith, "Ghosts vs. Children," *Survey,* LI (March 15, 1924), 673–76; *American Child,* VI (May 1924), 1, and VI (June 1924), 1. While the vote was neither strictly political (13 Republicans and 56 Democrats opposed the measure) nor sectional, 48 of the 69 negative votes were cast by Southerners.

13. U.S. *Congressional Record,* 68th Congress, 1st Session (1924), part 10, p. 10142; Davidson, *Child Labor Legislation in the Southern Textile States,* p. 270; NCLC press release, June 23, 1924, NCLC Papers; *American Child,* VI (July 1924), 10–11. Six Republicans and 17 Democrats voted against the measure; 14 of the 23 negative votes came from Southerners.

14. Abbott, "Federal Regulation," pp. 419–20; NCLC, *Handbook on the Federal Child Labor Amendment*, pp. 12–13.

15. NCLC, *Handbook on the Federal Child Labor Amendment*, pp. 12–16; Abbott, *The Child and the State*, I, 536, 544–45; Florence Kelley to Grace Abbott, June 6, 1922, Grace Abbott to Felix Frankfurter, July 27, 1923, and Box 34, folders 6–10, Abbott Papers; Florence Kelley, "The Federal Child Labor Amendment: Ten Answers to Ten Questions," *Survey*, LIII (October 15, 1924), 78; NCLC press release, May 1, 1924, NCLC Papers; *American Child*, VI (November 1924), 1, and VI (December, 1924), 1. In Congress, twenty-three suggested changes in wording were proposed and rejected.

16. Quoted in Johnson, "Child Labor Legislation," p. 446. Also see NCLC *Minutes*, June 16, 1924.

17. Abbott, "Federal Regulation," pp. 419–20. The 1924 Republican party platform stated:

> We commend Congress for . . . its prompt adoption of the recommendation of President Coolidge for a constitutional amendment authorizing Congress to legislate on the subject of child labor and we urge the prompt consideration of that amendment by the legislatures of the various states.

The 1924 Democratic party platform said that "without the votes of Democratic members of the Congress the Child Labor Amendment would not have been submitted for ratification." See Kirk H. Porter and Donald B. Johnson, eds., *National Party Platforms, 1840–1960* (Urbana, Ill., 1961), pp. 252, 262. On the other hand, *Survey* (LII [June 15, 1924], 342) predicted that "The familiar bogeys . . . of states' rights, the prohibition analogy, the grasping bureaucrats of Washington, the sacred right of the 17-year old farmer boy to pick blueberries on the hill, and all the rest—will no doubt troop from state capital to state capital to do their worst."

18. *New Republic*, XLII (May 20, 1925), 330.

19. Quoted in Sherman, "Rejection of the Amendment," pp. 7–8. Also see Davidson, *Child Labor Legislation in the Southern Textile States*, pp. 270–71; Herbert J. Lahne, *The Cotton Mill Worker* (New York, 1944), p. 115; Ned Weisberg, "The Federal Child Labor Amendment—A Study in Pressure Politics" (doctoral dissertation, Cornell University, 1942), pp. 24–25; *New York Times*, June 28, June 29, June 30, July 3, July 4, and August 23, 1924. In Georgia, the resolution rejecting the amendment stated in part that, if passed, the amendment

> would destroy parental authority and responsibility . . . would give irrevocable support to a rebellion of childhood which menaces our civilization, would give Congress not only parental authority, but . . . authority over education, would destroy local self-government . . . and create a centralized government far removed from the power of the people. . . . [It] is really intended to enslave the childhood of this republic.

Quoted in *American Child*, VI (August 1924), 5.

20. A detailed analysis of all the arguments used to discredit the amendment

is unnecessary; the arguments can be found in the congressional hearings and in innumerable articles, pamphlets, and editorials. No attempt will be made to cite all the sources consulted. For a good summary, however, see Johnson, "Child Labor Legislation," pp. 446–50, or John A. Ryan, *The Proposed Child Labor Amendment* (New York, 1924).

21. Stephen B. Wood, *Constitutional Politics in the Progressive Era* (Chicago, 1968), pp. 255–56; Donald Johnson, *The Challenge to American Freedoms: World War I and the Rise of the American Civil Liberties Union* (Lexington, 1963).

22. Quoted in *American Child*, VII (April 1925), 6. Also see James A. Ryan, "Child Labor Today," *American Child*, IX (March 1927), 4; Robert Bremner, *From the Depths: Discovery of Poverty in the United States* (New York, 1956), pp. 226–27.

23. Clarke A. Chambers, *Seedtime of Reform* (Minneapolis, 1963), p. 41; Vincent A. McQuade, *The American Catholic Attitude on Child Labor Since 1891* (Washington, D.C., 1938), pp. 182–83. Also, of course, there would be an increased financial burden on parishes if children were required to stay in school longer.

24. Robert K. Murray, *Red Scare* (New York, 1964), especially pp. 263–81. Senator William H. King, for example, declared on the U.S. Senate floor on May 31, 1924:

> Of course it is obvious that under the guise of the amendment Congress will in time take charge of the children the same as the Bolsheviks are doing in Russia, and control not only their labor and their education, but after a time determine whether they shall receive religious instruction or not, the same as the Bolsheviks do in Russia.

Quoted in *American Child*, VI (July 1924), 4.

25. Sherman, "Rejection of the Amendment," p. 9.

26. U.S. *Congressional Record*, 68th Congress, 1st Session (1924), part 10, p. 9963. Also see Josephine Goldmark, *Impatient Crusader: Florence Kelley's Life Story* (Urbana, Ill., 1953), pp. 117–19. Senator Thomas J. Walsh of Montana, one of the authors of the amendment and one of its leading supporters, answered these charges on the Senate floor. See U.S. *Congressional Record*, 68th Congress, 2nd Session (1925), part 2, pp. 1438–47. The fact that the Communist *Daily Worker* advocated immediate ratification of the amendment (December 1, 1924) helped to document the charges that it was a radical measure. Yet many radicals, especially Socialists, opposed the amendment. They felt that, since the elimination of child labor would lead to higher wages, passage of the amendment (and similar measures) would make wage earners all too content with the economic system—and thus postpone the social revolution these radicals desired.

27. Quoted in Sherman, "Rejection of the Amendment," pp. 9–10.

28. Quoted in Abbott, *The Child and the State*, I, 546–47. The amendment, said the *Manufacturers' Record*, was un-Christian and contrary to God's law:

"In the sweat of the brow shalt thou eat bread, and six days shalt thou labor"; it would annul the commandment that "Thou shalt honor thy father and thy mother." See *Manufacturers' Record*, LXXXVI (October 2, 1924), p. 45, and LXXXVI (November 13, 1924), p. 62.

29. Other members of the committee were C. S. Anderson of the Norton Co., Worcester, Mass., P. E. Glenn of the Exposition Cotton Mills, Atlanta, Ga., W. A. B. Dalzell of the Fostoria Glass Co, Moundsville, W. Va., and R. E. Wood of Montgomery Ward and Co, Chicago, Ill. See *New York Times*, August 18, 1924; Albion G. Taylor, *Labor Policies of the National Association of Manufacturers* (Urbana, Ill., 1927), pp. 130–31; Anne K. Brown, "Opposition to the Child Labor Amendment Found in Trade Journals, Industrial Bulletins, and Other Publications for and by Businessmen" (master's essay, University of Chicago, 1937). In part, industrialists' opposition to organized labor was transferred to the amendment. See, for example, *Manufacturers News*, XXV (August 30, 1924), p. 4, and (Aug. 20, 1924), p. 3.

30. *Manufacturers' Record*, LXXXVI (September 11, 1924), 2.

31. Congressman Israel Foster of Ohio disclosed the true nature of the organization on the House floor on February 17, 1925. See U.S. *Congressional Record*, 68th Congress, 2nd Session (1925), part 4, p. 4105. Also see *American Child*, VII (March 1925), 1; NCLC press release, October 1, 1925, NCLC Papers. Referring to Clark's work among farmers, J. S. Bahman, superintendent of the Anchor Duck Mills, Rome, Ga., wrote to Clark: "You are to be congratulated on the publicity you have furnished the opposition, and it is largely due to your efforts that this amendment was defeated." "While you have always performed services for the cotton mill interests," he went on, "the service you have just rendered in defeating the 20th Amendment is your greatest. . . ." Quoted in *Southern Textile Bulletin* (February 19, 1925), p. 18.

32. Johnson, "Child Labor Legislation," pp. 447–48; NCLC, *Handbook on Federal Child Labor Amendment*, p. 40; *New York Times*, November 22 and December 12, 1924, January 16, 1925; E. C. Lindeman, "Child Labor Amendment and the Farmers," *American Review of Reviews*, LXX (July 1924), 63. The editors of *Power Farming*, for example, declared:

> The proposed amendment would give to Congress the power to forbid any farm boy from milking a cow or even driving in a cow from the pasture until he is eighteen years old. Under its sweeping provisions it might and probably would be made illegal for sister Susie to wash a dish or sew on a button until after her eighteenth birthday.

Quoted in *Manufacturers News*, XXIV (February 1925), p. 7. Also see NCLC, *The Farmer and the Federal Child Labor Amendment* (New York, n.d.).

33. NCLC *Minutes*, February 6, 1924, November 20, 1925; Chambers, *Seedtime of Reform*, p. 40; NCLC, *Handbook on Federal Child Labor Amendment*, pp. 32–34; Box 1, NCLC Papers, contains the *Minutes* of the organization's meetings; NCLC press release, December 12, 1924, NCLC Papers.

34. NCLC *Minutes*, December 9, 1924; NCLC press releases, June 23 and

December 27, 1924, NCLC Papers; *American Child,* VI (November 1924) and VI (December 1924), *passim.* The Committee also temporarily discontinued its studies of agricultural child labor so as not to prejudice rural communities against the amendment.

35. *New York Times,* December 5 and December 24, 1923; Raymond G. Fuller, *Child Labor in Massachusetts* (Boston, 1926); Sherman, "Rejection of the Amendment," p. 12.

36. "Child Labor Must End!" *Nation,* CXIX (December 3, 1924), 590; Johnson, "Child Labor Legislation," pp. 446–47; W. A. Robinson, "Advisory Referendum in Massachusetts on the Child Labor Amendment," *American Political Science Review,* XIX (February 1925), 71; *New York Times,* November 17, 1924; NCLC *Minutes,* October 16, 1924.

37. Chambers, *Seedtime of Reform,* pp. 40–41; *New York Times,* July 19 and December 1, 1924.

38. *Pilot* (Boston), October 4 and October 11, 1924; Chambers, *Seedtime of Reform,* pp. 40–41; Abbott, "Federal Regulation," p. 421; "Catholics and Child Labor," *Nation,* CXX (January 21, 1925), 59; Aaron I. Abbell, *American Catholicism and Social Action* (New York, 1960), pp. 227–28; John A. Ryan, "Proposed Child Labor Amendment," *Catholic World,* CXX (November 1924), 166–74; William L. Chenery, "Child Labor—The New Alignment," *Survey,* LIII (January 1, 1925), 425. While a few prominent Protestant clergymen, such as Episocopal Bishop William Lawrence of Massachusetts, and some Protestant denominations, particularly in the South (such as the Southern Baptist Convention), opposed the amendment, many Protestant and most Jewish groups favored it.

39. Wiley H. Swift, "Misinformed Massachusetts," *Survey,* LIII (November 15, 1924), 177–78; "Massachusetts Referendum Vote Disapproves Amendment," *American Child,* VI (December 1924), 1; Sherman, "Rejection of the Amendment," pp. 13–14; *New York Times,* February 17 and February 20, 1925. David Clark wrote in the *Southern Textile Bulletin:* "We set out to beat the Federal Child Labor Amendment and have beaten it. If in the midst of their wailing and gnashing of teeth the pap-suckers and parasites vent some of their spleen upon us we are receiving that which we expected." See *Southern Textile Bulletin,* (February 5, 1925), p. 1.

President Calvin Coolidge's role in this affair was quite strange. The former Massachusetts governor had endorsed the measure on several occasions; yet when proponents of the amendment asked him to make a statement in its behalf during the referendum struggle in Masachusetts, he refused to do so. While anti-amendment forces flooded the state with stories that the President opposed the amendment, he remained silent. Then in December 1924, after the referendum, he publicly endorsed it. See, for example, Raymond G. Fuller to Calvin Coolidge, September 4, 1924, C. Bascom Slemp to Fuller, September 11, 1924, Slemp to Miss Minnie Farnsworth, September 9, 1924, Fuller to Edward Clark, October 24, 1924, Mrs. William L. Putnam to Coolidge, November 1, 1924, Mrs. William Z. Ripley to Coolidge, November 3, 1924, Slemp to Benjamin F. Offeck, December 8, 1924, Slemp to Miss Anna G. Frank,

December 22, 1924, and John Spargo to Coolidge, December 30, 1924, Calvin
Coolidge Papers, Manuscript Division, Library of Congress, Washington, D.C.
    40. "Excerpts from Governor Alfred E. Smith's Annual Message to the
Legislature, Jan. 7, 1925," NCLC Papers; Chambers, *Seedtime of Reform*,
p. 43.
    41. Florence Kelley to Mrs. (?) Kohn, September 28, 1928, NCL Papers.
Also see Jeremy P. Felt, *Hostages of Fortune* (New York, 1965), pp. 201–2.
    42. Florence Kelley to Mrs. (?) Rouse, January 7, 1925, NCL Papers.
    43. NCLC press releases, January 10, January 12, and February 6, 1925,
Lillian D. Wald Papers, Manuscript Division, New York Public Library, New
York City. The Committee declared:

> A popular referendum . . . , although on the surface a "democratic" method
> of handling the subject, is in reality merely another method of killing the
> Amendment in . . . [N.Y.] State.
>   We would be the first to welcome a popular referendum on the subject
> if we believed that both sides of this question could be presented with equal
> fairness to the voters. We do not believe that this is possible in New York
> State at this time—and we therefore believe that the matter should be voted
> upon by the legislators who have had the benefit of a public hearing and
> have had the opportunity to study all phases of the subject.

    44. Felt, *Hostages of Fortune,* pp. 194–216; *New York Times*, January 29,
1925. In the 1930's Smith came out openly against the amendment.
    45. Herbert Croly to Reuben Oppenheimer, January 1925, and Grace Ab-
bott to Oppenheimer, January 31, 1925, Abbott Papers.
    46. See Sherman, "Rejection of the Amendment," pp. 14–17; Felix Adler,
"The Child Labor Panic," *Survey*, LIII (February 15, 1925), 565–67; J. E.
Hulatt, Jr., "Propaganda and the Proposed Child Labor Amendment," *Public
Opinion Quarterly*, II (January 1938), 105–15. This certainly is not to imply
that all people who were against the amendment were deceived by the propaganda. Generally there were three types of opponents: (1) those who sincerely
opposed it because they believed that adoption of the amendment would violate
American principles; (2) those, sometimes equally sincere and sometimes not,
whose opposition was based on misinformation or misunderstanding of the
amendment; and (3) those who insincerely opposed the measure for reasons of
self-interest.
    47. This was clearly reflected in the NCLC's membership; in 1925 the organiza-
tion lost more than nine hundred members and more than $9,000 in membership
receipts. See NCLC *Minutes,* November 12 and November 20, 1925; *American
Child,* VII (November 1925), Supplement, 3.
    48. By the end of 1925 twenty-two states had rejected the amendment while
only Wisconsin was added to the other three that had ratified it. Montana's
approval of the measure in 1927 and Colorado's in 1931 were hardly commented
upon.
    49. Samuel McCune Lindsay to Owen Lovejoy, March 9, 1925, NCLC Papers.
    50. Owen Lovejoy, "It's Up to the States," *American Child*, VII (June

45. Herbert Croly to Reuben Oppenheimer, January 1925, and Grace Abbott to Oppenheimer, January 31, 1925, Abbott Papers.

46. See Sherman, "Rejection of the Amendment," pp. 14–17; Felix Adler, "The Child Labor Panic," *Survey*, LIII (February 15, 1925), 565–67; J. E. Hulatt, Jr., "Propaganda and the Proposed Child Labor Amendment," *Public Opinion Quarterly*, II (January 1938), 105–15. This certainly is not to imply that all people who were against the amendment were deceived by the propaganda. Generally there were three types of opponents: (1) those who sincerely opposed it because they believed that adoption of the amendment would violate American principles; (2) those, sometimes equally sincere and sometimes not, whose opposition was based on misinformation or misunderstanding of the amendment; and (3) those who insincerely opposed the measure for reasons of self-interest.

47. This was clearly reflected in the NCLC's membership; in 1925 the organization lost more than nine hundred members and more than $9,000 in membership receipts. See NCLC *Minutes*, November 12 and November 20, 1925; *American Child*, VII (November 1925), Supplement, 3.

48. By the end of 1925 twenty-two states had rejected the amendment while only Wisconsin was added to the other three that had ratified it. Montana's approval of the measure in 1927 and Colorado's in 1931 were hardly commented upon.

49. Samuel McCune Lindsay to Owen Lovejoy, March 9, 1925, NCLC Papers.

50. Owen Lovejoy, "It's Up to the States," *American Child*, VII (June

1925), 1 (reprinted in pamphlet form, *It's Up to the States* [New York, 1925]). Also see Owen Lovejoy, "The Crisis in Child Protection," manuscript dated June 9, 1925, NCLC Papers; H. Stephen Rauschenbusch, *The Child Labor Complication in 1925* (New York, 1925).

51. NCLC *Minutes*, May 20, 1925. This action was reaffirmed by the board on October 28, 1926. Also see NCLC *Minutes*, March 15, 1925; "The Next Year," *American Child*, VIII (October 1926), 1. "Apparently at present the American people do not want the federal government to regulate child labor," the Committee admitted publicly in June 1925. "Therefore there will be no authority for effective federal regulation in the very near future, probably not for four to six years at least." See *American Child*, VII (June 1925), 1.

52. Chambers, *Seedtime of Reform*, p. 44. "Why did I ever help to start the National Child Labor Committee?," asked Florence Kelley in disgust. See Florence Kelley to Lillian Wald, April 13 and April 4, 1927, Wald Papers. Grace Abbott felt the same way, even as late as 1929. See her exchange of correspondence with Felix Frankfurter in the Abbott Papers: Felix Frankfurter to Grace Abbott, May 31, 1928, January 7 and February 9, 1929; Grace Abbott to Felix Frankfurter, January 9, 1929.

53. *American Child*, VII (November 1925), Supplement, 1, and IX (January 1927), 5; Johnson, "Child Labor Legislation," pp. 451–55; NCLC press release, December 31, 1926, NCLC Papers; "Let the States Do It," *Survey*, LIX (October 15, 1927), 75–76; "1928's Record in Child Labor," ibid., LX (June 15, 1928), 337–38. There were, at best, a few minor advances for a year or two. Some of the more backward states took the poverty exemptions out of their fourteen-year age limit and prohibited night work for those under sixteen; others established an eight-hour day for fourteen- and fifteen-year-olds.

54. NCLC *Minutes*, October 9, 1925, and February 15, 1926; *American Child*, VIII (March 1926), 1–4, 7 ff., and VIII (July 1926), 2; NCLC press release, March 3, 1926, NCLC Papers; *Survey*, LV (March 15, 1926), 666; *New York Times*, March 5, 1926. Lovejoy was made a member of the Committee's board of trustees and served on its executive committee.

55. NCLC *Minutes*, February 15, 1926. Florence Kelley and Lillian Wald charged that Swift, a Southerner, opposed the child labor amendment—further proof of the NCLC's efforts to kill the measure. See Florence Kelley to Mrs. John Sherman, December 21, 1926, and Florence Kelley to John R. Commons, May 14, 1924, NCL Papers; Lillian Wald to Grace Abbott, October 30, 1926, Abbott Papers.

56. NCLC *Minutes*, February 15, 1926; Wiley Swift, "The Changing Order in Child Labor Work," *American Child*, IX (September 1927), 2.

57. Lillian Wald to Wiley Swift, October 28, 1926, Grace Abbott to Lillian Wald, November 1, 1926, Lillian Wald to Grace Abbott, October 30, 1926, Abbott Papers; Florence Kelley to Mrs. John Sherman, December 21, 1926, NCL Papers; Chambers, *Seedtime of Reform*, p. 46.

58. NCLC *Minutes*, October 28, 1926, January 7 and October 10, 1927; Lillian Wald to Grace Abbott, October 30, 1926, Abbott Papers.

59. *American Child*, VIII (October 1926), 2. The NAM's Junior Education

and Employment Committee was comprised of Howell Cheney, Cheney Bros.,
South Manchester, Conn., chairman; Garnett Andrews, Richmond Hosiery Co.,
Rossville, Ga.; E. M. Herr, Westinghouse Electric and Manufacturing Co.,
N.Y.; Simon Miller, Jacob Miller Sons and Co., Phila.; and W. A. Viall,
Brown and Sharpe Manufacturing Co., Providence, R.I.

60. *American Child,* VIII (October 1926), 2, and VIII (November 1926),
2; NCLC press release, November 11, 1926, NCLC Papers; Raymond G. Fuller,
Fourteen Is Too Early (New York, 1927). The Committee also published, at
this time, *School or Work in Indiana* by Charles E. Gibbons (the organization's
director of investigations who had replaced Clopper when he resigned in 1921),
a study of a sixteen-year age limit in successful operation.

61. The main differences between the NAM's program and the NCLC's standards were these: (1) The NAM called for a sixth-grade educational requirement, the NCLC an eighth-grade minimum. (2) The NAM merely endorsed a
forty-eight hour week, while the NCLC specified an eight-hour day and a six-
day week. (3) The NAM sanctioned work for children under sixteen until
9 P.M. while the NCLC sought to prevent those under sixteen from working
after 7 P.M.

62. Wiley Swift, "The Child Labor Position," *Survey,* LIX (October 15,
1927), 72–73; *New Republic,* LII (October 1927), 221–22.

63. Florence Kelley, "The Manufacturers' Plan for Child Labor," *Survey,*
LIX (October 15, 1927), 70–72; Florence Kelley to Broadus Mitchell, August
8, 1928, NCL Papers; Florence Kelley to Lillian Wald, December 7, 1927,
Wald Papers. Also see Florence Kelley to J. Minor, March 30, 1929, Florence
Kelley to G. Hall, April 2, 1929, NCL Papers; Florence Kelley, "Can the
Leopard Change Its Spots?," *New Republic,* LII (November 2, 1927), 289;
Box 42, NCLC Papers.

64. See Box 51, NCL Papers, especially Florence Kelley to Mrs. John Sher-
man, April 2, 1928; Florence Kelley, "The Manufacturers' Program Won't
Do," *Survey,* LX (June 15, 1928), 344–45; Dorothy Kenyon, *Manufacturers'
Child Labor Program* (New York, 1928); NCL, *National Education and Employ-
ment Program of the Junior Education and Employment Committee of the NAM*
(New York, 1929); NCLC *Minutes,* October 10, 1927.

65. NCLC, *The Long Road* (New York, 1944), p. 23.

66. *New York Times,* December 17, 1929. After twenty-five years, the first
chairman of the board of trustees, Felix Adler, was chairman emeritus. The
first permanent secretary, Samuel McCune Lindsay, was chairman of the board,
having replaced David Houston, who resigned in 1923. Of the fifteen original
incorporators of the Committee under the Act of Congress approved February
21, 1907, six—Felix Adler, Francis G. Caffey, Homer Folks, Lillian Wald,
Paul M. Warburg, and John W. Wood—were still members of the board.
V. Everit Macy, another founder of the organization, had recently resigned
from active membership on the board and had been elected an honorary life
member.

67. NCLC press release, June 24, 1929, NCLC Papers; *New York Times,*
December 15, 1929.

68. The 1930 White House Conference on Child Health and Protection took
an advanced position on child labor and education standards: a sixteen-year age
limit for all occupations, with no exemptions except for fourteen- and fifteen-
year-old children in domestic service or agriculture during vacation periods; and
compulsory education until age eighteen (part time from age sixteen to
eighteen if employed after completing eighth grade). The NCLC, while it supported these standards, felt they could not be attained in the near future. The
Committee, therefore, continued working for its own, somewhat lower, standards.
The higher ones, however, were of great educational value to the NCLC,
especially in states which still thought of a fourteen-year limit as a maximum
rather than a minimum standard. See NCLC, *The Long Road*, pp. 25–26.

69. NCLC *Minutes*, November 15, 1929, October 24, 1930, and February 9,
1931; NCLC press release, October 25, 1930, NCLC Papers; *American Child,*
XII (November 1930), 2, XII (December 1930), 2, and XIII (June 1931),
4. Dinwiddie had been secretary of the Associated Charities of Duluth, Minn.,
superintendent of Duluth's Department of Public Welfare, superintendent of
the Cincinnati Anti-Tuberculosis Association, and executive head of the National Child Health Council and the American Child Health Association. He also
directed a child health demonstration in various cities throughout the country,
carried on over a period of years by the Commonwealth Fund.

70. According to the 1930 census returns, approximately 700,000 children ten
to fifteen years of age, inclusive, were gainfully employed (about 230,000 of
them thirteen years of age or less)—a 37 per cent decline since 1920 despite
the larger total population. It was impossible, of course, to determine how much
of the decrease was due to the depression and widespread general unemployment
and how much to changed processes of production and protective legislation.
Counting the sixteen- and seventeen-year-old working children, however, the
number exceeded two million. Moreover, more than three million children aged
seven to seventeen, inclusive, were not attending school in 1930, of whom
1,332,872 were under sixteen. See NCLC, *Child Labor Facts* (New York, 1932);
"The Census of Working Children," *American Child,* XIV (November 1932),
1; ibid., XIV (January 1932), 2, and XIV (September 1932), 2; NCLC press
release, March 30, 1932, NCLC Papers; "Fewer Children at Work," *Survey,*
LXVII (November 15, 1931), 206.

71. Quoted in *American Child,* XV (May 1933), 1, and XV (September
1933), 4. The strikes actually were provoked when the children, who were
working for one to two dollars a week and had not been paid for three weeks,
were told there would be no payroll. Ibid., XV (January 1933), 4. Also see
"Labor in the Shirt Industry," *Monthly Labor Review,* XXXVII (September
1933), 501.

72. See, for example, Box 32, NCLC Papers; NCLC press releases, October
25, 1930, March 30, April 4, and November 28, 1932, May 26, 1933, NCLC
Papers; NCLC *Minutes*, December 15, 1931; *New York Times*, December 7,
1931, April 4, November 8, November 28, and November 29, 1932; "Can We
Use Unemployment to Reduce Child Labor?," *American Child,* XIII (September
1930), 2; Clare L. Lewis, "Child Workers in an Unemployment Period," ibid.,

XIII (January 1931), 1; "The Back-to-School Movement," ibid., XIII (October 1931), 2, XIV (March 1932), 2, and XIV (November 1932), 2; Courtenay Dinwiddie, "Their Fathers' Job?," *Survey*, LXV (December 15, 1930), 319–20, and "Unemployment Solutions: Elimination of Child Labor," *Proc. NCSW* (Minneapolis, 1931), pp. 276–83. The argument was not only that the elimination of child labor would reduce unemployment, raise wages, and increase the standard of living, but that in addition it would lead to more education, less illiteracy, increased vocational training and hence productivity, fewer industrial accidents, and better general health.

73. After virtually ignoring the subject for several years, in 1930, 1931, and 1932 the board discussed the amendment and on each occasion reaffirmed its earlier decision (May 20, 1925, and October 28, 1926) to concentrate on state legislation as opposed to the national measure. See NCLC *Minutes*, December 22, 1930, November 17, 1931, and November 21, 1932.

VIII
Depression Decade: Successes and Setbacks

1. *Minutes* of the meetings of the Board of Trustees of the National Child Labor Committee, May 26 and October 24, 1932, January 20, 1933, National Child Labor Committee Papers, Manuscript Division, Library of Congress, Washington, D.C. (hereafter cited as NCLC *Minutes* and NCLC Papers). Also see Grace Abbott, "Federal Regulation of Child Labor, 1906–38," *Social Service Review*, XIII (September 1939), 423; Grace Abbott to Arthur McKeogh, April 5, 1933, Abbott Papers, University of Chicago Library, University of Chicago, Chicago, Illinois (hereafter cited as Abbott Papers). Edward Keating, the editor of *Labor* who as a Congressman sponsored the first federal child labor law in 1916, was the only one attending the conference who felt the time was right to push for the amendment.

2. The nine states that ratified the amendment in regular session were Illinois, Michigan, New Hampshire, New Jersey, North Dakota, Ohio, Oklahoma, Oregon, and Washington. The five that acted favorably in special session were Iowa, Maine, Minnesota, Pennsylvania, and West Virginia. See *American Child*, XVI (January 1934), 1; Miriam Keeler, "What Child Labor Means Today," manuscript dated February 23, 1933, NCLC Papers. Only six states (Arkansas, Arizona, California, Colorado, Montana, and Wisconsin) had ratified the amendment between 1924 and 1933.

3. *American Child*, XV (March 1933), 3, and XV (April 1933), 2; NCLC *Minutes*, May 22, 1933; "The Next Trench," *Survey*, LXIX (November 1933), 383.

4. See, for example, William E. Leuchtenburg, *Franklin D. Roosevelt and the New Deal* (New York, 1963), pp. 57–58, 64–71; Arthur S. Link and William B. Catton, *American Epoch: A History of the United States Since the 1890's* (New York, 1963), p. 399.

5. NCLC press releases, July 20 and August 9, 1933, NCLC Papers; *New York*

Times, June 22, July 3, and July 20, 1933. At the time only four states had a sixteen-year minimum age for employment in industry, and three were western, nonindustrial states; nine states still permitted employment of children under fourteen years of age.

The Committee also worked for (1) strict regulation of the employment of learners or apprentices, lest employers use this as a loophole for the exploitation of minors (in some cases children worked, as learners, for several weeks without pay and then were fired and replaced by other learners who in turn worked without pay, etc.); and (2) careful regulation of the wage scales of young workers, lest employers hire low-paid juvenile workers in place of higher paid adults (or skilled workers under the guise of learners), thus defeating one primary purpose of the recovery program. See NCLC press release, August 9, 1933, NCLC Papers; "Child Labor Under the Recovery Program," *American Child,* XV (September 1933), 1. Also see Courtenay Dinwiddie, *Controlling Child Labor Through the Code Procedure* (New York, 1934), reprinted from *American Federationist* (January 1934).

6. NCLC, *Twenty-ninth Annual Report* (New York, 1933), p. 5. In 1933 the Committee published a report, *When Children Are Injured in Industry,* by Charles Gibbons and Chester Stansbury, which contained timely evidence of the need for strict regulation of hazardous occupations—one of the main reasons the Committee insisted on incorporation of an eighteen-year minimum in the codes. In this study, NCLC investigators followed up 167 children in Tennessee, Wisconsin, and Illinois who had received serious permanent industrial injuries about five years earlier, when they were under eighteen years old. The findings showed that in most cases the children came out quite badly. The compensation was rarely adequate for lifelong injury; money had to be spent to secure awards or pay for medical care; vocational rehabilitation or reeducation was not provided; when large awards were received, they were foolishly spent in the absence of guardianship provisions. Compensation laws clearly were poor substitutes for higher age limits in hazardous occupations.

7. NCLC, *Twenty-ninth Annual Report,* p. 5; "Child Labor Under the Recovery Program," *American Child,* XV (September 1933), 1; Miriam Keeler, "Child Labor and the NRA," manuscript dated February 1, 1934, NCLC Papers; "Child Labor Under the Industrial Codes," unsigned manuscript dated July 18, 1933, NCLC Papers; "No Child Labor," *Survey,* LX (July 1933), 259. Courtenay Dinwiddie estimated that the code removed some twenty thousand children under sixteen years of age from cotton textile mills. Dinwiddie, *Controlling Child Labor Through the Code Procedure,* p. 2.

8. "Child Labor Under the Recovery Program," p. 1; Dinwiddie, *Controlling Child Labor Through the Code Procedure,* p. 2.

9. *American Child,* XV (October 1933), 1-3, XV (November 1933), 3, and XV (December 1933), 3.

10. NCLC press release, October 28, 1933, NCLC Papers; *American Child,* XV (September 1933), 1, XV (November 1933), 3, and XVI (October 1934), 2; NCLC, *Thirtieth Annual Report* (New York, 1934), p. 5; Homer Folks, "Outlaw Child Labor," *Parents' Magazine,* X (February 1935), 13;

NCLC, *Handbook on the Federal Child Labor Amendment* (New York, 1937), p. 24. The child labor provisions of the codes continued to work. In 1934, for example, the Pennsylvania Department of Labor and Industry made a survey of the cotton garment industry and found that of twelve thousand employees only two were children under sixteen.

11. Dinwiddie, *Controlling Child Labor Through the Code Procedure*, p. 1; Courtenay Dinwiddie to Royal C. Taft, November 13, 1933, NCLC Papers; Courtenay Dinwiddie, "The Rise and Fall of Child Labor," *American Child*, XV (December 1933), 5. Also see ibid. (September 1933), 1.

12. *American Child*, XV (October 1933), 2, and XV (December 1933), 3.

13. *American Child*, XV (October 1933), 2; *New York Times*, October 30, 1933. Newspaper publishers deliberately misrepresented the NCLC's position on this matter. In Louisville, Ky., for example, newsboys were given mimeographed sheets to distribute to their customers which, among other things, said: "Reformers are attempting to prohibit through the NRA . . . boys under 18 years of age from being gainfully employed." See *American Child*, XV (November 1933), 2.

14. E. E. Keevin to Lewis E. Lawes, June 29, 1934, Franklin D. Roosevelt Papers, Franklin D. Roosevelt Library, Hyde Park, N.Y. (hereafter cited as FDR Papers); *American Child*, XVI (September 1934), 1, and XVIII (February 1936), 2. Also see Dorothy D. Bromley, "The Newspapers and Child Labor," *Nation*, CXL (January 30, 1935), 131–32.

15. Quoted in Bromley, "The Newspapers and Child Labor," pp. 131–32.

16. NCLC, *Thirty-first Annual Report* (New York, 1935), p. 12; Leon Whipple, "The Press Gets a Code," *Survey Graphic*, XXIII (April 1934), 194–95; Bromley, "The Newspapers and Child Labor," pp. 131–32.

17. "Newsboys at Work," *Survey*, LXXI (April 1935), 114–15. The NCLC also sought to make newspapers assume financial responsibility for the young workers they insisted on employing. Needless to say, this too did not improve the Committee's standing with the press. The attempt to have newspapers declared employers of children who were engaged in selling or delivering papers was resented. As the American Newspaper Publishers' Association frankly stated, this "would give direct ammunition to plaintiffs in carrier liability suits." Thus the newspaper industry continued to enjoy the double privilege of employing children and escaping all financial responsibility for their injuries.

18. "What the NRA Has Done for Child Labor," *American Child*, XVI (January 1934), 3, and XVI (October 1934), 3; NCLC, *Thirtieth Annual Report, passim*.

19. Ella A. Merritt, "Child Labor Under the NRA as Shown by Employment Certificates Issued in 1934," *Monthly Labor Review*, XLI (December 1935), 1477–91; U.S. Children's Bureau, "Effects of NRA Codes on Child Labor," manuscript dated June 5, 1935, NCLC Papers; Miriam Keeler, "Who Wants Child Labor?," manuscript dated March 26, 1935, NCLC Papers; NCLC, *Thirtieth Annual Report*, p. 5; *American Child*, XVI (January 1934), 3, and XVI (October 1934), 2.

20. In addition to the clothing trades (coats, suits, corsets, brassieres, dresses,

hats, underwear, etc.), the powder-puff, tag, toy, and a number of other industries that relied heavily on homework outlawed the practice in their codes.
This is not to say, however, that the evil was abolished entirely. Some industries refused to outlaw it, and even where it was prohibited enforcement was
difficult and violations continued. See NCLC, *Thirtieth Annual Report,* p.
8, and *Thirty-first Annual Report,* pp. 13–14.

    21. Samuel I. Rosenman, *The Public Papers and Addresses of Franklin D.
Roosevelt,* 13 vols. (New York, 1938–50), III, 415. The NCLC made a frantic
effort to get the President to retract, clarify, or amplify his comment so as
to negate the impression that there was no need for further child labor legislation or the amendment. As a result Roosevelt declared that, while child labor
was abolished, "whatever may be done to make its return forever impossible will
be agreeable and welcome." He also wrote, "I am in favor of the Child Labor
Amendment. A step in the right direction was achieved by demonstrating the
simplicity of its application to industry under the N.R.A." On another occasion
he stated that in "the child labor field the obvious method of maintaining
present gains is through ratification of the Child Labor Amendment. I hope this
may be achieved." See, for example, Stephen Early to Ray F. Jenney, January
8, 1934, and Franklin D. Roosevelt to Courtenay Dinwiddie, November 8,
1934, FDR Papers; Franklin D. Roosevelt to Mrs. LaRue Brown, January 25,
1934, and Franklin D. Roosevelt to Courtenay Dinwiddie, January 27, 1934,
NCLC Papers; *American Child,* XVI (March 1934), 1; Miriam Keeler, "The
Child Labor Amendment: Its History and Prospects," *Social Science,* X (July
1935), 259.

    22. NCLC, *Twenty-ninth Annual Report,* pp. 6-7, and *Thirtieth Annual Re-
port,* p. 2; NCLC press releases, October 28, 1933, and November 17, 1934,
NCLC Papers; NCLC *Minutes,* March 22, May 17, November 15, 1934; *American
Child,* XV (September 1933), 2; *New York Times,* July 15, 1933; Gertrude
Folks Zimand, "Will the Codes Abolish Child Labor?," *Survey,* LXIX (August
1933), 290–91; Folks, "Outlaw Child Labor," p. 13; "Ratify the Amendment,"
Survey, LXX (March 1934), 86.

    23. NCLC press releases, March 15, 1934, January 7, 1935, NCLC Papers.
For a list of the members see NCLC, *Handbook on the Federal Child Labor
Amendment,* p. 33.

    24. Walsh is quoted in NCLC, *Handbook on the Federal Child Labor Amend-
ment,* p. 43; members of the committee are listed on p. 34. See Box 135, Frank
P. Walsh Papers, Manuscript Division, New York Public Library, New York
City, especially the correspondence between Gertrude Folks Zimand (who
actually drew up the plan for the committee and asked Walsh to head it)
and Walsh, June 1935–November 1935 (hereafter cited as Walsh Papers).
Also see Box 56, NCLC Papers; *New York Times,* February 16, 1936; *New
York Sun,* February 17, 1936; NCLC *Minutes,* April 28, 1936; *American Child,*
XVI (April 1934), 3, and XVIII (March 1936), 1; *Albany* (New York)
Evangelist, February 21, 1936; *New York Catholic News,* February 22, 1936;
Jeremy P. Felt, *Hostages of Fortune* (New York, 1965), p. 212.

    25. *American Child,* XVI (December 1934), 2, XVI (March 1934), 2, and

XVI (April 1934), 3. Also see NCLC press release, February 17, 1934, NCLC Papers; *New York Post,* April 17, 1934; *New York Herald Tribune,* March 3, 1934. Especially vicious at this time were the attacks on Florence Kelley, who had died in February 1932. Both Newton D. Baker, an advocate of the amendment, and Alfred E. Smith, an opponent, rose to her defense. Baker declared:

> The fact about Florence Kelley is that she was wholly and altogether the most patriotic, humane, and enlightened intellect I have known. . . . She was willing to be slandered, she was willing to live on the verge of want, she was willing to talk down the proud and selfish in high places if she might in the least degree help the childhood of our nation.

And Smith added:

> If any statement that the late Florence Kelley was a Communist and that she devoted her life to social revolution and efforts to overthrow the government was made, that statement is not correct. Mrs. Kelley was for years at the head of the Consumers' League and favored all constructive legislation for the betterment of labor, practically all of which was enacted into law.

Quoted in *American Child,* XVI (March 1934), 2.

26. The flier, issued in 1936 by the Edmonson Economic Service (New York City), is in the Walsh Papers. Also see NCLC, *The Farmer and the Federal Child Labor Amendment* (New York, 1934); *American Child,* XVI (November 1934), 2, and XVII (March 1935), 1; Clarence E. Martin, "Shall Americanism Remain?," *Commonweal,* XIX (April 13, 1934), 649–51.

27. The organization allegedly resulted from a letter that appeared in the *New York Times* of December 28, 1933. The author, Nicholas Murray Butler, appealed to the Sentinels of the Republic, the crusaders, and "all those men and women who worked so hard and so successfully to repeal the Eighteenth Amendment" to join in the task of defeating the proposed child labor amendment. For a history of the organization, see *American Child,* XVII (March 1935), 4.

28. NCLC, *Handbook on the Federal Child Labor Amendment,* pp. 37–38; Keeler, "Child Labor Amendment—History and Prospects," p. 259; Gertrude Folks Zimand, "When Facts Are Not Enough," *Channels,* XVI (December 1938), 33–37; "The Real Fight over Child Labor," *Survey,* LXX (May 1934), 161; *American Child,* XVI (December 1934), 2. In a letter sent to all its members, the Sentinels declared: "As President Roosevelt, Mrs. Roosevelt, Postmaster General Farley, Secretary of Labor Perkins, and Governor Lehman are working for ratification, the necessity for active opposition is apparent." Quoted in *American Child,* XVI (May 1934), 2. The Committee's executive committee had twenty-three members; nine were lawyers and five were Catholic priests or Lutheran ministers.

29. NCLC, *Handbook on the Federal Child Labor Amendment,* p. 41; Bromley, "The Newspapers and Child Labor," pp. 131–32; Zimand, "When Facts Are

Not Enough," p. 35; *American Child,* XVI (September 1934), 1, and XIX (February 1937), 2–3.

30. Quoted in Zimand, "When Facts Are not Enough," p. 35. Also see NCLC, *Handbook on the Federal Child Labor Amendment,* p. 41; Bromley, "The Newspapers and Child Labor," pp. 131–32; *American Child,* XVII (March 1935), 2; and George Seldes, *Lords of the Press* (New York, 1938), a frontal attack on the American Newspaper Publishers' Association.

31. NCLC, *Thirtieth Annual Report, passim.* Also see Box 55, NCLC Papers. On April 21, 1934, and January 5, 1935, Marlene Pew, editor of *Editor and Publisher,* issued stinging rebukes to the newspapers for their opposition to the amendment.

32. Quoted in *American Child,* XVIII (October 1936), 2. Martin was quoted in the (New York) *Garment Worker,* September 8, 1933.

33. Guthrie, a Catholic, was on the executive committee of the National Committee for the Protection of Child, Family, School, and Church.

34. William D. Guthrie, "Report of the Special Committee to Oppose Ratification by States of Federal Child Labor Amendment and Promote Adoption of Uniform Child Labor Act," April 24, 1935, NCLC Papers; Non-Partisan Committee for Ratification of the Child Labor Amendment, "In Answer to the American Bar Association Committee on the Federal Child Labor Amendment," 1935, NCLC Papers; *New York Daily News,* January 6, 1935; Keeler, "Child Labor Amendment—History and Prospects," p. 260. Also see Paul L. Blakely, "Is There a Child-Labor Amendment?" *America,* LXXVI (April 21, 1934), 37–38. This attack on the amendment did not come as a complete surprise to the NCLC; in the fall of 1933 Owen Lovejoy reported to the board that such an attack was in the making. See NCLC *Minutes,* November 27, 1933. In large part the American Bar Association's case rested on the fact that, with regard to the Eighteenth Amendment, the Supreme Court held that a seven-year limitation, written into the measure, was reasonable. It did not imply, however, that in the absence of such a specific limitation, as in the case of the proposed child labor amendment, ratification over a longer period of time would be held unreasonable. As for the right of a state to ratify an amendment after rejecting it, there was no authoritative decision. However, the Fourteenth Amendment was adopted by votes of states which had first rejected and subsequently accepted the measure.

35. NCLC, *An Answer to the American Bar Association Committee on the Federal Child Labor Amendment: Ratify the Child Labor Amendment: A Statement by Lawyers* (New York, 1935). The *American Bar Association Journal,* in its April issue, published an article by C. C. Burlingham on "The Need for a Federal Child Labor Amendment"; it was reprinted and widely distributed by the NCLC. Also see *American Child,* XVII (April 1935), 1.

36. Later FDR's "court-packing" plan would be used against the amendment by frightening those who regarded the Supreme Court as a bulwark against any abuse of the amendment's broad grant of power, should it be passed. It is interesting to note that the liberal *New Republic,* on the other hand, argued that *failure* to achieve so mild a reform as the child labor amendment threatened the

American system. "Capitalism is a leaky ship; it must either be patched or re-placed by a new vessel," it declared. "What shall we say, then, of its crew, who refuse the slightest repairs and stick to their course ignoring the steadily deepening flood within the hold?" See "Who Wants Child Labor and Why?," *New Republic*, LXXVIII (April 25, 1934), 296–97. It should also be noted that three states—Connecticut, New York, and Pennsylvania—raised their mini-mum working age to sixteen in 1935. A number of others reduced hours, limited night work, and regulated homework. See NCLC, *Thirty-first Annual Report* (New York, 1935), p. 10.

37. *Schechter Poultry Corporation v. United States*, 295 U.S. 495 (1935); Alpheus T. Mason and William M. Beaney, *American Constitutional Law* (Englewood Cliffs, N.J., 1954), pp. 284–89.

38. "The Trend of Child Labor in 1936," *The Child*, I (July 1936), 17, and I (November 1936), 14; NCLC, *Handbook on the Federal Child Labor Amendment*, pp. 26–38; Abbott, "Federal Regulation of Child Labor," p. 426; NCLC, *Thirty-second Annual Report* (New York, 1936), p. 4; *American Child*, XVIII (February 1936), 3; XVIII (May 1936), 1; and XVIII (December 1936), 2.

39. NCLC *Minutes*, April 28 and November 16, 1936; "The Federal Child Labor Amendment," unsigned manuscript dated October 14, 1935, NCLC Papers. In August 1936 Congress enacted the Walsh-Healy Act, which provided that every contract in excess of $10,000 entered into with the federal govern-ment should include, among other things, a statement that no boys under sixteen years of age or girls under eighteen were to be employed. Enactment of this modest measure, which served only establishments that had government contracts, at least reestablished some of the basic standards of the NRA and kept alive the conception of a national industrial standard, providing the basis for more com-prehensive regulation in the future. See Arthur M. Schlesinger, Jr., *The Politics of Upheaval* (Boston, 1960), p. 509.

40. For a list of the organizations see NCLC, *Handbook on the Federal Child Labor Amendment*, pp. 32–33. Also see *American Child*, XVIII (January 1936), 2.

41. *New York Herald Tribune*, May 24, 1936; "Child Labor," unsigned manuscript dated July 1936, NCLC Papers; *American Child*, XVIII (September 1936), 4; Ned Weisberg, "The Federal Child Labor Amendment—A Study in Pressure Politics" (doctoral dissertation, Cornell University, 1942), p. 78.

42. *New York Times*, January 9, 1937; *Time Magazine*, XXIX (January 18, 1937), 13; NCLC press release, January 7, 1937, NCLC Papers; NCLC, *Thirty-third Annual Report* (New York, 1937), pp. 20–21; Courtenay Dinwiddie to Grace Abbott, January 4, 1937, Abbott Papers. Some earlier opponents of the amendment that began supporting it at this time were the *Louisville Courier-Journal*, the *New York Times*, the *New York Journal*, and the *Rochester* (New York) *Times-Union*. See *American Child*, XIX (February 1937), 1–3.

43. *New York Herald Tribune*, February 21, 1937; NCLC, *Thirty-third Annual Report*, pp. 20–21; *American Child*, XIX (March 1937), 1.

44. The *New York Herald Tribune*, a vigorous opponent of the amendment,

had exclusive rights to publish the poll, which was released the day before a legislative hearing on the measure at Albany. Its editors withheld publication of the poll until after the hearing, thus helping to defeat the measure. See *American Child*, XIX (March 1937), 1.

45. In *Hammer v. Dagenhart* the Supreme Court denied the power of Congress to control the movement of child-made goods in interstate commerce on two grounds. One was that the harmless character of the goods being transported was a significant factor; the other was that the production of goods intended for interstate commerce was "a matter of local regulation" and therefore beyond the power of Congress. Those two assumptions, however, were now swept away by these Court decisions: the first in the Kentucky Whip and Collar Co. case [299 U.S 334 (1937)], in which the Court declared "inadmissible" the contention that the usefulness and harmlessness of the goods being transported invalidated the Act forbidding their shipment; the second in the NLRA cases [301 U.S. 1 (1937)], in which the Court held that the fact that the employees concerned were engaged in production (which it had previously declared to be a matter for local regulation) was not determinative. The only question that remained, therefore, as the Court pointed out, was "the effect upon interstate commerce of the labor practice involved."

46. NCLC *Minutes*, March 23, 1937; *New York Times*, November 7, 1937; Grace Abbott to William Green, December 14, 1937, Abbott Papers; *American Child*, XIX (May 1937), 2, and XIX (October 1937), 1.

47. NCLC, *Thirty-third Annual Report, passim.*; Abbott, "Federal Regulation of Child Labor," p. 426; "Child Labor," *Survey*, LXXIII (April 1937), 110, and "Strings to the Child Labor Bow," ibid., LXXIII (July 1937), 225. In addition, several other constitutional amendments with lower standards were introduced in Congress. Of the substitute measures, the only one that received serious consideration was the so-called Vandenberg Amendment; it was reported out by the Senate Judiciary Committee without a hearing. However, it never came to a vote in either house. The Vandenberg Amendment differed from the pending one in its omission of the word *regulate*, substitution of the phrase *employment for hire* for "labor," and reduction of the age minimum from eighteen to sixteen.

48. A law forbidding the sale of goods from any state that were wholly or in part manufactured under conditions which would violate another state's child labor law would present fantastic enforcement difficulties. Industrial firms would have to operate under forty-eight different standards, depending upon the destination of the goods being manufactured. Prison-made goods were produced for a competitive market in only a few public institutions and involved a very limited number of articles. It would not be difficult, therefore, for a state to keep track of the manufacture of such goods. In the case of child labor, though, the problem was far different. See NCLC *Minutes*, March 23, 1937; *New York Times*, January 26, 1938; Abbott, "Federal Regulation of Child Labor," p. 426.

49. Quoted from Jeremy P. Felt, "The Child Labor Provisions of the Fair Labor Standards Act," p. 9, paper delivered at the Annual Meeting of the Organization of American Historians, Dallas, Texas, April 20, 1968.

50. Katharine Lenroot to Grace Abbott, April 23, 1937, and Courtenay Dinwiddie to Grace Abbott, May 6, 1937, Abbott Papers; NCLC *Minutes*, March 15
and March 23, 1938. Samuel McCune Lindsay resigned as chairman of the
NCLC board of trustees in 1935. He was succeeded by Homer Folks, who
held the post until 1944.

51. *New York Times*, January 26 and February 17, 1938; "Child Labor,"
Survey, LXXIII (April 1937), 110.

52. "Statement of the National Child Labor Committee on the Fair Labor
Standards Bill Submitted to the Senate Committee on Education and Labor and
House of Representatives Committee on Labor by Courtenay Dinwiddie, June
8, 1937," NCLC Papers; NCLC *Minutes*, October 18 and December 7, 1937,
March 15, April 29, and December 7, 1938; Gertrude F. Zimand to Grace
Abbott, December 9, 1937, Abbott Papers. For a good, brief account of the
politics involved see Felt, "The Child Labor Provisions of the Fair Labor
Standards Act," pp. 10–12.

53. Quoted in Felt, "The Child Labor Provisions of the Fair Labor Standards
Act," p. 2. Also see NCLC *Minutes,* December 7, 1938; Joseph Hackman and
Paul H. Douglas, "The Fair Labor Standards Act of 1938, I," *Political Science
Quarterly*, LIII (December 1938), 491–515; John S. Forsythe, "Legislative
History of the Fair Labor Standards Act," *Law and Contemporary Problems*,
VI (Winter 1939), 464–90.

54. *American Child*, XX (June 1938), 2, and XX (November 1938), 1.
Also see *American Child*, XXIII (October 1941), 2; Mary B. Dahl, "The End
of Homework," *Survey Graphic*, XXXII (June 1943), 252–55. At the time
only ten states had a sixteen-year minimum age for work during school hours.
Eight states (through exemptions in their statutes) still permitted children under
fourteen to work in industry during school hours. Six states still permitted
children between fourteen and sixteen to work nine to eleven hours a day,
and nine states allowed such children to work until 8 P.M. or later. Thirty-one
states practically had no regulation of the employment of sixteen- and seventeen-
year-olds in hazardous occupations.

55. *American Child,* XXI (January 1939), 2, and XXI (May 1939), 3;
NCLC, *The Why and How of Amending the Federal Child Labor Law* (New
York, 1949); "Jobs and Workers," *Survey Midmonthly, LXXX* (May 1944),
168–69.

56. Beatrice McConnell, "One Year of Federal Child Labor Control," *Ameri-
can Child*, XXI (October 1939), 1; NCLC, *Thirty-sixth Annual Report* (New
York, 1940), pp. 15–16, 18–19; Dorothy Bradbury, *Five Decades of Action
for Children* (Washington, D.C., 1962), p. 52; Homer Folks, *Changes and
Trends in Child Labor and Its Control* (New York, 1938), p. 24; Beulah
Amidon, "New Floors and Ceilings: The Wages and Hours Administration
Reaches a Second Stage," *Survey Graphic, XXVIII* (December 1939), 728–33.
As in the case of the previous federal child labor laws, close cooperation between
local and state authorities and the Children's Bureau in enforcing the federal
statute strengthened the hands of local authorities in protecting children under
state laws.

57. Furthermore, beginning in 1949 the FLSA was strengthened by a series of amendments to be discussed in the next chapter.

58. There had been a decided occupational shift among child workers during the 1930's; the overwhelming majority moved from manufacturing to mercantile and personal service industries, thus leaving only a small percentage of working children within the law. See Homer Folks, *Changes and Trends*, pp. 15–17, 24; *American Child*, XX (February 1938), 3, and XX (November 1938), 2; NCLC, *Thirty-third Annual Report*, pp. 29–30; NCLC *Minutes*, December 7, 1938.

59. Courtenay Dinwiddie to the Board of Trustees, January 17, 1938, and Franklin D. Roosevelt to James E. Murray, June 13, 1938, Abbott Papers.

60. Abbott, "Federal Regulation of Child Labor," pp. 424–30; "The Fight to Ratify," *Survey*, LXXIII (March 1937), 79. The NCLC did all it could to get the cases before the Supreme Court, hoping for a favorable ruling and thus the end of this argument. See NCLC *Minutes*, October 18 and December 7, 1937; Courtenay Dinwiddie to Grace Abbott, February 3, 1938, Abbott Papers.

61. *Coleman v. Miller* [307 U.S. 433 (1939)]; *American Child*, XXI (June 1939), 1; "Child Labor," *Survey Mid-monthly*, LXXV (August 1939), 250.

62. NCLC, *The Federal Child Labor Amendment: What It Is, Why It Is Needed, Who Supports It, Answers to Objections* (New York, 1940).

63. *United States v. Darby* [312 U.S. 100 (1941)]; Mason and Beaney, *American Constitutional Law*, pp. 305–7; "The Significance of the Supreme Court Decision," *American Child*, XXIII (March 1941), 1.

64. Link and Catton, *American Epoch*, pp. 404–7; Leuchtenburg, *Franklin D. Roosevelt and the New Deal*, pp. 48–52.

65. Courtenay Dinwiddie to the Board of Trustees, May 14, 1934, January 21, 1935, NCLC Papers; "Children Out of the Beet Fields," *Survey*, LXX (December 1934), 388.

66. *United States v. Butler* [297 U.S. 1 (1936)]; Mason and Beaney, *American Constitutional Law*, pp. 330–36.

67. Charles E. Gibbons, "The Beet Fields Revisited," *American Child*, XVIII (September 1936), 1; "Child Beet Workers," *Survey*, LXXII (October 1936), 311; Grace Abbott, ed., *The Child and the State*, 2 vols. (Chicago, 1947), I, pp. 591–97.

68. NCLC *Minutes*, May 26 and November 24, 1941; Gertrude F. Zimand, *Children Who Work on the Nation's Crops* (New York, 1942). On the other hand, a bill to suspend the child labor provisions of the Sugar Act suddenly moved from an inactive to a very active status. It was rushed through the House in record time without a hearing; only quick action by the NCLC prevented it from going through the Senate. See *American Child*, XXIV (March 1942), 2, and XXIV (December 1942), 2; NCLC, *Thirty-ninth Annual Report* (New York, 1943), p. 17.

69. Although mechanized farming had reduced the need for hand labor in some crops or certain crop operations, the seasonal demand for workers con-

tinued to exceed the supply of available local labor in many areas and for many crops where mechanization was incomplete or impractical. Thus children continued to engage in a large number of different operations on farms. They thinned, hoed, pulled, and topped sugar beets; weeded cabbage and other vegetables; gathered string beans, lima beans, peas, tomatoes, walnuts, cranberries, strawberries, and other berries; picked prunes and other orchard fruits and hops; chopped and picked cotton, etc. The main arteries of migratory agricultural labor were the Atlantic coastal route; the Pacific coastal route; the Mississippi Valley, following the different fruit crops; the West and Northwest, working on the beet crop; and the Northern and Northwestern grain migration route. See, for example, *American Child*, VII (July 1925), 1; VII (November 1925), 1–2; IX (April 1927), 2; X (October 1928), 2; XII (April 1931), *passim.;* Gertrude Bender, "Eastern Children Also Follow the Crops," ibid., XXI (February 1939), 1; Agnes E. Benedict, "Young Nomads," *Survey*, LVII (December 15, 1926), 376–77; NCLC, *Thirty-fourth Annual Report* (New York, 1938), pp. 11–27; NCLC, *Pick for Your Supper: Migratory Child Workers in the West Coast States* (New York, 1939); NCLC, *Children in Strawberries* (New York, 1940).

70. By paying large landholders to reduce productive acreage, the AAA, for example, drove many tenant farmers and sharecroppers from the land.

71. NCLC *Minutes*, November 27, 1939; NCLC, *Thirty-sixth Annual Report,* pp. 9–10; Courtenay Dinwiddie to F. C. Harrington, March 3, 1939, Abbott Papers; *American Child*, XXI (May 1939), 2, and XXI (December 1939), 2.

72. *American Child*, XXIII (April 1941), 1, and XXIII (May 1941), 4. Among the migrants who appeared before the Tolan Committee were a Mr. and Mrs. Johnson. Originally from North Dakota, they had later worked in Missouri and Arkansas, and were at the time working in Michigan. The Johnsons reported that they had six living children, none of whom had been in school until they came to Michigan, when five of them entered first grade. See Gertrude F. Zimand, *Children Who Work on the Nation's Crops* (New York, 1942), p. 5.

73. See Sidney Baldwin, *Poverty and Politics: The Rise and Decline of the Farm Security Administration* (Chapel Hill, 1968). Also see Leuchtenburg, *Franklin D. Roosevelt and the New Deal*, p. 141; NCLC, *Thirty-sixth Annual Report*, pp. 37–46.

74. NCLC *Minutes*, November 27, 1939; NCLC, *Thirty-sixth Annual Report*, pp. 9–10; *American Child*, XXII (October 1940), 3, and XXIII (November 1941), I; Courtenay Dinwiddie, "Must the Night Fall?," ibid., XXII (December 1940), 1, and *How Good Is the Good Earth?: A Venture in Re-Discovery* (New York, 1942); Gertrude F. Zimand, "Child Labor Today Bears Watching," *Public Health Nursing*, XXXIII (October 1941), 572.

75. Needless to say, few members of Congress were concerned with the problems of the voteless and often inarticulate migrants and sharecroppers. Thus the Tolan Committee's proposals to extend social security to migrants and provide federal grants-in-aid to the states to assist non-settled people were also

ignored. See Courtenay Dinwiddie, *Food, the Little Farmer, the War and the Future* (New York, 1943).

IX
World War II and After

1. "According to the Census," *American Child*, XXIII (November 1941), 1; Gertrude F. Zimand, "School Attendance and Child Labor in the United States," manuscript dated May 1942, in the author's possession.

2. The "employed" in the 1940 census were those who were working or actively seeking work during the week in March when the census was taken; in previous years the "employed" were those "usually" gainfully employed. For the first time, then, those who worked full time on the crops seven or eight months a year but did not begin work until, say, April, were not counted. Also, in 1940 the census authorities, over the protestations of the NCLC, decided not to count child laborers between the ages of ten and thirteen. This omission removed the only factual base that existed for estimating the number of children under fourteen years old at work in agriculture.

3. Reports on the issuance of employment certificates for 1941 showed (in areas where comparable legal restrictions existed in both 1940 and 1941) an increase of over 80 per cent in the number of fourteen- and fifteen-year-old children legally leaving school for work. Coupled with this increase in legal child employment, there was a tremendous rise in illegal child labor. See, for example, *American Child*, XXIII (December 1941), 1; XXIV (March 1942), 2; XXIV (October 1942), 3; XXV (May 1943), 2; NCLC, *Thirty-eighth Annual Report* (New York, 1942), p. 4; Zimand, "School Attendance and Child Labor," p. 13.

4. See, for example, Gertrude F. Zimand, *Child Workers in Wartime* (New York, 1942), or *Child Manpower—1943* (New York, 1943).

5. *American Child*, XXIV (February 1942), 2; NCLC, *Thirty-eighth Annual Report*, pp. 5–6; *Minutes* of the meetings of the Board of Trustees of the National Child Labor Committee, November 24, 1941, January 28, 1942, National Child Labor Committee Papers, National Committee on Employment of Youth, New York City (hereafter cited as NCLC *Minutes*). NCLC *Minutes*, April 1904–October 1945, are in the Manuscript Division of the Library of Congress; beginning with those for November 5, 1945, the *Minutes* are located at the National Committee on Employment of Youth, New York City. Also see Zimand, *Child Workers in Wartime*, pp. 12–13.

6. The text of the paragraph was as follows:

It is essential that children and youth be sound and well-prepared in body and mind for the tasks of today and tomorrow. Their right to schooling should not be scrapped for the duration. Demands for the employment of children as a necessary war measure should be analyzed to determine whether full use has been made of available adult man power and to distinguish between actual labor shortage and the desire to obtain cheap labor. The education and wholesome development of boys and girls should be the first consideration in making decisions with regard to their employment and other contributions to our war effort.

Dinwiddie, by the way, served as chairman of the Commission's Committee on Legislation. See "Children's Charter in Wartime," *American Child*, XXIV (April 1942), 2; Zimand, "School Attendance and Child Labor," p. 14, and *Child Manpower—1943*, p. 35; NCLC, *Thirty-ninth Annual Report* (New York, 1943), pp. 11–12.

7. Interestingly, in most cases, the industries that called for a relaxation of child labor standards were those that had traditionally relied on the practice, such as shrimp canning, for example. NCLC, *Thirty-ninth Annual Report*, p. 16, and *Forty-fourth Annual Report* (New York, 1948), p. 6; NCLC *Minutes*, April 28, 1942.

8. Illegal employment increased by about 400 to 500 per cent. See Ella A. Merritt and Floy Hendricks, "Trend of Child Labor, 1940–44," *Monthly Labor Review*, LX (April 1945), 756–75; Albion G. Taylor, *Labor Problems and Labor Law* (New York, 1950), pp. 242–43; Zimand, *Child Manpower—1943*, pp. 8–9; *American Child*, XXVI (March 1944), 3; Beatrice McConnell, "The Employment of Minors," *Proceedings of the National Conference of Social Work* (New York, 1943), pp. 158–69 (hereafter cited as *Proc. NCSW*); NCLC, *Forty-fourth Annual Report*, p. 6.

9. Full-time employment in intrastate industry at age fourteen was permissible in all but fourteen states; part-time employment in non-manufacturing establishments was allowable at any age in ten states and, with the exception of a few occupations with a fourteen-year minimum, in thirteen others. Students could work full time after school hours in thirty-nine states. Over half the states had no night work or hours provisions for sixteen- and seventeen-year-old children. See McConnell, "The Employment of Minors," pp. 163–64; NCLC, *Thirty-ninth Annual Report*, p. 9, and *Forty-first Annual Report* (New York, 1945), pp. 7–8; Taylor, *Labor Problems and Labor Law*, pp. 242–43; *American Child*, XXV (January 1943), 1, and XXVI (November 1944), 1; Elizabeth S. Magee, "Impact of the War on Child Labor," *Annals of the American Academy of Political and Social Science*, CCXXXVI (November 1944), 101–9; Leonard W. Mayo, "The Findings of the National Commission on Children and Youth," *Proc. NCSW* (Buffalo, 1946), pp. 371–78.

10. NCLC, *Child Labor Manifesto* (New York, 1944); NCLC *Minutes*, September 24 and November 18, 1943, February 7, 1944; NCLC, *Thirty-ninth Annual Report*, pp. 5, 23, and *Fortieth Annual Report* (New York, 1944), p. 39. In the midst of its wartime efforts the Committee suffered a severe loss when its general secretary for thirteen years, Courtenay Dinwiddie, suddenly died in the fall of 1943. Gertrude F. Zimand, the organization's able associate general secretary, was elevated to the top spot. A few months later, Eduard

C. Lindeman, a member of the board of trustees since 1921, was appointed chairman when Homer Folks resigned at the age of seventy-seven.

11. NCLC, *Thirty-ninth Annual Report*, p. 8. The war extracted a heavy price from American children even though they were spared the horrors of bombing, military invasion, and starvation. Many were forced to live in new and sometimes strange communities under crowded conditions. Many were neglected in the absence of fathers in the service or mothers on war jobs. Some were orphaned as war casualties mounted. Others, of course, were prematurely burdened with work too heavy for their strength.

12. NCLC, *Forty-first Annual Report* (New York, 1945), p. 5, and *Forty-second Annual Report* (New York, 1946), pp. 7–8; NCLC *Minutes*, November 5, 1945. Also see Eduard Lindeman to Alice Hamilton, December 5, 1945, National Consumers' League Papers, Manuscript Division, Library of Congress, Washington, D.C.; *American Child*, XXVI (December 1944), 1; Sol Markoff, "Employment of Children and Youth at the Mid-Century," *Social Service Review*, XXV (June 1951), 143–55. The overall picture of child employment in 1945 did not change greatly from that of the preceding year. Employment of fourteen- to seventeen-year-old children remained at about the 1944 level of three million, in contrast to around 900,000 in 1940. The big change in 1944–1945, however, was that for the first time in several years there was no marked increase in child labor. In addition, there was only a negligible drop in high school enrollment, and a decrease in the number of working papers issued—all indications that child labor had reached its peak and that the leveling-off process had begun. See NCLC, *Forty-first Annual Report*, pp. 3–4.

13. Mrs. Zimand graduated from Vassar in 1916, Phi Beta Kappa. In college she was a member (and former chairman) of the Suffrage Club, the Settlement Association, and the Intercollegiate Student Conference, and chairman of the Socialist Club (which she helped to found) and the debating society. At commencement she was awarded prizes for the highest standing in her class in history and mathematics. Except for her service for a year in France (1917–1918) as a mmeber of the American Committee for Devastated France (for which she was awarded the medal of the Reconnaissance Française), and for three years (1923–1926) as a social worker and faculty member in the Department of Social Science at the University of Cincinnati, she served the NCLC continuously from 1916 until her retirement in 1955. See Savel Zimand, ed., *Gertrude Folks Zimand: A Tribute* (n.p., 1967).

14. Gertrude F. Zimand, "Talk Before the Annual Meeting of the Illinois Child Labor Committee," manuscript dated January 25, 1946, National Child Labor Committee Papers, Columbia University School of Social Work, New York City. In the late 1920's Mrs. Zimand and acting general secretary Wiley Swift had suggested that the NCLC begin to turn its attention to the problems youths face during the transition from school to industrial life. They urged the Committee to concern itself with fourteen- to eighteen-year-olds, who needed some sort of constructive program that would both provide them with maximum educational opportunities for all of life, including work, and minimize the

industrial hazards (physical and mental) they faced when legally employed. See, for example, NCLC press releases, April 29, 1928, June 24, 1929, National Child Labor Committee Papers, Manuscript Division, Library of Congress, Washington, D.C. (hereafter cited as NCLC Papers); NCLC *Minutes*, April 22, 1929; Gertrude F. Zimand, "Child Labor and the Future," *New Republic,* LIV (March 21, 1928), 150–53; *American Child*, XII (January 1930), 2; NCLC, *Child Labor Facts* (New York, 1933), p. 22.

15. Both studies were conducted by Harold J. Dillon, who took a leave of absence from the Connecticut State Department of Education to work for the NCLC; later he resigned from his Connecticut position and became a full-time NCLC staff member. During the first five years of Mrs. Zimand's secretaryship, eighteen new members were added to the Committee's board of trustees, many of whom were educators.

16. The real question, of course, was, Were such programs educational, and thus good, or were they merely another form of child labor which the NCLC should combat? See Harold J. Dillon, *Work Experience in Secondary Education—School-Work Programs* (New York, 1946); *American Child*, XXVII (February 1945), 1; "Work Experience in Secondary Education," ibid., XXVIII (May 1946), 1; Florence Taylor, "Has Work Experience a Place in Secondary Education?," *High School Journal*, XXIX (November–December 1946), 241–51.

17. Harold J. Dillon, *Early School Leavers: A Major Educational Problem* (New York, 1949); *American Child*, XXIX (April 1947), 1, and XXXI (October 1949), 1; Florence Taylor, *Child Labor Fact Book, 1900–1950* (New York, 1950), pp. 22–23. More than one million sixteen- and seventeen-year-old boys and girls were not attending school, and about 70 per cent of them were working.

18. See, for example, NCLC, *Forty-second Annual Report*, p. 27, and *Forty-sixth Annual Report* (New York, 1950), p. 40; NCLC *Minutes*, January 10 and October 13, 1949; NCLC, *Look Before You Leap* (New York, 1946); NCLC, *Why Stay in School* (New York, 1948); NCLC, *Just a Minute . . . Are You Thinking About a Job?* (New York, 1953); NCLC, *Two Is a Team, When School and Employment Service Work Together* (New York, 1955).

19. NCLC *Minutes*, December 16, 1946, February 3 and April 7, 1947, March 22, 1951; Taylor, *Child Labor Fact Book*, pp. 22–23; *American Child*, XXX (April 1948), 1; XXXI (March 1949), 2–3, and XXXVII (January 1955), 1; Gertrude F. Zimand, "Major Activities Since Last Board Meeting," manuscript dated May 4, 1950, NCLC Papers. For the issues and politics involved in federal aid to education, see R. Freeman Butts and Lawrence Cremin, *A History of Education in American Culture* (New York, 1953), pp. 534–38, 580–84.

20. Where there were sixteen-year minimums for employment, they usually exempted fourteen- and fifteen-year-olds for agricultural or domestic work; the Committee sought to erase these exemptions as well. It also worked for increased appropriations for enforcement of child labor and compulsory education laws. NCLC, *The Case for Sixteen Year Employment Laws* (New York, 1947); *American Child*, XXVII (January 1945), 1.

21. "Loopholes in the Child Labor Law," *Survey*, LXXXV (April 1949), 224; NCLC, *The Why and How of Amending the Federal Child Labor Law* (New York, 1949); Gertrude F. Zimand, "Present Trends in Child Labor and Youth Employment," manuscript dated December 1948, Gertrude Folks Zimand Papers, Social Welfare History Archives Center, University Libraries, University of Minnesota, Minneapolis, Minnesota (hereafter cited as Zimand Papers); *New York Times*, November 28, 1952, November 20, 1953; *American Child*, XXXI (January 1949), 1, and XXXII (November 1950), 1. With the tremendous increase in the use of farm machinery, especially tractors, by the late forties and early fifties there was a shockingly high toll of serious and often fatal accidents to children working on farms. Agriculture, in fact, became one of the most hazardous industries; its accident frequency and severity rates were considerably higher than for industry as a whole. See *American Child*, XXXV (January 1953), 2.

22. NCLC *Minutes*, January 11, 1951; *American Child*, XXXIII (January 1951), 2–3. Following the outbreak of the Korean War in 1950, child labor again increased, and efforts were made by opponents of regulation to break down legislative standards. The NCLC insisted (as it had done during World Wars I and II) that there be no relaxation of existing federal or state child labor laws and that the laws be strictly enforced. The Committee also urged that states whose legal provisions were below the standards generally recognized as necessary for the protection of children enact immediate legislation to fill the gap. See *American Child*, XXXIII (January 1951), 1; NCLC, *Forty-seventh Annual Report* (New York, 1951), pp. 1–2, 19.

23. U.S. Department of Labor, *Growth of Labor Law in the United States* (Washington, D.C., 1962), pp. 43–44; *American Child*, XXXI (February 1949), 1; XXXI (October 1949), 2, and XXXII (October 1950), 2; Taylor, *Child Labor Fact Book*, pp. 20–21.

24. As of 1953 only twenty-three states and the District of Columbia made any attempt to regulate the work of newsboys. The usual minimum age in those states was twelve years or lower for street selling, and ten years or lower for route delivery. Hour regulations usually permitted boys of those ages to work until 8 or 9 P.M. and to start work at 5 A.M. or earlier. While some municipal ordinances covered newsboys, generally the provisions were equally inadequate. Wisconsin and Louisiana were the only states that had enacted legislation to bring newsboys under workmen's compensation.

25. NCLC *Minutes*, October 24, 1951; NCLC, *Forty-seventh Annual Report*, pp. 15–16.

26. See, for example, NCLC, *Forty-sixth Annual Report* (New York, 1950), pp. 15–16, 19–20; *Forty-seventh Annual Report*, p. 17, and *Forty-eighth Annual Report* (New York, 1952), pp. 13–14, 19; NCLC *Minutes*, January 26, 1950; Howard E. Thomas and Florence Taylor, *Migrant Farm Labor in Colorado: A Study of Farm Families* (New York, 1951); NCLC, *Colorado Tale* (New York, 1951); *New York Herald Tribune*, February 27, 1952; *American Child*, XXX (November 1948), 3; XXXII (February 1950), 2; XXXII (March 1950),

1; XXXIV (February 1952), 2; XXXIV (March 1952), 3; XXXVIII (November 1956), 3; XXXIX (January 1957), 1.

27. NCLC *Minutes*, March 8, 1954.

28. *American Child*, XXXIII (March 1951), 1.

29. NCLC *Minutes*, March 8, 1954; NCLC, *Fifty-first Annual Report* (New York, 1955), pp. 15–16; Gertrude F. Zimand, "The NCLC—1954," *American Child*, XXXVI (May 1954), 5 ff.

30. NCLC *Minutes*, April 15, October 20, and November 19, 1953.

31. Dwight D. Eisenhower to F. Ernest Johnson, April 9, 1954, Zimand Papers.

32. NCLC, *Fiftieth Annual Report* (New York, 1954), pp. 14, 18. For the best account of the event see *American Child*, XXXVI (May 1954), *passim*.

33. Quoted in *American Child*, XXXVI (May 1954), 1, 3. A year later, after thirty-nine years of service, Mrs. Zimand retired; she was replaced by her assistant, Sol Markoff. See *American Child*, XXXVII (November 1955), 1; NCLC *Minutes*, March 15, May 3, and October 21, 1955.

34. NCLC, *Fiftieth Annual Report*, p. 4; NCLC, *The Changing Years, 1904–1954* (New York, 1954), p. 3.

35. NCLC *Minutes*, November 10, 1955, February 26, 1956. The issue had come up repeatedly since the early 1920's, especially in the early 1950's. See NCLC *Minutes*, January 26 and May 11, 1950. Aside from inadequately conveying the scope of the Committee's activities, the name National Child Labor Committee was losing meaning and appeal. Many people felt that child labor had been eliminated; as a result, the Committee was losing members and financial contributions.

36. See NCLC *Minutes*, October 9, 1956–December 11, 1958, especially April 3, 1957, and May 7, 1958; *American Child*, XL (January 1958), 1; Eli E. Cohen to the author, July 25 and September 10, 1969.

37. The National Committee on Employment of Youth and the National Committee on the Education of Migrant Children are housed at 145 East Thirty-second Street, New York City. Eli E. Cohen, who came to the National Child Labor Committee on January 1, 1958, with long experience in the field of vocational guidance, serves as executive secretary of both.

38. As Jeremy P. Felt recently pointed out (in "The Child Labor Provisions of the Fair Labor Standards Act," paper delivered at the Annual Meeting of the Organization of American Historians, Dallas, Texas, April 20, 1968), the apparent rise in violence, juvenile delinquency, and urban unrest suggests some danger that child labor may increase once again. To a growing number of people the problem of today's youth, many of whom would have been child laborers in an earlier day, seems to be too much free time; the youngsters either cannot or will not find jobs. At last a partial solution to the nation's current domestic problems, these people say, might be what would amount to a revival of child labor. Such a simplistic solution—aimed chiefly at keeping ghetto youths off the streets—is mingled with more serious efforts to achieve a long-range program for disadvantaged youth.

A Note on Sources

SINCE THE TEXT of this work has been extensively documented, it seems un-necessary to list each item separately in a conventional bibliography. Rather, the general character of the sources will be discussed briefly and those that were most useful, both primary and secondary, will be indicated. Most of them have been cited; some have not. All have been helpful.

The most important source for this study was the collection of National Child Labor Committee Papers in the Manuscript Division of the Library of Congress —some 2,800 items occupying twenty-two linear feet of shelf space. Ranging over the years 1904–1953, they include correspondence, official records (in-cluding *Minutes* of board meetings), reports, convention proceedings, press releases, and newspaper and magazine clippings related to child labor and the Committee. The papers are well organized, carefully indexed, and easy to use.

Only slightly less important than these NCLC Papers were the Committee's *Annual Reports,* the *Child Labor Bulletin,* the *American Child,* and its several hundred other publications. While much of this material can be found scat-tered about in various libraries, the most complete set is located at the office of the National Committee on Employment of Youth, 145 East Thirty-second Street, New York City. While the NCLC Papers at the Library of Congress (especially the *Minutes* of board meetings) were essential for an understanding of policy-making decisions and differences of opinion within the Committee, these publications were indispensable for an understanding of its activities.

A number of other manuscript collections were quite important. The Alexander J. McKelway Papers at the Library of Congress provided an understanding of McKelway's thought and a clear picture of many of his and the Committee's child labor activities, particularly in the South, as well as the creation of the U.S. Children's Bureau and the passage of the first federal child labor law.

The National Consumers' League Papers, also at the Library of Congress, contain many items bearing on child labor and the NCLC, its relation to the NCL, and especially Florence Kelley's feelings about the Committee and some of its personnel.

The Edgar Gardner Murphy Papers at the University of North Carolina Library are essential for an understanding of Murphy's thought and his child labor activities, notably his opposition to the Beveridge bill. The Grace and Edith Abbott Papers at the University of Chicago Library contain a great deal of useful material on the NCLC, its relationship to the Children's Bureau, and especially their joint struggle for passage of the child labor amendment and its adoption by the states.

Other manuscript collections possess items of interest. At the Library of Congress, the Theodore Roosevelt Papers yielded useful material on the Beveridge bill, as did, of course, the Albert J. Beveridge Papers. Interesting items on the creation of the Children's Bureau and selection of its first chief can be found in the William H. Taft Papers. In the Woodrow Wilson Papers is a revealing correspondence between the President and Alexander McKelway, particularly concerning the Keating-Owen bill. Among the Calvin Coolidge Papers are several helpful items on the child labor amendment, especially the fight for its adoption in Massachusetts.

At the New York Public Library, the Lillian D. Wald Papers contain pertinent items on a variety of topics. The Frank P. Walsh Papers have the best collection of material on the Catholic Citizens Committee for Ratification of the Federal Child Labor Amendment. The National Civic Federation Papers reveal telling items on the opposition to federal child labor legislation, especially the Beveridge bill. The Franklin D. Roosevelt Papers at Hyde Park, New York, were important for an understanding of the Committee's role in drafting NRA industrial codes and the child labor provisions of the Fair Labor Standards Act. Finally, the NCLC Papers at the Columbia University School of Social Work, which touch upon a wide range of matters, were also worthy of study.

Because the NCLC Papers at the Library of Congress include some fifty containers of scrapbooks with newspaper clippings related to child labor and the Committee, newspapers in themselves were not too important for this study. When I did seek newspaper coverage or opinion of some event, I usually used the *New York Times,* chiefly because of its extensive index.

On the other hand, a major source for this study was periodical literature. Most important were the *Annals of the American Academy of Political and Social Science,* which published all the NCLC's early reports, convention proceedings, and the like as well as a great deal of other material on child labor, and the *Survey,* official publication of the social work profession. Other journals that deserve special mention for their significance to this study are: *The Commons, Charities, Charities and The Commons, Charities Review,* the *Outlook,* the *Nation,* the *New Republic,* and the *Social Service Review.*

Although government documents and publications were not widely used, some were extremely important. Among these are the *Congressional Record,* the

Proceedings of various White House Conferences on Children, and U.S. Senate Document No. 645, *Report on the Condition of Women and Child Wage-Earners in the United States,* 19 vols. (Washington, D.C. 1910–13). In addition, two U.S. Children's Bureau publications were quite useful: Grace Abbott's *Administration of the First Federal Child Labor Law* (Washingotn, D.C., 1921) and Dorothy Bradbury's *Five Decades of Action for Children: A History of the Children's Bureau* (Washington, D.C., 1962).

Similarly, although publications of voluntary organizations other than the NCLC were not widely used, some proved most helpful, if not essential. Among these were the *Proceedings of the National Conference of Charities and Correction* (later *Social Work,* then *Social Welfare*). In addition, two books of documents were very useful: Grace Abbott, ed., *The Child and the State,* 2 vols. (Chicago, 1947), I, especially 259–563, and Kirk H. Porter and Donald B. Johnson, eds., *National Party Platforms, 1840–1964* (Urbana, Ill., 1961).

Although there is no single book on the entire child labor movement, I profited enormously from works by some earlier writers who dealt with limited aspects of the subject. Most important were Elizabeth H. Davidson, *Child Labor Legislation in the Southern Textile States* (Chapel Hill, 1939), a study of child labor reform until the mid–1930's in North and South Carolina, Georgia, and Alabama; Jeremy P. Felt, *Hostages of Fortune: Child Labor Reform in New York State* (New York, 1965), largely a history of the New York State Child Labor Committee, 1903–1942; and Stephen B. Wood, *Constitutional Politics in the Progressive Era* (Chicago, 1968), a sociolegal history of the first and second federal child labor laws of 1916 and 1919.

Of help, too, were Edward N. Clopper, *Child Labor in City Streets* (New York, 1912); Fred S. Hall, *Forty Years, 1902–1942: The Work of the New York Child Labor Committee* (New York, 1942); Herbert J. Lahne, *The Cotton Mill Worker* (New York, 1944); and Vincent A. McQuade, *The American Catholic Attitude on Child Labor Since 1891* (Washington, D.C., 1938).

The following more general works were also useful in many ways: Robert H. Bremner, *From the Depths: The Discovery of Poverty in the United States* (New York, 1956); Clarke A. Chambers, *Seedtime of Reform: American Social Service and Social Action, 1918–1933* (Minneapolis, 1963); Lawrence Cremin, *The Transformation of the School: Progressivism in American Education, 1876–1957* (New York, 1961); Josephine Goldmark, *Impatient Crusader: Florence Kelley's Life Story* (Urbana, Ill., 1953); Maud King Murphy, *Edgar Gardner Murphy: From Records and Memories* (New York, 1943).

In addition, several articles and chapters in books were quite helpful. Among the most important were Edith Abbott, "Early History of Child Labor," *American Journal of Sociology,* XV (July 1908), 15–37; Grace Abbott, "Federal Regulation of Child Labor, 1906–1938," *Social Service Review,* XIII (September 1939), 409–30; John Braeman, "Albert J. Beveridge and the First National Child Labor Bill," *Indiana Magazine of History,* LX (March 1964), 1–36; Elizabeth S. Johnson, "Child Labor Legislation," in John R. Commons, et al., *History of Labor in the United States,* 4 vols. (New York, 1918–35), III,

403–56; John W. Larner, Jr., "The Glass House Boys: Child Labor Conditions in Pittsburgh's Glass Factories, 1890–1917," *Western Pennsylvania Historical Magazine*, XLVIII (October 1965), 355–64; and Richard B. Sherman, "The Rejection of the Child Labor Amendment," *Mid-America*, XLV (January 1963), 3–17.

Other useful articles were Edith Abbott, "Grace Abbott—A Sister's Memories," *Social Service Review*, XIII (September 1939), 351–407; Hugh C. Bailey, "Edgar Gardner Murphy and the Child Labor Movement," *Alabama Review*, XVIII (January 1965), 47–59; Dorothy D. Bromley, "The New Move to End Child Labor," *Current History*, XXXVIII (August 1933), 564–70, and "The Newspapers and Child Labor," *Nation*, CXL (January 30, 1935), 131–32; Sol Cohen, "The Industrial Education Movement, 1906–17," *American Quarterly*, XX (Spring 1968), 95–110; Robert J. Doherty, Jr., "Alexander J. McKelway: Preacher to Progressive," *Journal of Southern History*, XXIV (May 1958), 177–90; Dewey W. Grantham, Jr., "The Progressive Movement and the Negro," *South Atlantic Quarterly*, LIV (October 1955), 461–77; J. E. Hulatt, Jr., "Propaganda and the Proposed Child Labor Amendment," *Public Opinion Quarterly*, II (January 1938), 105–15; Alton DuMar Jones, "The Child Labor Reform Movement in Georgia," *Georgia Historical Society Quarterly*, XLIX (December 1965), 396–417; Miriam Keeler, "The Child Labor Amendment: Its History and Prospects," *Social Science*, X (July 1935), 257–60; Sol Markoff, "Employment of Children and Youth at the Mid-Century," *Social Service Review*, XXV (June 1951), 143–55; and Paul S. Taylor, "Hand Laborers in the Western Sugar Beet Industry," *Agricultural History*, XLI (January 1967), 19–26.

Finally, I profited from reading unpublished master's essays and Ph.D. theses. Included among these were Louis L. Athey, "The Consumers' Leagues and Social Reform, 1890–1923" (doctoral dissertation, University of Delaware, 1965); Anne K. Brown, "Opposition to the Child Labor Amendment Found in Trade Journals, Industrial Bulletins, and Other Publications for and by Businessmen" (master's essay, University of Chicago, 1937); Alice E. Padgett, "The History of the Establishment of the U.S. Children's Bureau" (master's essay, University of Chicago, 1936); Ben E. Salinsky, "A History of Federal Child Labor Legislation" (master's essay, University of Wisconsin, 1931); John G. Van Osdell, Jr., "Cotton Mills, Labor, and the Southern Mind" (doctoral dissertation, Tulane University, 1966); and Ned Weisberg, "The Federal Child Labor Amendment—A Study in Pressure Politics" (doctoral dissertation, Cornell University, 1942).

Index

McKelway, Alexander J. *(cont.)*
131; on child labor in the South, 85–
86, 87; and Children's Bureau bill, 119;
counters Southern defense of child labor,
104–105; death, 137; dispute with
Julia Lathrop, 133–134; on federal aid
to education, 157; and federal child
labor legislation, 123–124, 127; South-
ern opposition to him, 100–101; sup-
ports Beveridge bill, 89, 91–92; urges
Wilson to support Keating-Owen bill,
130
Macy, V. Everit, 57, 60, 64
Mann Act. *See* White Slave Act.
Manufacturers' and Farmers' Journal, 27
Manufacturers' Record, quoted, 173, 283–
284 n28
Markham, Edwin, 48, 99
Martin, Clarence E., 199
Mason, Lucy R., 204
Maternity and Infancy (Sheppard-Towner)
Act, 167
Maurice, Frederic, 28
Medalie, George Z., 199
Memphis Commercial Appeal, 127
Messengers. *See* Night messengers; Street
trades and child labor.
Migrant child labor, 10, 151, 210–212,
223, 224–225, 229, 299–300 n69. *See
also* Agriculture; Fair Labor Standards
Act; Farm Security Administration; Na-
tional Child Labor Committee.
Miller, R. M., 82–83
Miller, Simon, 281 n11
Milwaukee Journal, 194
Mines and child labor, 71–75
Model child labor bill (1904), 70, 115,
263 n53
Montgomery Advertiser, 91
Moore, Sir Henry, quoted, 26
Moore, Henry W., 281 n11
Murphy, Edgar Gardner, 57, 58; begins
organized anti-child labor movement,
50–54; calls for national child labor
committee, 55–56; creates Alabama
Child Labor Committee, 54; on NCLC
executive committee, 60; opposes Beve-
ridge bill and resigns from NCLC, 90–
92; quoted, 245 n21, n23

National Association of Manufacturers,
103, 127; denounces FLSA, 204; and
National Education and Employment
Program, 181–183; opposes Child Labor
Amendment, 166, 173, 175, 177
National Catholic Welfare Council, 163–
164, 176
National Child Health Organization, 156
National Child Labor Committee: begins

work, 69–71; and Beveridge bill, 87–
93; broadens activities to include whole
field of human conservation, 154–156;
changes direction in favor of youth
employment work, 225–226; and child
labor in agriculture, 152–154, 180; on
Child Labor Amendment, 164, 169, 174–
175, 179, 190, 195–202, 207–208; and
child labor in canneries, 107–109; and
Child Labor Day, 76; and child labor
in glass factories, 76–79; and child labor in Southern cotton textile mills, 81–
87, 98–105; and child labor in the street
trades, 109–114; on child labor in tenements, 148; and Children's Bureau bill,
93, 96–98; early organization and membership, 60–67, 247 n43; and education,
including federal aid for, 156–158, 222,
278 n27, n30; evaluation of, 12–13,
230–233; and federal child labor legislation, 123–140, 146; fiftieth anniversary,
226–228; and FLSA, 203–206, 209,
223–224; founding of, 58–59; and FSA,
211; incorporated, 75, 246 n39, 250 n20;
and Jones-Costigan Act, 209; and migrant child labor, 210–212, 224–225,
229; and name change, 158–159, 228–
229, 306 n35; and NRA codes, 190–
195, 291 n5; and Pennsylvania coal
mines and breakers, 71–75; postwar
program, 219–227; and selection of
Children's Bureau chief, 119; today,
229; twenty-fifth anniversary, 183–184,
288 n66; and World War I, 134; and
World War II, 216–219
National Citizens Council on Agricultural
Life and Labor, 225
National Citizens Council on Migrant La-
bor, 225
National Civic Federation, 103, 105; and
organized labor, 260 n24
National Committee for the Protection of
Child, Family, School, and Church, 197,
294 n27
National Committee for Rejection of the
Twentieth Amendment, 173, 175, 284
n29
National Committee on the Education of
Migrant Children, 229
National Committee on Employment of
Youth, 228–229
National Conference of Charities and Cor-
rection, 55, 121, 123
National Congress of Mothers and Parent-
Teacher Associations, 279 n2
National Consumers' League, 34–35, 60–
61, 70, 204; attacks NAM, 183; en-
dorses Palmer-Owen bill, 125; and
"Standard Child Labor Law," 47
National Council of Catholic Women, 176

A Note on the Author

Walter I. Trattner was born in New York City and studied at Williams College, Harvard University, and the University of Wisconsin. His articles on the history of social welfare in America have appeared in major scholarly journals, including the *Journal of American History* and the *Social Service Review,* and he is the author of *Homer Folks: Pioneer in Social Welfare* (1968). Mr. Trattner is now Associate Professor of History and Social Welfare at the University of Wisconsin–Milwaukee.

DATE DUE

APR 22			
MAY 10			
MAR 1 8			
MAY 1 0			
APR 1 8			
MAY 1 0			
MAR 1 1 1987			
MAR 2 5 1987			
APR 2 1 1987			
MAY 6 1987			
GAYLORD			PRINTED IN U.S.A.